2 to 22 DAYS
IN
NEW ZEALAND

THE ITINERARY PLANNER
1991 Edition

ARNOLD SCHUCHTER

John Muir Publications
Santa Fe, New Mexico

Originally published as *22 Days in New Zealand*

John Muir Publications, P.O. Box 613, Santa Fe, NM 87504

© 1988, 1991 by Arnold Schuchter
Cover © 1988, 1991 by John Muir Publications
All rights reserved.
Printed in the United States of America

Schuchter, Arnold (Arnold L.)
  2 to 22 days in New Zealand : the itinerary planner / Arnold
  Schuchter. — 1991 ed.
    p. cm.
  Rev. ed. of: 22 days in New Zealand.
  Includes index.
  ISBN 0-945465-58-0
  1. New Zealand—Description and travel—1981- —Guide-books.
I. Schuchter, Arnold (Arnold L.). 22 days in New Zealand.
II. Title. III. Title: Two to twenty-two days in New Zealand.
DU405.5.S38   1991
919.304'37—dc20   90-27014
                                                                                          CIP

Typeface Garamond Light
Design Mary Shapiro
Cover Map Michael Taylor
Maps Janice St. Marie
Typography Copygraphics, Inc., Santa Fe, New Mexico
Printer McNaughton & Gunn, Inc., Saline, Michigan

Distributed to the book trade by:
W. W. Norton & Company, Inc.
New York, New York

CONTENTS

How to Use this Book		1
Itinerary		31
Day 1	Arrive in Auckland	36
Day 2	Around Auckland	45
Day 3	Tour of Waitakere Range and North Shore	53
Day 4	Auckland to the Bay of Islands	57
Day 5	Russell—Bay of Islands—Waitangi—Kerikeri	69
Day 6	West of the Bay of Islands—South to Coromandel Peninsula	73
Day 7	Coromandel Peninsula—Rotorua	80
Day 8	Rotorua—Lake Taupo	91
Day 9	Lake Taupo—Tongariro National Park—Wanganui	102
Day 10	Wanganui—Wellington	112
Day 11	Wellington	116
Day 12	Wellington to Christchurch	120
Day 13	Christchurch Region	127
Day 14	Christchurch—Queenstown	134
Day 15	Queenstown	142
Day 16	Queenstown—Te Anau	147
Day 17	Te Anau—Milford Sound	154
Day 18	Te Anau—Wanaka	158
Day 19	Wanaka to Fox and Franz Josef Glaciers	166
Day 20	Franz Josef—Hokitika—Greymouth	171
Day 21	Greymouth—Arthur's Pass National Park—Christchurch	176
Day 22	Christchurch—Banks Peninsula	179
Index		183

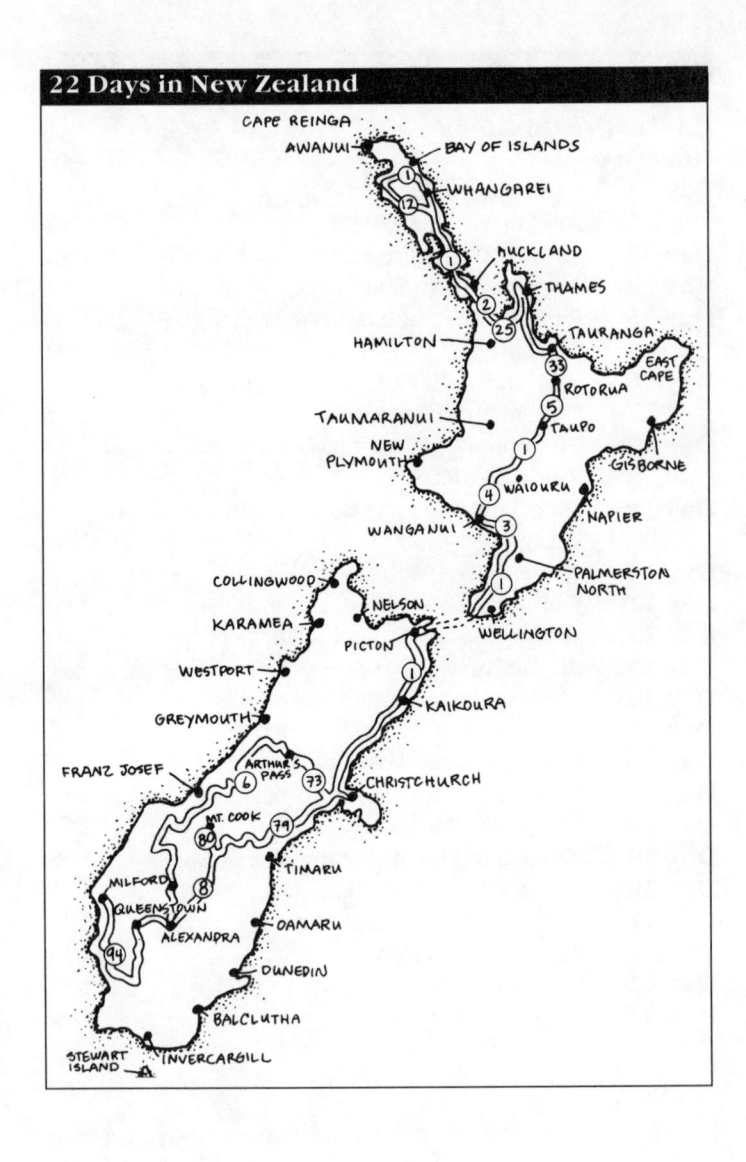

22 Days in New Zealand

HOW TO USE THIS BOOK

New Zealand's coastlines are fringed with coves, bays, rocky cliffs and headlands, fiords, steep mountains, calm and surf-swept golden and black sand beaches. Volcanic and alpine mountains form the centerpieces of national parks no more than a few hours' drive from either coastline, and in many instances only minutes away. These parks include one out of every 13 acres in the nation, preserved for the benefit of all nature lovers. The South Pacific Ocean on the east and the Tasman Sea on the west unify New Zealand's contrasting coasts on two islands as large and as different from each other as the British Isles or Japan. Sheep also unify the diverse New Zealand landscape—a profusion of 70 million gentle woolly creatures speckling every pasture and hillside, innocently inducing in travelers an uncanny sense of déjà vu with almost every new roadway.

Following the do-it-yourself tour described in this book, you will:

- Acclimate to Kiwi country by covering the gamut of urban, coastal, island, and mountain "bush" activities in the Auckland region.
- Tour the glorious Bay of Islands and then giant kauri forests on the west coast of historic Northland, with an optional trip to its northern tip, Cape Reinga and Ninety Mile Beach.
- Travel south to Wellington passing through scenic Coromandel Peninsula, explore Rotorua-Taupo-Tongariro's volcanic mountains and trout-filled lakes and rivers, and maybe jetboat on the beautiful Wanganui River from the "Garden City" of the same name, with the option of touring a riverside winery.
- Cross Cook Strait on the Inter-Island Ferry from Wellington through the South Island's fabulous Marlborough Sounds.
- Leave the "sun belt of the South Island" from the ferry port of Picton and head down the Kaikoura Coast to

a marvelous variety of attractions in the Christchurch region and the South Island's most picturesque and "British" city.

- Travel from Christchurch over Burke's Pass and past glacial lakes to Mt. Cook National Park.
- Pass through Mackenzie Country, rimmed by the Southern Alps, over Lindis Pass to the spectacular mountains, lakes, and rivers of Queenstown, Te Anau, Fiordland National Park, and world-renowned Milford Sound.
- Drive through the beautiful Wanaka/Mt. Aspiring National Park region over Haast Pass to the west coast's Fox and Franz Josef Glaciers.
- Return to Christchurch over Arthur's Pass after exploring some of the west coast's beautiful glacial lakes, as well as greenstone and gold mining attractions, to complete your tour on beautiful Banks Peninsula in a tiny Victorian harbor town touched by French culture and history.

For each day, this book provides:

1. A **suggested schedule** of where to go, in what order, how long to stay there, what to see, and how to travel between destinations.

2. The most unique and scenic **sightseeing highlights**, rated: ▲▲▲ "Don't miss"; ▲▲ "Try hard to see"; and ▲ "Worthwhile if you can make it."

3. My recommendations for **where to eat** and **where to stay**, in all budgetary ranges but mainly for budget-minded travelers.

4. **Itinerary options**, activities, and side trips, usually requiring more time or money.

5. **Maps** of all areas covered in this tour.

Customize your own itinerary. This guide can be followed literally for 22 days, or you can select any day or combination of days as your itinerary, or even take only one itinerary option in one chapter and make it your entire vacation. Some travelers want to "see it all"; others prefer to concentrate their time in a few selected areas with a large variety of activities, or a single, unique sporting/outdoors activity such as deep-sea fishing, diving,

How to Use this Book

white-water rafting, or perhaps just relaxing. Each "Day" in this book is **modular**—within certain limitations, days in this itinerary can be rearranged to suit your travel preferences and travel time. With the exception of about five days spent in three cities (Auckland, Wellington, and Christchurch), most sightseeing and activities on both islands center on coastlines, mountains, lakes and rivers.

2 to 22 Days in New Zealand is for the young at heart who love the outdoors. Seeing the best of New Zealand's diverse landscapes and coastal waters makes for three weeks of very full days. The itinerary guides you step by step through each one of these days to experience a full range of the finest this marvelous country has to offer.

New Zealand's natural beauty needs to be seen on foot (walking, hiking, "tramping," trekking, climbing, and even golfing), by water transport (rowboat, sailboat or yacht, cruiser, ferry, hydrofoil, catamaran, jetboat, canoe, and raft), by air (light plane, helicopter, pontoon plane, skiplane, and balloon), underwater and underground. In addition to miles of interconnected tracks for hiking enthusiasts, I will tell you about routes for short and easy walks in and around cities, other touring bases, and scenic spots. Pack a comfortable pair of walking shoes.

Throughout this book, I describe special-interest sporting activities for those who wish to take advantage of the incomparable opportunities New Zealand presents. Anglers, for example, will have an incredible variety of world-class choices. On the North Island, there's deep-sea and sport fishing in the Bay of Islands, Hauraki Gulf, and the Bay of Plenty. New Zealand is one of those rare places where "fish stories" probably are true. Believe everything you've heard about trout fishing in the North Island's Rotorua-Taupo lake system and the Tongariro River and its tributaries; or on the South Island, Lakes Rotoiti and Rotoroa (and dozens of nearby rivers), Hanmer Springs' Hurruni and Waiau rivers, the Raikaia and Rangitata rivers south of Christchurch, the legendary Mataura, Oreti, and Aparima in the southeast, and sport-fishing in Marlborough Sounds.

New Zealand is golfers' heaven. You can spend your entire vacation moving from green to glorious green, with small or no green fees, each setting more beautiful than the last: Auckland's Muriwai, Bay of Island's Waitangi, Rotorua's Arikikapakapa (with boiling mud pool "traps" and hot pool "hazards"), Christchurch's Russley or Shirley, Dunedin's Otago Golf Club, and dozens of others.

Cost and Budget Considerations
The good news (for other than Kiwis) is that, at this writing (mid-1990), the United States-New Zealand exchange rate has stayed about the same since 1987. US$1 buys NZ$1.68 or US$.59 buys NZ$1. Stated another way, in US$, the price of anything purchased in New Zealand is about 60 percent less than NZ$. For example, the NZ$50 room is US$30. If you're used to paying $50 for a motel room in the United States, that's over NZ$83.

The offsetting bad news for U.S. visitors to New Zealand is that, in addition to inflationary pressures in New Zealand over the past few years, New Zealand's Goods and Services Tax (GST) of 12.5 percent applies to accommodations, meals, car rentals, and other travel-related items. Some accommodations include the GST in their quoted rates; others don't and you have to ask and make your own mental calculations to figure out the total rate. In this guide, I indicate whether GST is included or extra in the rates quoted by accommodations.

Prepare yourself for New Zealand to be a more expensive destination than it was a few years ago and in comparison to traveling in the United States. The trans-Pacific airfares have gone up and so has everything else. For example, even mid-priced hotel packages in Auckland, Rotorua, and Queenstown (such as the Quality Inn and Holiday Inn) run close to or over US$100 per person per day (with breakfast and a brief tour of the town), with a two- or three-day minimum. For a single, the price for the same package is over US$150-$175 per day. However,

How to Use this Book

almost all of the accommodations (and restaurants) suggested in this guide cost *much less.*

New Zealand still can and should be a moderate-cost destination, in cities and outside, for travelers who plan ahead using this guide and then actually spend their NZ$ very carefully. Here's a summary of useful tips to save quite a bit of money:

1. Fly to New Zealand in "shoulder season" (especially early March or late October) as close as possible to the end or beginning of New Zealand's warmer and summer months (November-February).

2. If you plan to fly more than once in New Zealand, definitely consider a heavily discounted **Mt. Cook Kiwi Air Pass** or an **Air New Zealand Freedom Pass**, which you must purchase before leaving the United States.

3. If you're going to rent a car or motor home, do so after a careful comparison of rates offered by New Zealand and U.S. car/camper van/motor home rental companies. Differences in daily and weekly rates can be considerable.

4. Travel on the rail and bus services of **InterCity** (with good Newmans and Mt. Cook Landline connections) or with other discount bus-rail packages and save a bundle. Rub elbows with Kiwis, travel by train on coastal and mountain routes often hidden from highways, save driving wear and tear—and save money.

This guide is set up so that you can preplan your trip day-by-day at home and then figure out how to make it work as a bus-rail journey (or by car if you prefer, which, admittedly, is much more convenient). For example, the money-saving **Travelpass** (see below) includes 15 days of travel over a 22-day period, which fits this book's entire itinerary. InterCity even will plan your entire trip in advance: read this guide, select the places you want to see, day by day, and send the list to Passenger Management, InterCity, Private Bag, Wellington. InterCity will return a bus-train itinerary to fit your plan.

Following the suggestions in this guide, book your own accommodations directly to suit your budget, travel style, and tastes. See Where to Stay, below, for detailed information.

A more expensive money-saving option, shop for a **fly-drive accommodations package** including car rental by the week and hotels/motels. One of the lowest cost, good quality, weekly car/hotel/motel package (for example, Continental Newmans Vacations) is about US$104 per day for 2 persons (share twin).

All prices in this book are shown in **New Zealand dollars (NZ$)**. Without GST, a single person traveling with a moderate budget plan, enjoying just a few recommended splurges, can expect to spend: NZ$50-$60 for a comfortable room or B&B anywhere in New Zealand; NZ$30-$45 per day for meals, plus tea time and snack extras; a generous average of NZ$60-$70 per day for sightseeing excursions, ferry fares, admission fees, bike or canoe rentals, horse trekking, whitewater rafting, cable car trips, and special entertainment event costs (including one or perhaps two flightseeing spectaculars), a limited guided trek into the bush country, and other very special outings highly recommended in this guide; and NZ$15 per day for entertainment and miscellaneous.

These figures add up to an average expenditure per person of about NZ$200 per day (with GST), without international or domestic transportation—a 22-day budget of NZ$4,400. Even with good planning and discounts, the cost can be higher for one person car rental. Expect to pay NZ$455 per week (with GST and insurance). You probably will spend another NZ$200 per week for fuel. Add NZ$2,100 for car-related costs for 22 days to the NZ$4,400 costs above, totaling NZ$6,500 or US$3,835 plus about US$1,000 for trans-Pacific airfare, for a total of US$4,835.

A second person would share the NZ$2,100 car-related cost, add to accommodations costs but also share them, and add to meal costs. Based on the cost assumptions above for accommodations, meals, car rental, activities, and airfare, two persons from the United States traveling together in New Zealand for 22 days would spend a total of about NZ$10,000 (US$5,950) plus another US$2,000 for airfare (US$7,950). These figures do not include souvenirs or other purchases. However, as a consolation, this "excursion" budget could include skiing for a day or two, a deep-sea fishing day trip (shared with half a dozen other people), and other activities in New Zealand's glorious outdoors.

Entry Requirements
As an American citizen, you need a passport valid for at least three months beyond the date of your expected departure from New Zealand. No visa is required if you plan to stay less than three months. No inoculations are required. Each person over 17 can bring into New Zealand 200 cigarettes and 50 cigars, 4.5 liters of wine or beer, one bottle of spirits or liquor, and goods valued at NZ$500 (US$300) for your use as a gift. Bring in as much money as you like. Prohibited items include food, plants, animals or animal products, insects, other squirming objects (except children), and drugs other than over-the-counter and prescriptions.

Entry permission requires a round-trip ticket on confirmed passage out of New Zealand; NZ$1,000 (at least US$600 per person per month of stay in New Zealand including traveler's checks and credit cards with available credit), with advance paid-for accommodation bookings acceptable in lieu of cash or credit; and the required documents to enter your next destination. Technically, you can be asked to prove that you have at least US$1,000 with you in cash, traveler's checks, or valid credit cards. I've never experienced this type of welcoming "investigation" and, chances are, neither will you.

Currency
New Zealand has one, two, five, ten, twenty, and fifty dollar notes, and one, two, five, ten, twenty, and fifty cent coins. As of this writing, a New Zealand dollar is worth US$.59, but the relative value of both dollars changes

daily. Traveler's checks can be exchanged for New Zealand currency at any bank without a fee and even earn you a slight premium over exchanging U.S. dollars. Trading banks are open from 9:30 a.m. to 4:00 p.m. Monday through Friday but not on Saturdays, Sundays, or public holidays. American Express, Bankcard, Diners Club, MasterCard, and Visa credit cards are welcomed at large and medium-sized hotels, tourist shops, and higher-priced restaurants, but you'll enjoy more flexibility with a supply of both U.S. and New Zealand traveler's checks and, off the beaten path, about NZ$100 in cash.

Seasons, Holidays, and Hours
New Zealand's seasons are opposite those of the United States. Spring is September through November; summer, December through February; autumn, March through May; and winter, June through August. The climate is temperate. Seasonal variations are noticeable but only extreme in the mountains and the far southern part of the South Island. You can gaze at snow on the mountains of both islands from their mild coastlines. Winter on the North Island tends to be wet, but the weather is only dismal for a few midwinter days in the Auckland region. On the South Island, when wet weather hits the mountains, frequently with fierce winds, watch out for rapidly flooding rivers and streams or blizzards that happen before you can say, "Let's get out of here!"

In July, the coldest month in Auckland, the average temperature is 58 degrees Fahrenheit. July also has the most days of rain (12), so the dampness (70% humidity) can make it seem colder. January, the warmest month in Auckland, is also one of the driest (6 inches of rainfall) but still humid (64%). Christchurch, a little colder in midwinter (51 degrees) and a little cooler in midsummer (71 degrees), also has high humidity (57-70%).

There are substantial variations throughout each island. It rains twice as much in the Bay of Islands as on the southeast coast south of Gisbourne. Most of the north and east coasts of the South Island are drier than the North Island. The west coast can be quite wet and colder than on the east side of the Southern Alps.

Combine a summer (December to February) trip to New Zealand with a trip to southeastern Australia (Sydney to Adelaide) or Tasmania. If any place in the South Pacific compares to New Zealand for concentrated natural beauty, it is the island of Tasmania. Or plan a winter trip to New Zealand for skiing (July-August) with a visit to Australia's Queensland, Northern Territories, or Western Australia during some of their best weather, and perhaps to Victoria and Tasmania for more skiing. John Gottberg's *22 Days in Australia* tells you how to economically explore the other wonders "down under."

Unless you plan to ski or you are en route to the northern half of Australia, don't travel to New Zealand in the winter. Fall and especially spring and summer are more beautiful and drier. But in the summer months, when school is out and New Zealanders are on holiday, accommodations, transportation, and tourist attractions are scarce and heavily booked, prices go up, and you have to scramble and pay more for less.

National and School Holidays: For travel planning purposes, the significance of New Zealand's national holidays is that the country shuts down. Don't arrive on one or try to travel anywhere. Stay put. Don't drive if you are low on gas. Take a walk, hike, sail or whatever you like, purchasing food the day before. Don't bother looking for restaurants or pubs except maybe a stray milk bar in the hinterlands. Be prepared for these holidays:

New Years Day—January 1
Waitangi Day—February 6
Good Friday, Easter Monday
(Anzac Day)—April 25
Queen's Birthday—June 1 (first Monday in June)
Labor Day—October 26 (fourth Monday in October)
Christmas Day—December 25
Boxing Day—December 26

If the holiday falls on a Tuesday through Thursday, it shifts to the previous Monday; on Friday though Sunday to the following Monday. Also watch for local holidays in every part of the country, such as January 29 in Auckland and January 22 in Wellington, which can be equally hazardous to your travel plans. The main school and family vacation period is from mid-December to the end of January. Schools are also closed for two weeks in May and in the beginning of August.

Time Zones: The most confusing aspect of the trip to New Zealand is the difference in day, date, and time back home. You cross the International Date Line and "lose" a day, gaining it back on your return. Fortunately, New Zealand has just one time zone—12 hours ahead of Greenwich Mean Time. New Zealand's time zone is 20 hours ahead of Pacific Time. If you're on the West Coast of the United States, New Zealand is tomorrow and 4 hours earlier (12:00 noon on Saturday in Los Angeles is 8:00 a.m. Sunday in Auckland). Fly out of Los Angeles on Saturday, and you'll arrive on Monday in Auckland. On the return trip, you'll actually be home "before you leave." New Zealand observes Daylight Saving Time, advancing one hour from the last Sunday in October to the first Sunday in March.

Don't leave the United States on Friday, or you'll arrive in Auckland on Sunday when many of the city's tourist attractions, information centers, and restaurants are closed. Instead, leave on Thursday or Saturday.

Shopping Times and Business Hours: Most stores are open from 9:00 a.m. to 5:30 p.m. Monday through Thursday, until 9:00 p.m. on Friday in major cities, and on Saturday until noon. Only tourist shops in season and dairies will be open Sunday. Offices, businesses, and post offices are open weekdays from 8:00 a.m. to 5:00 p.m. Banks are open from 10:00 a.m. to 4:00 p.m. Monday through Friday.

What to Bring

Be prepared for any kind of weather at any time of year, with wet-weather gear, a windproof jacket, light and heavier sweaters (which can be purchased in New

Zealand) and some medium-weight clothing, shorts, a swimsuit, sunglasses and sun screen (expensive in New Zealand), comfortable walking/hiking shoes and good socks. Men who plan to eat out at a splurge restaurant or visit nightclubs should bring an appropriate jacket, shirt, and tie. Women, bring a dress or skirt and blouse. And, of course, bring your 35mm camera with plenty of film, which costs less in the United States.

If you're taking an electric appliance, such as a hair dryer, bring a voltage transformer and a three-pin flat adapter plug with the top two pins set at an angle. New Zealand runs on 230 volts AC, though many hotels and motels provide 110-volt AC sockets.

On trans-Pacific airline flights you are limited to two checked bags per person, so if you have a lot to pack or expect to bring back bulky purchases use the largest suitcases you can find. Pack light, and take no more than two sets of anything.

Flying to New Zealand

Continental Airlines, Air New Zealand, Qantas, American, United Airlines, UTA, and French Airlines have direct service from the United States. They all offer essentially the same fares for three seasons: low season (May 1 to the end of September), US$1,200 round-trip; shoulder season (March-April), US$1,400; and high season (December through February), US$1,630. Check with each airline—and especially with your travel agent—for special promotional fares and packages. Ask specifically about rental car and accommodation packages.

Book your New Zealand flight far enough ahead to take advantage of advanced purchase excursion (APEX) fares. Without a special promotional fare, off-season APEX fares with stopover privileges in three destinations besides New Zealand (Hawaii, Fiji, Cook Islands, Tahiti, or Australia) cost about US$1,295. Ideally, to make travel time adjustments in easy stages, break your journey en route each way in Hawaii, Fiji, or Tahiti on an Apex fare with stopover privileges. Unless you plan to take advantage of stopover privileges, try to avoid a change of planes in Hawaii or a stop in Tahiti; either poses the risk of delay in the event that the connecting flight to Auckland is late.

Traveling by Car, Camper Van, or Motor Home
Looking at New Zealand on a globe or in an atlas, merely a tiny sliver in the vast South Pacific next to the far larger Australian continent, easily leads to the illusion that North and South Islands can be covered comfortably in a car in a matter of days. However, New Zealand is 1,000 miles long, with 5,700 miles of coastline. There's a good network of roads but no freeways. The 22-day itinerary is based on an *average* speed of 40 mph or less.

Rental cars rented by themselves are *very* expensive, normally costing NZ$64 to $129 (US$38-$77) per day (plus GST and NZ$12 per day insurance) with unlimited mileage (most car rental companies offer unlimited mileage); NZ$577 to $859 per week (US$343-$511); and NZ$1,964 to $2,690 per month (US$1,169-$1,600). Even when packaged with hotels/motels, in packages that require two persons traveling together, the car rental cost within the package for a subcompact shift vehicle is over NZ$84 (US$50) a day (including GST and insurance).

The three standout local exceptions, renting late-model Japanese cars, are: **Maui Rentals** (100 New North Rd., Auckland, tel. 09/793-277, or 23 Sheffield Crescent, Christchurch, tel. 03/584-159), renting an Econocar for NZ$45.50 (US$27) and standard compact at about NZ$61 with GST and insurance (about US$36), which should be rented before leaving the U.S. through Air New Zealand (if you fly with them) or through NZTP; **Percy** at NZ$76 (Auckland, Rotorua, Wellington, Picton, Christchurch, and Queenstown); and **Letz Rent A Car** (51-53 Shortland St., Auckland, tel. 09/390-145, or book in the U.S. for a lower rate at 800-445-0190/U.S. and 800-551-2012/CA) for NZ$95 per day with GST and insurance (about US$57). Be prepared to pay a security bond of NZ$275 when you pick up the car. (Under typical Comprehensive

How to Use this Book 13

Collision Damage coverage, in the event of an accident you are responsible for the first NZ$275.)

If you plan to take the **Inter-Island Ferry** from Wellington to Picton, you can drop your vehicle off in Wellington and pick up another in Picton or Christchurch, or take the vehicle with you on the ferry for NZ$91-$117. Car rental companies will book the ferry for you and pay for the ticket when you book your car. You pay them for the booking when you pick up your car. Usually booking ahead is only necessary from December 30-January 20. There is no exchange charge for the one-way car rentals and no drop-off charges.

Air New Zealand's Hot Pac and car rental companies offer car-accommodations (plus continental breakfast) combinations that give you a seven day/six night rate of NZ$753 single or NZ$447 pp, twin share, which is NZ$106 per night (US$63 single and US$76 two persons per night).

With the increasingly high cost of accommodations and meals in New Zealand, consider renting **Maui Rentals' Hi-Top Campa** (2-berth: double bed and overhead bunk) at NZ$69 to $107 depending on the season—figure NZ$100 per day (US$59) plus US$13 insurance per day and a $500 security bond returned when you turn in the motor home. The next best rate, for a larger motor home, is the Maui Campa, which accommodates four adults and one child at NZ$85 to $124 daily.

To these motor home rental costs add the overnight costs of about NZ$10 pp at motor camp caravan sites with power connections and 100 percent higher fuel costs than in economy cars. Motor homes can get over 20 miles per gallon, but there's a lot of acceleration and deceleration built into the New Zealand road system. Gas is expensive in New Zealand, about NZ$1 per liter or NZ$4 a gallon.

Traveling in a motor home still costs close to NZ$170 (US$100) per day for two or more (including fuel and motor camp stops every night), which is more than two persons should budget for a car rental, fuel, and moderately priced accommodations. But motor home touring has other advantages besides cost, which experienced caravaners already know: more flexibility in departure and arrival days and times around New Zealand; opportunities to stay over in more out-of-the way spots in the great outdoors, in the motor home, or camping out; cooking and eating more fresh Kiwi lamb chops, seafood, vegetables, and fruits while en route (note that broilers are not included in standard motor home equipment); conveniently transporting more Kiwi woolens, arts and crafts, and other gifts and souvenirs; and not having to carry your belongings into new accommodations every night or couple of nights.

Traffic keeps to the left-hand side of the road. Start out driving on uncrowded local streets, rather than main highways, to get used to left-hand drive. For the first day, pay very careful attention until left-hand drive becomes comfortable and automatic. Each morning remind yourself about left-hand drive before you start driving.

Immediately learn the "right-hand rule": always give way to traffic approaching on your right except for a car directly in front that intends to turn right. The maximum speed limit is 100 kilometers per hour (roughly 60 mph), or 50 kph (30 mph) in built-up areas. An "L.S.Z." (Limited Speed Zone) sign means no speed limit—use your good judgment.

Don't drink when driving! New Zealand laws are even tougher than those in the United States. Watch out for sheep and cows, school buses, and children. Keep your gas tank full, use chains when required, don't try to drive across flooding rivers, and have a safe and enjoyable trip.

Traveling by Coach and Train
Hiring a car or camper van is extremely helpful but not necessary for touring New Zealand using this guide.

Without a car you do have a problem following all of the 22-day schedule in this guide. Using buses and trains, you'll have a time, rather than a transportation, problem

How to Use this Book 15

going to suggested attractions and activities in and between the itinerary's main destinations. You can rent a car or camper van in certain locations (Auckland, Wellington, Picton, Christchurch, Dunedin, and Queenstown) in order to cover more ground in a shorter time or to reach a few places that are otherwise inaccessible.

The **InterCity rail, bus, and ferry network** covers most of New Zealand. InterCity's **Travelpass** must be purchased before you leave the United States, except for the 15- and 22-day low season, February-December, pass. It covers three periods of unlimited travel time in either high or low season: 8 days of travel in a 14-day period for NZ$275 (US$163), 15 days of travel in 22 days for NZ$355 (US$211), or 22 days within a 31-day period for NZ$440 (US$262). The more days you travel, the bigger the discount, from NZ$34 (US$18) per day in the 8 days to NZ$20 (US$12) per day in the 22 days. How can you beat unlimited travel for US$12 per day? These passes can be used on any **Newmans** coach and **Delta Coachline. Mt. Cook Line**'s (in the U.S., 800-468-2665) **Kiwi Coach Pass**, good on Mt. Cook Landline, which also must be purchased through your travel agent before leaving the United States, costs about the same per day: 7 days for NZ$230; 10 days for NZ$285; 15 days for NZ$380; and 25 days for NZ$545. The price of these Kiwi Coach Passes varies during January-September and October-December periods (higher).

Traveling by Air
Three major carriers—Air New Zealand, Mt. Cook Airlines, and Ansett Airlines—provide ample air services between all major cities and tourist centers. Purchase a Mt. Cook Lines (Suite 1020, 9841 Airport Blvd., Los Angeles, CA 90045, tel. 213-684-2117) **Kiwi Air Pass** before leaving the United States and you can travel in the same circular direction around New Zealand (with reservations), continuously or with unlimited stops (air and land services on Mt. Cook Coach Lines) within 30 calendar days following your first flight, for NZ$754 (US$499)

adults and NZ$630 children (US$375). These fares vary in high and low seasons and do not include Milford Sound sightseeing. Considering that in the same travel period, car rental would cost no less than US$770 plus about US$300 (2,500 miles) for gas to drive for just 22 days around New Zealand, using the Kiwi Air Pass may be a practical alternative to driving, especially if you plan the trip carefully. Call 800-468-2665.

Air New Zealand (800-262-1234) offers a **Freedom Pass** in conjunction with **Mt. Cook Air** and **Mt. Cook Coach Lines** that is very much like the Kiwi Air Pass, covering four and six "sectors" for NZ$395 (US$235) to NZ$550 (US$327). These fares vary in high and low seasons. The coupons are good for 60 days from the date of the first flight and must be purchased before leaving the United States. Air New Zealand's **Visit New Zealand Pass Fares** also provide similar sector discounts without the air/land tie-in with Mt. Cook.

When you decide what you want to see and do in New Zealand, talk to Air New Zealand's Hot Pac Desk about booking a Freedom Pass. Ask for copies of their very useful Hot Pac brochures—"go as you please" and "the good night book"—with valuable information on car, accommodations, and sightseeing packages and discounts. The Freedom Pass also has to be purchased before leaving the United States.

Ansett New Zealand also offers discount coupons for flying multiple "sectors" of New Zealand (without the coach option). The **Ansett Air Pass** (booked through **Qantas**, 800-227-4500, along with your Qantas flight or through your travel agent separately) offers discount coupons for 4, 5, 6, 7, and 8 flight sectors covering New Zealand at a cost of NZ$475 to $815. These fares are competitive with Mt. Cook Lines' Kiwi Pass and Air New Zealand's Freedom Pass but don't include a coach option. Ansett New Zealand's **Good Buy Special Fares, Good Buy 43, Saver Plus Fares**, and **See New Zealand Fares**, with discounts ranging from 30 to 55 percent, have various prepurchase and usage restrictions.

Where to Stay

The variety, number, and quality of accommodations choices in New Zealand should be a joy to every traveler. First, a brief overview of common features of many Kiwi accommodations, followed by a description of the variety of accommodations you'll find in New Zealand to suit all requirements, tastes, and price levels.

In general, expect telephones in rooms or on the premises and available for your use, washing machines and dryers or drying rooms somewhere on the premises (usually free of charge), good heating when needed, and early afternoon check-in (2:00 p.m.) and early check-out (10:00 a.m.) times. Tea and coffee are either in your room, with milk and sugar, or accessible in a public area or kitchen, at no charge. Good to excellent heating is central or in individual rooms, unless cabins, hostels, and lodges indicate otherwise, and frequently you'll have electric blankets in the room. Where crockery, linens, utensils, and other items for daily use are not included in the rate, such as in no-frills tourist flats, they are available for rent at a minimal charge.

Rooms based on per person rates usually give discount rates for children under 12: 5-12 years, half price; 2-4 years, 25 percent off; and under 2, free. These discounts apply so universally that they are not mentioned in the guide. Backpackers sometimes get special discount rates in no-frills private hostel, lodge, or motor camp accommodations.

Rates in primary tourist destinations usually go up in high season (Dec.-Mar.) or peak season (school vacations, winter at ski resorts, deep-sea fishing months along the coast, etc.). The highest rates are from mid-December through January, everywhere; Easter; and school holidays in May and August. AVOID THESE TRAVEL TIMES IF POSSIBLE! OTHERWISE BOOK AHEAD! If you arrive in Kiwiland without bookings, look to the **New Zealand Tourist and Publicity Bureau Offices (NZTP)** throughout the country for free booking advice or, for a small fee, to make your accommodations and transportation bookings.

Youth hostels are neat and no-frills, have common showers, kitchens, and laundries, TV or other lounges, bulletin boards with information on activities, and range from old houses to very modern facilities. Breakfasts and sometimes dinners are available, extra. YHA hostels shut down daily from 10:00 a.m. to 5:00 p.m., then close for curfew at 11:00 p.m. Bookings are held until 7:00 p.m. so you have two hours to check in or lose your bed unless you've paid in advance. Do so through the YHA National Reservation Centre, P.O. Box 1687, Auckland (tel. 09/794-224). Enclose a money order or bank draft and an international Reply Coupon. Rates usually don't exceed NZ$15 for seniors (over 18). Members can buy discount cards in New Zealand which offer 9 nights for NZ$99 (9/99) or 20 nights for NZ$200 (20/200)—another way to save money. YHA members also qualify for discounts on car rentals, transportation, excursions, and so on.

If you're not a YHA member, join for $10 to $25 (junior/senior rates) through **American Youth Hostels, Inc.**, P.O. Box 37613, Washington, D.C. 20013, or for NZ$20 seniors and a NZ$10 joining fee in New Zealand when you get to Auckland (Australia House, 36 Customs St. East). Pick up a copy of the invaluable *New Zealand YHA Handbook* with detailed information on each YH location.

YMCAs and YWCAs are a very attractive budget option in major cities and towns, starting at about NZ$17-$20 per person. Since many students live in them, these facilities frequently are less crowded during peak season when school is out and offer more privacy, with some private or shared rooms.

B&Bs are called guest houses or private hotels in New Zealand. Usually there's hot and cold running water (H&C). If hot running water is important to you, as it is to most travelers, always ask (H&C available?) just to be sure. Most often, bathroom and shower are shared (ask) by some rooms and private in others for a higher rate. (Do without a private bath and shower and often you can save up to 20% on the room rate.) Two kinds of breakfasts are served: continental and fully cooked. Dinners may be available on request (ask). Rates run from NZ$35 to $65 single, NZ$45 to $75 share twin/double (with and without GST).

B&Bs are hard to find. Because of space limitations, only a small fraction of New Zealand's better B&Bs are identified in this guide. For more B&B information, contact **New Zealand Home Hospitality Limited** (tel. 800-351-2323, and in California, 800-351-2317; in Nelson, tel. 054/82-424).

Stay at a traditional New Zealand **working farm** (sheep, dairy, beef, deer, goats, or horticulture) or in a country house or other nonfarm homestay, in a choice of hundreds of homes, by purchasing vouchers that include breakfasts and dinners (and lunches if you stay two nights or more) for NZ$75 per night single, NZ$62 pp twin/double, NZ$40 children under 13, NZ$27 children under 5. Reservations can be made through U.S. travel agents, Air New Zealand's Hot Pac, or contact:

Farm Holidays Ltd., P.O. Box 1436, Wellington, tel. 04/723-2126;

Farmhouse Holidays, Kitchener Rd., Milford, Auckland, tel. 09/492-171;

New Zealand Farm Holidays, Private Bag, Parnell, Auckland, tel. 09/394-780;

Farm Home and Country Home Holidays, Box 31-250, Auckland, tel. 09/492-171;

Hospitality Haere Mai, P.O. Box 56175, Auckland, tel. 09/686-737;

Home Stay/Farm Stay, P.O. Box 630, Rotorua, tel. 073/24-895, including nonfarm homes throughout the North Island;

Town and Country Home Hosting, Box 143, Cambridge, tel. 27-6511;

Rural Tours, P.O. Box 228, Cambridge, tel. 07-127;

Rural Holidays New Zealand, P.O. Box 2155, Christchurch, tel. 03/61-919;

Friendly Kiwi Home Hosting Service, P.O. Box 5049, Port Nelson, tel. 054/85-575;

N.Z. Home Hospitality, P.O. Box 309, Nelson, tel. 054/82-424 or in the U.S., 800-351-2323, also offering nonfarm homestays throughout both islands;

Hand New Zealand Travel Hosts, 279 Williams St., Kaiapoi, tel. 6340, for home hosting.

Get a copy of the *New Zealand Accommodation Guide* from the NZTP office in the United States or Auckland for a listing of individual farms and home hosts.

Motel flats/tourist flats (complete apartments) usually include two bedrooms, a living room, a fully equipped kitchen, and a bathroom with shower for NZ$35-$49 double (low-price), with a pool and spa on the premises. Medium-priced motels cost NZ$50-$69. Serviced motels—rather Spartan motel rooms—cost slightly less than tourist flats.

New Zealand's **motor camps** are really eye-openers for Americans and other foreigners. It's difficult not to become an enthusiastic fan of New Zealand's budget motor camps. Occupying large, sometimes huge sites, motor camps often are situated in the best lakeside, seaside, or mountain locations, with marvelous (normally expensive) views. The tree-filled, well-maintained grounds usually contain a remarkable assortment of inexpensive and moderately priced accommodations. Many are listed in these pages.

Two-thirds of the steps in the ladder of no-frills accommodations are represented in motor camps: campsites; caravan sites with power; on-site caravans; rustic bunkhouses and cabins of all sizes with 2 to 10 beds, including tourist cabins with H&C and kitchens; no-frills one- and two-bedroom tourist flats with separate bedrooms and kitchen facilities; and the central kitchens, bathrooms and showers, laundries, lounges, pools and spas, and other facilities. They offer plenty of opportunities for meeting and getting to know Kiwis and other travelers.

There are two types of accommodations that call themselves motels—motel flats and serviced motels.

Motel flats are fully equipped apartments with one or two bedrooms, a kitchen with everything you'd ever want to use (at home or while traveling), a bathroom with shower, TVs, radios, and telephones, a laundry room with automatic washer and dryer. Cost: an average of NZ$65 double, and usually about NZ$12 for extra adults. Stay in Best Western motel flats for your entire stay and save about NZ$6 per day (10 percent). Purchase Best Western New Zealand Accommodation Passes (Best Western International, Marketing Services, P.O. Box 10203, Phoenix, AZ 85064) and two can stay at any Best Western for NZ$56 including GST.

Serviced motels offer one sparsely furnished room and bathroom, like standard motel rooms you know, with a tea and coffee maker. If you're a AAA member, which I advise for drivers, stop by any AAA office for their *Accommodation, Camping and Breakdown Guide to the South Island, Accommodation and Camping Guide South Island, AAA North Island Outdoor Guide, New Zealand Holiday Parks Guide to N.Z. Camp Caravan and Cabin Accommodation*, and the directory of the Camp & Cabin Association.

At the other end of the budget spectrum are luxury and first-class hotels, many operated by international hotel chains, and sporting lodges that offer unique facilities and experiences for fishing and hunting enthusiasts. Book hotel reservations at the time you make international air reservations in order to obtain discount packages or discounts offered by the airlines. Superior and luxury class hotels in New Zealand are easy to locate and book through their U.S. sales centers.

The only more expensive hotels that you'll find in these pages are **Tourist Hotel Corporation (THC) of New Zealand** facilities in some of the best locations in New Zealand: Waitangi Peninsula, Tongariro National Park, Mt. Cook, Queenstown, Milford Sound, Wanaka, Franz Josef Glacier, and others. Rates range from NZ$75-$150 (plus GST), high in New Zealand but moderate in U.S. dollars considering the locations. Frequently THC hotels have special and package rates. Contact the Southern Pacific Hotel Corporation (800-421-0536), or in

New Zealand, Wellington, tel. 04/729-179, or toll-free from Auckland, tel. 09/773-689.

Where and What to Eat
The New Zealand eating experience that should not be missed is a Maori *hangi* (feast) in Rotorua, which features many steamed dishes and Maori entertainment.

Surprisingly few restaurants do justice to the quality of New Zealand meat or seafood. In or out of restaurants, the foods to look for are: roast spring lamb (especially October-January), steaks and roast beef, farm-raised venison, tasty and inexpensive meat and savory pies (egg and bacon, mincemeat), and great seafood—five varieties of blue cod, fresh plump bluff oysters in the winter and small sweet Auckland rock oysters, Marlborough scallops in spring and summer, crayfish, marinated mussels year-round, smoked and fresh salmon, John Dory, orange roughy, grouper, kingfish, flounder, snapper, and squid. Look for melons in summer, kiwi fruit in winter and spring, fresh vegetables and all kinds of berries.

Stay at a bed-and-breakfast and the quantity of good food may even carry you until dinner. Otherwise wait until tea time (after 10:00 a.m.) to snack with your tea or coffee. I recommend eating places for light lunches in each city and town (about NZ$6-$8), but look carefully at each day's schedule to see if an economical takeout picnic lunch at a park or beach wouldn't be more fun. Tourist spots are full of pubs and take-aways, and every town of any size has its Cobb & Co. with reasonable prices. Many of the best dinner spots are unpretentious BYOs (bring your own wine). Most "splurge" restaurants are licensed to serve liquor, except on Sundays, and dress-up is expected. You don't have to tip anywhere, but if the service is good, a tip is appreciated.

Information Sources
Information to supplement this book is available from the New Zealand Tourist and Publicity (NZTP) Office nearest you: Suite 1530, 10960 Wilshire Blvd., Los

Angeles, CA 90024, tel. 212-447-8241; Suite 810, 1 Sansome Street, San Francisco, CA 94104; Suite 530, 630 Fifth Avenue, New York, NY 10111, tel. 212-698-4680.

If you're planning a visit longer than 30 days, contact the consulate in the same buildings as the NZTP.

New Zealand Travel Offices, providing information and complete travel services, are located in:

Auckland, 99 Queen Street, tel. 09-798-180
Rotorua, 67 Fenton Street, tel. 073-85-179
Wellington, 25-27 Mercer Street, tel. 04-739-269
Christchurch, 65 Cathedral Square, tel. 03-794-900
Dunedin, 131 Princes Street, tel. 024-740-344
Queenstown, 49 Shotover Street, tel. 0294/28-238

Every city and larger town has a public relations office (PRO) and visitors information center. AAA members can collect maps and information for every square kilometer of New Zealand, and also book everything, at the New Zealand Automobile Association:

Auckland, tel. 09/774-660
Wellington, tel. 04/851-745
Christchurch, tel. 03/791-280
Dunedin, tel. 024/775-945

To call any of these numbers from the United States, dial the country code (64), then the area codes. When dialing within New Zealand, include the zero before the city's code.

Suggested Reading

Supplement *2 to 22 Days in New Zealand* with other travel guidebooks for background and detail. Two completely different New Zealand travel guides stand out: the photographs, historical and cultural treatment, and interesting and balanced travel narrative of Insight Guides' *New Zealand* (APA, 1990) and the detailed information in Jane King's *New Zealand Handbook* (Moon Publications, 1990), in a class by itself for thoroughness. Both books include extensive and balanced reading lists. Travelers watching their budgets especially owe Ms. King a debt of gratitude. Her book's detail and travel options even surpass those in Tony Wheeler's excellent *New Zealand: A Travel Survival Kit* (Lonely Planet, 1990).

For hikers and walkers, Jim Du Fresne's *Tramping in New Zealand* (Lonely Planet, 1989) is indispensable for trip planning, background information, and handy maps. The best (and only) cycling guide that covers North and South Islands is Bruce Ringer's *Cycle Touring in New Zealand* (The Mountaineers, Seattle, 1989).

Susan Poole's *Frommer's New Zealand on $45 a Day* (Simon & Schuster, 1990) is also a bargain. *Fodor's New Zealand 1987* covers only tourist highlights in a super-condensed text. Sunset's *New Zealand Travel Guide* (Lane Publications, 1990) is well organized and readable, with a good collection of maps and photos.

The NZTP is your best source for information on fishing, sailing, jet boating, rafting, skiing, and horseback riding. For information on New Zealand's more than 400 golf courses, contact the New Zealand Golf Association, P.O. Box 11842, Wellington. For a listing of public tennis courts, contact the New Zealand Lawn Tennis Association, P.O. Box 11541, Wellington. The New Zealand Boardsailing Association, P.O. Box 37213, Parnell, Auckland has everything you want to know about windsurfing and the New Zealand Surfriders Association, P.O. Box 737, New Plymouth, covers surfing information. With over 1,000 canoeable rivers and lakes, you'll want suggestions from the New Zealand Canoeing Association, P.O. Box 5125, Auckland. North Island diving locations are plentiful; contact the New Zealand Underwater Association, P. O. Box 875, Auckland. Hikers can get excellent information and maps of the 10 national parks and 21 forest parks from the New Zealand Forest Service, Private Bag, Wellington. Before climbing any of the 30 peaks in New Zealand over 9,000 feet, contact the New Zealand Mountain Guides Association, P.O. Box 20, Mt. Cook. For information on bird-watching tours, contact either the World Wildlife Fund, 22 Brandon St., Wellington, or the Royal Forest and Bird Protection Society of New Zealand, 26 Brandon Street, Wellington.

How to Use this Book

Claire Jones's *New Zealand's Bay of Islands: The Land and Sea Guide*, published by Roger and Evelyn Miles (owners of Rainbow Charters, Opua), provides detailed touring information, business telephone numbers, nautical charts, and superb photos of the Bay of Islands. It is only available in New Zealand.

Flora and Fauna

When New Zealand broke away from Australia and Antarctica, about 70 million years ago, its geographic isolation ensured a unique assortment of animals and plant life not found elsewhere. Dense forests with 112 native tree species and thick undergrowth supported 250 species of native birds, many flightless, which grazing animals and predators introduced by settlers reduced dramatically. Many of the species released by European settlers, such as cats, weasels, deer, opossums, pigs, and hares, live in Urewera National Park, the North Island's largest forest.

The most famous survivor is the flightless, nocturnal kiwi, New Zealand's national emblem, named after its piercing whistle, "keee-weee." You're more likely to hear than see the kiwi in the bush, especially in the night, so look for it in nocturnal houses such as at Auckland's zoo. The kiwi is only one of several remaining flightless birds, including the kakapu, kea, waka, and the very rare blue and iridescent green takahe, thought to be extinct until a colony was rediscovered in South Fiordland. All of these birds live in Fiordland, along with the rare southern crested grebe and the Fiordland crested penguin.

At lower elevations, you'll find New Zealand's version of pampas grass, toe toe, along with rimu, northern rate and tawa forest, fading to beech, totara, and tawari above 2,600 feet. This vegetation shelters three species of parrot—kaka, morepork, and red-crowned and yellow-crowned parakeet—and the white-breasted kereru, New Zealand's only native pigeon, easily sighted here or in Tongariro National Park because it makes a loud flapping noise when it flies.

The kaka is a very shy brown and green parrot, quite unlike the personality of the daring kea, a flightless parrot which lives mainly in the Southern Alps. The scavenging kea will tear anything in your campsite or on your car that it can get its hooked beak into. Equally bold but not as common, the flightless weka may be seen trashing campsites on the west coast of the South Island and on the east coast of the North Island, around Ginsborne.

In each of the mountain areas you'll visit on the North and South Islands, variations in climate (wet side and dry side) and altitude produce distinctive vegetation zones. In Tongariro National Park (Day 9), Urewera National Park, and Egmont National Park on the North Island, and the Southern Alps from Arthur's Pass National Park to Fiordland National Park, a green canopy of broadleaf rain forests, with thick undergrowth, passes through several different forest zones to shrub, tussock, and alpine herb zones, sprinkled with buttercups and daisies, until only lichen can survive below permanent snowlines.

From north to south there are many different birds, but always they are abundant. Native songbirds, like the tui and bellbird, can be heard below the 3,000-foot level in Tongariro's rain forests, their rapturous songs managing to crest above the noisy cicadas, except at the deafening summer crescendo. Watch for the blue duck, an endangered species, near streams flowing swiftly through the broadleafs, small and huge fern trees (up to 30 feet high), vines, and other exotic greenery. In Westland National Park (Day 20), tuis and bellbirds are joined by fantails, tomtits, oyster-catchers, terns, godwits, and white herons breeding in coastal wetlands from October to February.

In Fiordland National Park and Mt. Aspiring National Park, bird-watchers can look for banded dotterels, black-billed gulls, black-fronted terns, yellow hammers, shining cuckoos, yellow heads, song thrushes, and dozens of others.

There are more than 150 species of ferns in New Zealand, growing everywhere together with mostly white or cream colored flowers, including 60 species of orchids. Stewart Island alone has 30 species and a wealth of other native plants and rare birds.

About 500 species of alpine flowers are found only in New Zealand. Above the 3,000-foot level, the tiny green rifleman and silver eye inhabit the beeches, safely below the subalpine tussock shrublands that are minutely searched for small birds and animals by native falcons. In December and January, birds of Tongariro's tussockland fly over vast acreage of alpine flora blooming white with touches of purple or mauve orchids. In December you'll see the pohutukawa (New Zealand Christmas Tree) bloom, and in spring the parasitic rata's red blossoms and the bright yellow kowhai blossoms. Aging gnarled pohutukawas form the backdrop of Auckland's sandy bays tucked between headlands on the eastern shoreline.

New Zealand's native kauri is a conifer, botanically in the pine and fir family of less magnificent trees found in Australia, Malaysia, and Pacific Islands. The kauri's lower branches and bark shed leaving a massive crown of leathery leaves as high as 150 feet above the large mound of humus covering its root system. Settlers and shipbuilders depleted most kauri forests of these giants that require about 800 years to mature. However, surviving and now protected kauri groves still can be seen west of Auckland in the Waitakera Ranges (Day 3), around Russell (Day 5) and west of Kerikeri (Day 6), north of Dargaville (Day 6) and on the Coromandel Peninsula (Day 7).

No discussion of New Zealand flora and fauna would be complete without mentioning the islands' most common mammals—sheep. More than 70 million sheep dot the countryside, about 20 sheep for every New Zealander. New Zealand is the third largest producer and the second largest exporter of wool in the world. Sheep are raised for wool in the hill country, with lamb and mutton production in the low country. From 1850 to 1880, while Maori tribes and the government on the North Island were at war over land, huge tracts of the South Island's tussockland were rapidly being occupied by Australian merino sheep farmers. Sheep scab disease, a plague of rabbits, and the discovery of gold in the 1860s slowed expansion of sheep grazing. But the introduction of refrigeration and refrigerated cargo ships in the early 1880s spurred lamb raising for overseas meat consumers.

At the Agrodome in Rotorua, the sheep station in Queenstown, and other locations, sheepherders put talented sheepdogs through their paces with vocal and whistled commands. And professional sheep shearers show how shearing is done.

New Zealand's Volcanic Legacy
Volcanoes dominate the Auckland-Coromandel Peninsula landscape from air, sea, and land. Symmetrical Rangitoto Island, guarding the entrance to Auckland's Waitemata Harbour, erupted a mere 200 years ago. Auckland itself is situated on a plateau marked by 60 volcanic cones around which early Maori settlements clustered for defense. The volcanic ramparts of the Waitakeres rise to the west, descending to black sandy beaches on the western shores pounded by Tasman Sea breakers. Today these are parks and reserves, among the best view points. The Coromandel Ranges are volcanic stumps rising steeply east of the Firth of Thames. Volcanic remnants still exist, and on Day 6 you'll dig hot water pools around Hot Water Beach.

Polynesian voyagers from "Hawaiki" landed their canoe, *Te Awara*, at Maketu (south of what is today Tauranga—Day 7) on the Bay of Plenty in the middle of the fourteenth century. According to legend, Ngatoroirangi traveled south to Tongariro and, when close to freezing to death in a snowstorm, called on his sisters in Hawaiki to bring warmth. His route south is marked by geothermal activity, from the active volcano Whakaari (White Island) through the geysers, steaming cliffs, bubbling pools of mud, and hot springs spurting from the ground around Rotorua and Lake Taupo, to the active volcanoes of Tongariro National Park. The Maori had been using the healing properties of local mineral hot pools, the "healing springs," five hundred years before tourists were first drawn to Rotorua's thermal wonders, especially

How to Use this Book

the Pink and White Terraces of Lake Rotomahana, produced by hydrothermal changes in the pumice and destroyed by the eruption of Tarawera in 1886.

Maori Art, Crafts, and Settlements

The earliest history of New Zealand is linked to ancestors of the Maoris from eastern Polynesia. Maori mythology has Kupe discovering Aotearoa about A.D. 950, followed about four hundred years later by the armada of canoes to which Maori tribes trace their genealogies. Archaeological remains suggest that as early as A.D. 1000, Maori hunters of huge, now-extinct flightless birds (moa) roamed the coastal South Island. The giant moa offered plentiful food, and forests yielded huge trees (kauri) for carving dugout canoes and construction of dwellings. Later as the moas became rare, tribal and subtribal groups settled in villages.

Pas were fortified settlements built by a large family or part of a tribe which housed the local chief and his war band and also served as a dwelling place, a food storage facility, a center for craftsmen, and a refuge against attack. Located on a defensible high point, coastal headland, or edge of a swamp, the pa and its surroundings were fortified with earthworks, scarping on the sides and ditches, with living quarters on artificial terraces. Pas were built and used from the late fifteenth or early sixteenth century to the early 1800s. They can be seen in the Bay of Islands, Kerikeri, Russell, the Auckland isthmus, the Bay of Plenty, Waikato, and Taranaki (southwest) and Hawke's Bay (southeast) on the North Island.

In the years that followed European settlement, the Maski opened a period of constructing communal meeting houses (*whare whakairo*) for social purposes and to discuss many problems: fighting with settlers, British, and other tribes; land disputes; disease; guns. These meeting houses are highly ornamented displays of Maori wood-carving skills. See, for example, the Tama-te Kapua at Ohinemutu, in Rotorua; Poho-o Rawiri, the largest meeting house in New Zealand, near Gisbourne; Te Hauki

Turanga in the National Museum (originally built in Poverty Bay); Hotunui in the Auckland Museum; and the Waitangi Treaty House on the Waitangi Peninsula.

The greenstone rocks that you can see in Auckland and Hokitika factories on the South Island's west coast are only found in New Zealand in the Arahura and Taramakau riverbeds flowing from the Southern Alps to the Tasman Sea. Greenstone was so revered by Maori tribes for tools, ornaments, and weapons that they trekked over the Alps to the west coast to collect it and fought wars for it.

When Captain Cook arrived in Northland in 1769, Maori culture and arts were at their peak. No tour of New Zealand would be complete without seeing some examples of traditional Maori art and crafts from this classic period, housed primarily in North Island museums. In the last hundred years, much of the native genius infusing the most marvelous artistic aspect of Maori culture has suffered inevitable attrition in the process of conflict with and assimilation by *pakehas* (Europeans). However, the Maori's unique visual arts legacy still lives on, fostered by intensifying Maori and national efforts to sustain and revive the traditions.

Maori culture and artistic accomplishments are most visible on the North Island and in Rotorua, supplemented by exhibits at national and regional museums and meeting house sites.

ITINERARY

DAY 1 Arrive in Auckland in the morning, get set up in your accommodations, then relax and enjoy a leisurely visit to Queen Street, the spine of downtown, and side streets climbing the hillsides. Have a snack lunch at the waterfront, then visit the Auckland Visitor's Bureau, the NZ Government Tourist Bureau, or AA New Zealand for information, brochures, maps, and reservations as needed for North and South Island accommodations, transportation, and excursions. After dinner, call it quits early to beat jet lag.

DAY 2 Downtown Auckland's attractions can be seen in a full morning. Start with city views from either One Tree Hill or Mt. Eden. If you feel energetic and the weather is pleasant, walk along portions of the Coast-to-Coast Walkway from Waitemata Harbour to Manakau Harbour. Visit the Parnell District for lunch, followed by a walking tour among its Edwardian and Victorian houses. Afterward head down to the harbor for a cruise in the Hauraki Gulf Maritime Park. Briefly visit the Old Auckland Customhouse before taking a 20-minute ride on the Devonport Ferry to the North Shore for sunset views from North Head or Mt. Victoria, followed by dinner in Devonport. Return to downtown Auckland on the ferry.

DAY 3 Take the Waitakere Range Scenic Drive, west of Auckland, to Pahi's black sand beach along the Tasman Sea. For lunch and wine tasting, visit Henderson Valley vineyards in the western suburbs. Then drive east to the North Shore's beaches and bays en route to the Waiwera hot mineral pools, 30 miles north of Auckland. After a relaxing dip, head back to Auckland for dinner.

DAY 4 Leave early for the Bay of Islands and make scenic side trips on the way north. Head for the car ferry to Russell at Opua. Indulge in a delicious local seafood dinner. In the evening, enjoy a few hours at the Duke of Marlborough Pub, relaxing and listening to big-game-fishing conversation. Stay overnight in Russell.

DAY 5 After a leisurely breakfast in Russell, take an all-morning Cream Trip cruise to the outer limits of the Bay of Islands, including a picnic lunch. In the afternoon, head for Kerikeri via Paihia, historic Waitangi, and beautiful Haruru Falls. Sightsee before dinner at the Stone Store Restaurant. Stay overnight in Kerikeri.

DAY 6 Today will be a long day of driving and sightseeing. Check out early and head to the west coast to see the Waipoua Kauri Sanctuary's huge and ancient kauri trees. Further south, on the way back to Auckland, stop at Dargaville's Northern Wairoa Museum and the outstanding Otamatea Kauri and Pioneer Museum in Matakoke. Drive 75 miles southeast of Auckland to Thames on the Coromandel Peninsula. Check in and enjoy a late but leisurely dinner at the Brian Boru hotel.

DAY 7 From Thames, head north along the rugged coast for breakfast overlooking the harbor in Coromandel. Afterward you have a choice of heading east on unpaved Highway 309 through stunning mountain scenery across the peninsula or heading north to view the breathtaking coastal scenery from Colville to Fletcher Bay. Stop to dig your own thermal hot pools and have a picnic lunch. After lunch move on to Whitianga, renowned for big game fishing, diving, and underwater photography, and then to even more spectacular coastline from Mercury Bay to Waihi Beach. From Waihi Beach, follow the Bay of Plenty through Tauranga and Mount Maunganui. Then turn inland from the Bay of Plenty's beaches to Rotorua.

DAY 8 In Rotorua explore an incredible assortment of geysers, hot springs, steaming cliffs, and boiling mud pools. In beautiful forest parks, visit trout pools fed by enormous quantities of spring water. Learn about Maori culture, arts, and crafts and enjoy a Maori hangi feast and entertainment.

DAY 9 Leave early in the morning for a drive to Aratiatia Rapids and Huka Falls on the Waikato River and a visit to the geothermal power project to the south, all on the way to Taupo. After lunch in Taupo, drive to Turangi to fish or just watch trout from behind glass in a trout hatchery.

Itinerary

Then drive along Tongariro National Park to Ohakune and up the slopes of Mt. Ruapehu. Afterward, continue driving to Wanganui, one of the most picturesque cities in New Zealand, aptly called the "Garden City."

DAY 10 Sightsee in Wanganui, then have a picnic lunch in beautiful Virginia Lake Park. After lunch take a paddle wheeler trip to Holly Lodge East Winery and from there a jet boat ride to Hipango Park. After returning to Wanganui, drive south past a string of scenic beach settlements along the Tasman Sea to New Zealand's capital city of Wellington.

DAY 11 Set in a green amphitheater on a sparkling harbor, Wellington is at its best viewed from the heights of Mount Victoria or from 24-mile Marine Drive and Miramar Peninsula, stopping along the way for a picnic lunch. Spend the afternoon touring downtown Wellington. In the late afternoon, take the cable car up to Kelburn terminal for a stroll through the Botanic Gardens followed by dinner in one of Wellington's excellent restaurants.

DAY 12 Sail early on the Inter-Island Ferry (with breakfast on board) across Cook Strait from Wellington to Picton at the head of Queen Charlotte Sound in Marlborough Sound. The trip to Christchurch takes five to six hours. Dinner in this English city setting is followed by a stroll along the beautiful Avon River.

DAY 13 Tour the inner city and outskirts of Christchurch. Perhaps rent a canoe and follow the Avon for a tour of local architecture, stopping for a riverside picnic lunch. In the afternoon, make a round-trip on the scenic North and South Summit Road to Lyttelton Harbour. Have dinner on Summit Road or return to your hotel to get ready for dinner and an evening of entertainment at the Christchurch Arts Centre.

DAY 14 This morning travel south across sheep-covered plains from Christchurch through Fairlie and Burke's Pass, past the blue-green and turquoise glacial Lakes Tekapo and Pukaki to Mt. Cook National Park. Trampers, climbers, rafters, and skiers will find a feast of activities. After lunch, if at all possible, take a ski-plane flightseeing trip to the Tasman Glacier. On returning, drive through the tussock-covered expanses of the Mackenzie Basin, with a brief stop at Lake Oahu. Follow the Southern Alps over Lindis Pass to Queenstown, gateway to the wonders of Fiordland.

DAY 15 After breakfast and booking excursions in the Queenstown center, start the day with a leisurely cruise on beautiful Lake Wakatipu on the coal-burning *T.S.S. Earnslaw*. A trip to Queenstown would not be complete without a jetboat or white-water rafting trip on one of Otago's gold-bearing rivers. After lunch in Arrowtown, a pretty relic of the gold mining era, take a horse trek to Moke Lake or spend an exciting afternoon traveling by four-wheel vehicle up Skippers Canyon above the Shotover River. In the evening, take the gondola ride from the town center up to Bob's Peak for dinner and spectacular views.

DAY 16 With an early start from Queenstown, head for Te Anau and Lake Manapouri. The first stop in Te Anau is the Fiordland National Park Headquarters. After a picnic lunch in one of Lake Te Anau's most picturesque inlets, visit Te Anau Caves' glowworm caves, or take a launch tour of the West Arm followed by a bus or floatplane trip to Doubtful Sound for a two-hour launch cruise. In the evening have a relaxing dinner in Te Anau or the vicinity.

DAY 17 Rudyard Kipling aptly described Milford Sound as "the eighth wonder of the world." It is three memorable hours from Te Anau to Milford through Eglinton and Hollyford valleys and the Homer Tunnel, culminating in a magnificent one- or two-hour Milford Sound launch cruise with views of Mitre Peak and Sutherland Falls. If possible, stay overnight at the THC Milford Sound Hotel. Finish the day with dinner in Te Anau or have a camper's meal along one of the tracks.

DAY 18 Backtrack to Queenstown and, in good weather, drive up the unpaved road to the top of the Crown Range, then through Cardrona Valley in time for lunch in Wanaka. Climb up Mt. Iron for the view. There's still time for superb trout or salmon fishing in Lakes Wanaka or Hawea, kayaking on the Motatapu River, horse-trekking or, in winter, afternoon skiing on Cardrona. The Wanaka waterfront and nearby Glendhu Bay are great places for after-dinner sunset strolls.

DAY 19 Leave Wanaka very early for a full day's drive down Makarora Valley, over Haast Pass and then to the National Park Centre at Fox Glacier in South Westland. Move on to Franz Josef Glacier for dinner and overnight.

DAY 20 Have a hearty breakfast and leave by minibus for the 2½-hour Franz Josef Glacier Valley Walk. Later, on the way up the narrow Westland coastal strip to Hokitika, visit Lake Matheson, Lake Kaniere Reserve or some of the other beautiful small lakes en route. Spend the afternoon in the Hokitika area visiting relics of the gold mining era, factories cutting greenstone (the Maori sacred gemstone), and several superb viewpoints, before driving to Greymouth for the night.

DAY 21 Visit Shantytown's reconstruction of an 1860's gold mining town near Greymouth. Then drive on to Highway 73, Arthur's Pass Road, the most spectacular of the South Island's alpine crossings, passing through Arthur's Pass National Park. Plan for a lunch stop near Arthur's Pass Village, scenic walks on several inspiring trails, and perhaps a last trout fishing excursion at Pearson Lake. Descend to Christchurch to check in and prepare for dinner in Christchurch.

DAY 22 In the morning head for Banks Peninsula, with beautiful coastal stretches dotted with sleepy towns. Enjoy lunch and sightseeing in Akaroa. On the way back to Christchurch in the afternoon, stop at Okains Bay and several other villages on the peninsula. Celebrate the conclusion of the trip this evening with a deluxe dinner at Grimsby's near Christchurch.

DAY 1
ARRIVE IN AUCKLAND

Welcome to New Zealand! Ease into the comfortable Kiwi life-style and pace. Spend the day in Auckland settling into your hotel and getting acquainted with the central city, Parnell, and the harborfront. While you're on Queen Street, stop at the New Zealand Tourist and Publicity travel office (NZTP) to book future accommodations, transportation, sightseeing and other tours in the Auckland region and elsewhere in New Zealand, and gather information and maps for the rest of your trip.

Suggested Schedule

Arrive at Auckland International Airport. Take a bus or taxi downtown or directly to your accommodations and check in.

Enjoy a relaxing breakfast or lunch in Parnell before exploring the city.

Book future accommodations, transportation, and excursions at the NZTP office.

Ease into Auckland's nightlife with the expectation of an early start the next morning.

Auckland Orientation

Auckland straddles a narrow isthmus between two harbors, Manakau on the west and Waitemata on the east merging into Hauraki Gulf. The Harbour Bridge across Waitemata Harbour links the city with the rapidly growing North Shore. Over a quarter of New Zealand's population (850,000) lives in Auckland, mostly in single-story houses, an urbanized network of villages sprawling over a hilly region of volcanoes. A large Maori community and immigrants from Europe, Asia, and the Pacific Islands give Auckland a cosmopolitan flavor. With over 70,000 Polynesians, Auckland is the world's largest Polynesian center. Niueans and Cook Islanders, Samoans and Tongans add interest and vitality to city life.

See the city tomorrow from several vantage points: the twin cones of Mt. Victoria and North Head across the Waitemata Harbour; One Tree Hill and Mt. Eden, part of a Coast-to-Coast Walkway from Waitemata Harbour to Manakau Harbour; and the Waitakere Scenic Drive west of the city. Discover Auckland's beautiful parks, especially Victorian Albert Park in the city center and Cornwall Park, with sheep and cattle grazing on its slopes, which merges with One Tree Hill.

Lower Queen Street is downtown Auckland's main street. From the Ferry Terminal on wide and busy Quay Street, Queen Street is filled with shops, arcades, and offices. The street has little charm but plenty of choices. From the Ferry Terminal, catch the ferry to Devonport on the North Shore or, from nearby wharves, launch trips to Hauraki Gulf Island. Queen Elizabeth Square at the bottom of Queen Street contains the central post office, downtown complex (more stores and the city's duty-free shop) and offices.

Browse in craft shops, antique stores, art galleries, and boutiques in the suburbs of Parnell along Parnell Road, with its renovated Victorian and Edwardian buildings, as well as in Remuera, Ponsonby, Victoria Park Market's food and craft market, and colorful Karangahape Road, opposite Grafton Bridge, where many Pacific Islanders shop.

If you arrive on Saturday, Auckland's downtown is best seen before noon, when many shops, cafes, and restaurants close. If you arrive on Sunday, take the day off like everyone else. Depending on the weather, join the droves heading for beaches and the ocean. Otherwise, get lost in the fabulous War Memorial Museum.

From Airport to Accommodations
Auckland International Airport lies 13 miles south of the city. The terminal contains the Travellers' Information Centre (tel. 275-7467), which is open Monday to Sunday,

Auckland

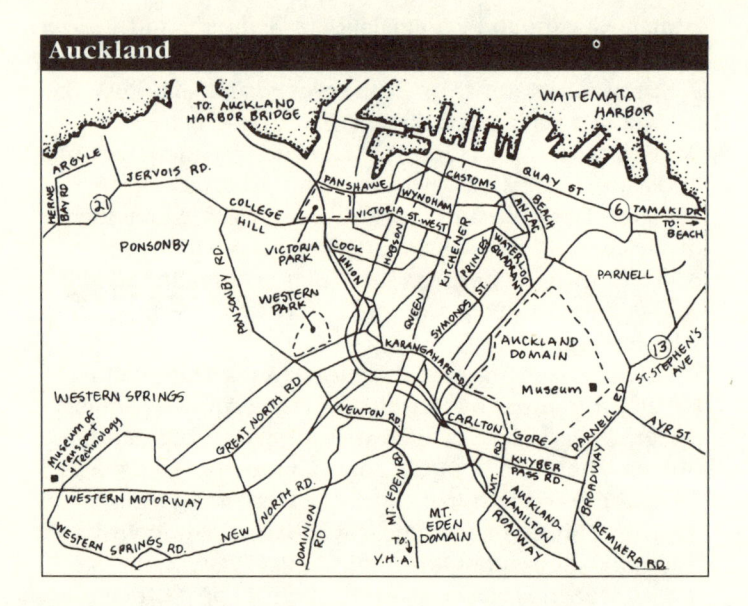

6:30 a.m. to 11:00 p.m., a bank, a post office, a rental car desk, and even a rental shower. Between 6:00 a.m. and 9:00 p.m., coaches leave regularly for the Downtown Airline Terminal at the corner of Quay and Albert streets. The fare is NZ$12. On request, the driver will drop you off at city hotels on the direct bus route. Taxi fares to downtown are about NZ$30 on weekdays and slightly higher on weekends. Touristop Tourist Services Ltd. in the Downtown Airline Terminal is open all week from 8:30 a.m. to 4:30 p.m. (tel. 775-783). Deplaning in Auckland on the weekend without a room reservation can be a problem. The Travellers' Information Centre at the airport will book accommodations, or, when you arrive in downtown Auckland, turn immediately to the New Zealand Government Tourist Bureau (NZGTB), 99 Queen Street (tel. 798-180), for booking assistance (8:30 a.m. to 5:00 p.m. weekdays and 9:30 a.m. to noon on Saturdays). NZGTB has a NZ$2 booking fee. The Automobile Association, 33 Wyndham Street (tel. 774-660), can be just as helpful if you bring your U.S. AAA membership card. The

Auckland Youth Hostel (YH) office, open from 8:30 a.m. to 4:30 p.m., is in Australis House, 36 Customs Street East (794-224), very close to the Bus Terminal.

In addition to the NZGTB, the Auckland Visitors' Bureau, 299 Queen Street at Aotea Square, has all the maps, information, and guidebooks you could possibly need for the next few days, including brochures on Auckland's latticework of signposted walkways, parks, reserves, botanic gardens, and dozens of gulf islands.

City Transportation

A car is convenient but not essential to see Auckland. You don't have to rent a car until Day 3. Buses of the Auckland Regional Authority (ARA) and suburban companies run frequently to most in-town and outlying locations from the Downtown Bus Centre (tel. 797-119 between 6:00 a.m. and 11:00 p.m. for information) on Commerce Street behind the main post office and other downtown locations. In addition to the main ARA terminal, there are four suburban centers: in New Lynn, Onehunga, Panmure, and Otahuhu. Timetables and tickets can be obtained from kiosks at these locations or The Bus Place (131 Hobson St., Mon.-Fri., 8:15 a.m. to 4:30 p.m.). Call Buz-a-Bus (tel. 797-119 between 6:00 a.m. and 11:00 p.m. weekdays), tell them where you want to go, and they'll provide timetable information.

Ask about 10-trip tickets and family passes for about NZ$5. Busabout Day Pass, which can be bought from a bus driver, costs NZ$4.30 adults, NZ$2 children (or, for two days, NZ$7 adults, NZ$3.60 children) for unlimited ARA bus travel after 9:00 a.m. on weekdays and anytime on weekends and holidays.

For cycle touring, stop by the Visitors Bureau and pick up a bike route map covering about 30 miles around Auckland. Most bike shops around town rent bicycles. On weekends bike rentals are available at The Domain, along the waterfront and in Devonport on the North Shore.

Where to Shop

Parnell's upmarket shopping in one of Auckland's oldest districts benefits from imaginative restoration creating boutiques for fashions, pottery, glassware, jewelry, antiques, various craft items, along with a variety of good quality restaurants and pleasant shops for snacks and refreshments. On and near Parnell Road are historic church buildings, St. Stephen's and St. Mary's, and some fine old nineteenth-century buildings that are open to the public. From November to March, see the lovely rose gardens in nearby Sir Dove-Meyer Robinson Park.

Ponsonby's exclusive boutiques stand side-by-side with shops catering to the daily needs of local Polynesians. On Karangahape Road (called "K Road" by local residents) many shops are stocked with Polynesian foods. On Sunday at noon there's a popular market at the corner of K Road and Ponsonby Road. While in the Ponsonby District for shopping or dining, visit Renall Street which has about 20 preserved nineteenth-century cottages, privately owned and not open to the public but worth seeing from the outside.

Visit the Otara Shopping Centre car park on Saturday morning for more Polynesian shopping activity.

Cook Street and Victoria Park are busy and entertaining bazaar-style markets. The Cook Street Market is in Aotea Square on Friday from 9:00 a.m. to 8:00 p.m., Saturday from 10:00 a.m. to 4:00 p.m. and Sunday from 10:00 a.m. to 3:00 p.m. Victoria Park Market, Victoria Street West, from 9:00 a.m. to 7:00 p.m. seven days a week, gathers weavers, potters, leather workers, and other crafts people in the midst of a fruit and vegetable market.

Where to Stay

Hostels and YMCA: Close to Parnell Village, **Parnell Hostel** (2 Churton St., Parnell, Auckland, tel. 09/790-258) has very comfortable rooms (even with a harbor view), communal bathrooms, delightfully colorful decor and dining area, lots of New Zealand travel literature and videos, and pleasant outdoor seating in a large yard/garden. Rates are NZ$14 per night for adults and half for juniors (incl. GST).

Take the Three Kings city bus a few miles south of the city's center to the **Mt. Eden Youth Hostel** (5A Oakland Rd., off Mount Eden, tel. 09/603-975). Seniors pay NZ$13, juniors half (incl. GST) for one of 46 beds in nine rooms.

Book ahead at these hostels during busy December to March months.

At the corner of Pitt Street and Greys Avenue, the five-story **Auckland YMCA** (tel. 09/303-2068) provides both men and women (separate floors, no couples, and over age 17) with spartan luxury within a long walk from downtown. Small carpeted single or shared rooms are furnished with desks and reading lamps. Each floor has a laundry and shower. On-premises parking is handy. NZ$30 per person the first night, then NZ$22 per night thereafter; rates include breakfast and dinner. Office hours are 8:00 a.m. to 9:00 p.m. Monday through Friday, 9:00 a.m. to 9:00 p.m. weekends.

Bed & Breakfasts: Ascot Parnell (36 St. Stephens Ave., Parnell, Auckland 1, tel. 09/399-012) has lost none of its charm and casual elegance. Conveniently located near Parnell Village, so energetic walkers can make it to the city center and take the bus back. Off-street parking is provided. Spacious guest rooms in the beautifully restored and maintained 1910 house all have private baths (and direct-dial phones). Singles at NZ$58 and doubles at NZ$79, each additional adult NZ$19 (plus GST), include a cooked or continental breakfast. Children under 12 NZ$10. Book well in advance of your trip.

Just a short walk from Queen Street in downtown, the friendly **Aspen Lodge** (62 Emily Pl., Auckland, tel. 09/796-698) is a little hotel with 26 small, clean rooms, NZ$40 single and NZ$55 double (incl. GST). Bathrooms are shared; there are no kitchens, but help-yourself all-you-can-eat-breakfasts are excellent. Airport buses stop at the door; buses and trains are nearby.

More than half of Day 2 is spent on the North Shore (over the Harbour Bridge or by a delightful ferry ride). Consider making the North Shore your base in Auckland, within easy walking distance from Devonport's shops and restaurants, North Head, Mt. Victoria, waterfront parade and Cheltenham Beach, at Jackie Cozby's pink Victorian **Devonport Manor** (7 Cambridge Terrace, Devonport, Auckland, tel. 09/452-529). Joggers will appreciate the park across the street. The four bright, cheerful guest rooms each have a queen-size bed and share a bath at NZ$55-$75 (incl. GST) per person. The higher rates are worth it. Jackie's breakfasts also are unsurpassed among Auckland's B&Bs. Spoil yourself in the Cambridge Suite, with a fireplace and private bath, for NZ$88-$100 per person (incl. GST).

Budget Hotels: Centrally located **Smart Budget Hotel** (City Road and Liverpool Street, off Queen St., P.O. Box 68-441, Auckland, tel. 09/392-801) offers attractive, no-frills, small rooms, with separate male and female bathrooms on each floor, for NZ$50 single, NZ$80 double (plus GST), without breakfast. If you want a private bathroom, check out the centrally located **Park Towers Hotel** (3 Scotia Pl., Auckland, tel. 09/392-800), and pay at least NZ$20 more per night. Both hotels (under the same ownership) have decent restaurants.

Motel Flats: The original and newer Executive Block of the **The Barrycourt Motor Inn** (a Best Western, 10-20 Gladstone Rd., off St. Stephens Avenue, tel. 09/33789) has everything you want, from kitchens to phones and color TVs, spa pools, a swimming pool, even a tanning salon. One- and two-bedroom units cost from NZ$75 to $160. The Portland Road bus stops in front so you don't need a car. The very good Gladstone's restaurant is on the premises (see Where to Eat, below).

Just a short walk from Mt. Eden, leave your car parked at the **Mt. Eden Motel** (47 Balmoral Rd., Mount Eden, Auckland 3, tel. 09/687-187), and take the nearby bus into and around town for your first two days. One- and two-bedroom units, with full kitchens and private bathrooms (color TVs and telephones), are NZ$70 single and NZ$84 double, NZ$12 per additional person (plus GST). This 26-unit motel has an outdoor pool, indoor jacuzzi, two saunas, and guest laundry. Robyn and Jim Baker will gladly answer any questions about touring Auckland and New Zealand.

Where to Eat
Auckland's restaurants are underrated and getting better. The only negative dining news is the GST of 12.5 percent added to your bill. Auckland's restaurants compare favorably to Wellington for variety and quality in all price ranges. Concentrations across price and quality are found in the Parnell and Ponsonby roads areas, the latter tending to be more expensive. Pick up a free Auckland Dining Guide at hotels or the NZTP office.

Victoria Park Market, on Victoria Street across from Victoria Park, has pies, hot dogs, pastas, salads, and a variety of other standard and ethnic foods for hungry budget travelers. At **Rick's Cafe American** (tel. 399-074) in the market you can count on the potato skins and spare ribs served in Bogart decor. For comparable variety and inexpensive food, the **Plaza Arcade** at 128 Queen Street has 12 international food shops spanning cuisine from Bali to Britain. The Mexican food favorite in Auckland now is **The Hard to Find Cafe** (47 High Street, tel. 734-681); BYO and NZ$10-$14 depending on your appetite for the best in town. After the long climb up Mt. Eden—or even if you drive—try a bowl of **Chez Daniel**'s onion soup at 597 Mt. Eden Road, tel. 689-676. Nearby **La Bella Napoli** (401 Mt. Eden Road), just a half block from the Youth Hostel, continues to satisfy the appetite and pocketbook of YH residents.

Inside and outside, the attractively decorated and inexpensive **La Trattoria** (259 Parnell Road, tel. 795-358) is perfect for homemade pasta and other Italian dishes.

The ten-course buffet lunch for NZ$14, 12:00 noon to 2:30 p.m. weekdays, at the **New Orient Restaurant** (Strand Arcade, tel. 797-793) is delicious and less expensive than meals in other Chinese restaurants. Avoid disappointment with seafood fare by heading for the **Union Fish Company**'s old brick warehouse (16 Quay Street, tel. 796-745), replete with maritime decor. You can fit the meal to your pocketbook there, but an even better seafood value is the tiny **Harborside Seafood Bar and Grill**, Ferry Building, Quay Street, tel. 732-770.

Ponsonby Road is the hands-down winner as the street with the greatest number and variety of excellent restaurants—mostly expensive. Jervois Road and Herne Bay, in Upper Ponsonby, add to Ponsonby's culinary clout. The epicurean safari on Ponsonby Road follows ascending street numbers. Take your choice. How could you leave New Zealand without at least one first-rate game dish with the right wine? **Colin Brown's Gamekeeper**, 29 Ponsonby Road, tel. 789-052 is one of the best choices. Try stuffed calamari at **Franco's One on the Side**, 42A Ponsonby Road, tel. 790-471; a loin of lamb dinner outside on a summer night at the **Bronze Goat**, 108 Ponsonby Road, tel. 768-193; lunch in **Oblio**'s garden conservatory, 110 Ponsonby Road, tel. 763-041; Sunday brunch and jazz at **Carthews**, 151 Ponsonby Road; a seafood dinner before an evening of partying at **Peppermint Park**, 161 Ponsonby Road, tel. 768-689; fish of the day immersed in the **Jungle Cafe**'s greenery, 222 Ponsonby Road, tel. 767-888; and last but not least, seafood chowder at **Fed Up**, 244 Ponsonby Road, tel. 768-469.

DAY 2
AROUND AUCKLAND

A full morning in Auckland covers the best view points, parks, and museums, followed by lunch and a walking tour in the Parnell District. Afterwards take a 1½-hour cruise in the Hauraki Gulf. Return for brief downtown sightseeing before taking a 20-minute ferry ride to the North Shore for sunset sightseeing and dinner. Return to Auckland by ferry in the late evening.

Suggested Schedule

7:00 a.m.	Early breakfast.
8:00 a.m.	Catch a bus from the Downtown Bus Terminal to Cornwall Park and One Tree Hill or Mt. Eden Domain for easy walking and views.
10:30 a.m.	Tour the Auckland Domain, War Memorial Museum, and Winter Garden possibly on an Auckland City Council guided walk.
12:00 noon	Lunch in Parnell.
1:30 p.m.	Mt. Cook/Auckland Harbor cruise.
4:00 p.m.	Return to downtown and visit the Old Auckland Customhouse.
5:00 p.m.	Ferry to Devonport for a walk to sunset sightseeing at North Head and nearby Mt. Victoria.
6:30 p.m.	Dinner in Devonport at Rickerby's or Rocks Restaurant.
8:30 p.m.	Return to city by ferry.

Transportation
The Ferry Building Information Centre has all harbor information and timetables. The Devonport Ferry Service departs seven days a week from the Queens Wharf, the terminal behind the Ferry Building on Quay Street, crossing the harbor in 20 minutes to Devonport on the North Shore, for NZ$3.25 adults, NZ$1.65 children (round-trip). The ferry leaves Queens Wharf every hour

on the hour and leaves Devonport Wharf on the half-hour (until 11:30 p.m., Monday through Saturday). Fuller's Captain Cook Cruises, Ltd. (tel. 394-901), on Quay Street, offers a variety of cruises around the harbor: morning tea cruises, 9:45 to 11:30 a.m. (NZ$25); volcanic island cruise, 9:45 a.m. to 2:30 p.m. (NZ$38); lunch cruise, noon to 2:15 p.m. (NZ$36); afternoon tea cruise, 2:30 to 4:00 p.m. (NZ$25).

Sightseeing Highlights
▲▲▲**The Domain** is a beautiful park setting for the War Memorial Museum, Winter Garden, Fern Glen, Planetarium, and Herb Garden. The Auckland City Council's (tel. 792-020) free two-hour guided walk around the central city, featuring The Domain, is an excellent introduction to the city.
▲▲▲**The War Memorial Museum** (390-443) on a grassy hilltop in Auckland Domain, has outstanding views of Waitemata Harbour and the North Shore. Even if you're not fond of museums, don't miss its outstanding display of Maori and Pacific Island artifacts, natural history exhibits covering the gamut of New Zealand's flora and fauna, sea life, geology and paleontology, maritime history exhibits, and a planetarium (Saturday and Sunday shows). The Museum's "Centennial Street" is a reconstruction of an Auckland shopping street of 1866. September to May, open 10:00 a.m. to 5:00 p.m. (4:15 p.m. in winter), Monday through Saturday, and Sunday 11:00 a.m. to 5:00 p.m.; June to August, 10:00 a.m. to 4:15 p.m. Admission free.
▲▲**Winter Garden** on the museum grounds in The Domain holds over 10,000 South Pacific plants in a Cool House and an amazing variety of hothouse plants in the Tropical House and the Fernery (10:00 a.m.-noon and 1:00-4:00 p.m. daily, no admission fee).
▲▲**Mt. Eden**, Auckland's highest point (643 feet), offers the finest views over the city, surrounding water, and the Waitakere Ranges. Walk or drive up Mountain Road to the summit. This volcano crater was used as an ancient Maori

fortress, and defense terraces and storage pits can still be seen around the sides. Mt. Eden is part of the Coast-to-Coast Walkway. It is closer to the downtown than One Tree Hill. Seeing both Mt. Eden and One Tree Hill requires a very early start. Catch a bus from the Downtown Bus Terminal to either vantage point.

▲▲**One Tree Hill and Cornwall Park**—The terraced volcanic cone rises above Cornwall Park, which includes Acacia Cottage, Auckland's oldest wooden building (1841). Walk or drive past sheep-filled fields to the summit of what was once the home of the region's largest Maori fort (pa). By day or at night, view Auckland and its twin harbors from One Tree Hill's summit.

▲▲▲**Hauraki Gulf**—Islands in the Hauraki Gulf Maritime Park, extending from the Poor Knights Islands (see Day 4) to the Alderman Islands off the Coromandel Peninsula, can be reached by ferries, launches, yachts, or seaplanes from Auckland's harborfront. Stop between 9:00 a.m. and 3:00 p.m. at the Hauraki Gulf Maritime Park Information Centre, tel. 799-972, at the back of the Ferry Building for current time schedules and prices. There are about 100 islands out there, from the nearest, Rangitoto, an uninhabited volcano, to the farthest and largest, Great Barrier Island, covering 70,000 acres. Favorites include Rakino, Pakatoa, Mototapu, Waiheke, and Motuihe, with its excellent beaches and walks that draw thousands of people on summer days. Views from Waiheke's hilltop and the summit of Rangitoto are the best in the gulf. Walking up Rangitoto is well worth the effort. Wear sturdy footwear, sun lotion, and sunglasses. Beach lovers, try Onetangi on Waiheke Island or Medlands Beach on Great Barrier Island.

▲**The Old Auckland Customhouse**, at the corner of Custom and Albert streets near the harborfront, has been renovated in French Renaissance-style into a shopping emporium with a restaurant, bar, and cinema. See the downtown Auckland branch of the Clevedon Woolshed, with its great selection of knitwear, weaving, sheepskins, accessories, and gifts.

▲▲ **The Devonport Ferry** to the North Shore is one of the best ways to see Auckland from the water. The ferry service includes the *Kestrel*, built in 1905 and beautifully refurbished. Walk up to North Head for a good viewing point or up nearby Mt. Victoria (250 feet) for panoramic views. From Queen's Wharf terminal on Quay Street, the ferry leaves every hour on the hour from 7:00 a.m. to 11:00 p.m. Monday through Saturday, until 9:45 p.m. on Sunday. One-way fare is NZ$3 adults, NZ$5 round-trip.

Where to Eat
Take an evening ferry trip to Devonport for a stuffed leg of rabbit dinner and scrumptious desserts at **Rickerby's**, Fleet Street, Devonport, tel. 457-072. For reasonable seafood dishes with great harbor views in Devonport, try **Rocks**, 33 King Edward PDE, tel. 451-455. Also on the North Shore, **J.C.'s**, Beach Road, Rothesay Bay, tel. 478-8123, has superb dishes, decor, and service. All three restaurants offer a great way to end a day of exploring nearby beaches and the harbor.

Itinerary Options
The **Coast-to-Coast Walkway** is marked by signs between the Waitemata Harbour on the east coast and the Manukau Harbour on the west. The Walkway connects Albert Park, Auckland University, Auckland Domain, Mt. Eden, One Tree Hill, and other points of interest, keeping to reserves wherever possible. At an easy pace, the eight-mile walk can be done in four hours, near bus routes all the way.

Extended Inner City Walking Tour (2 hours)
Starting at **Albert Park** by the **University Tower** on Princes Street, about two blocks from Queen Street, walk under the park's towering trees (toward Wellesley St.) to the **Auckland City Art Gallery** (tel. 377-700 or 390-831) at the corner of Grey's Avenue and Queen Street, open 10:00 a.m. to 4:30 p.m. daily, no admission charge. Continue past the stone **Auckland Town Hall**,

through **Vulcan Lane** shopping mall and Queen Street to the **Old Customhouse** on Custom Street West (see above). Stroll around the restored Customhouse (9:00 a.m.-5:00 p.m. Mon.-Thurs., until 5:30 p.m. Fri. and Sat., noon-5:30 p.m. on Sun.) to see some of New Zealand's best craft shops selling pottery, quilts, woodwork, glassware, and porcelain. Breakfast, lunch, and dinner are served at the **Cellar Cafe**. If you decide to head back to Albert Park, stop at Walker & Hall's Queen Street store to see their antique jewelry, sweaters at the Canterbury Stores and the New Vision Ceramic Arts in the **Great Northern Arcade**, fishing gear in Tisdale's on Queen Street, and superbly carved greenstone jade in the **War Memorial Museum Shop**.

From this point, for an even more ambitious and pleasant walk, with bus stops en route in case you get tired, from the Post Office in Quay Street walk about 4 miles eastward to **Mission Bay**, an attractive swimming beach with fine lunch spots. Two miles out you'll pass the remarkable underground **Kelly Tarlton's Underwater World**, open daily 9:00 a.m. to 9:00 p.m, NZ$8 adults, NZ$4 children ages 4-12, children under 4 free, tel. 589-318, at Orakei Wharf on Tamaki Drive. Three linked former municipal sewage tanks were converted into a 395-foot-long aquarium above and around the viewer seen from a conveyor belt or adjacent footpath.

From the Customs House you can turn east on Customs Street and turn right to the mall at the foot of Queen Street and retrace steps up Queen Street past department stores and shops back to Albert Park. As an alternative, take a right on West Victoria Street heading west from Queen Street and walk six blocks. Across from **Victoria Park** is the Victoria Park Market where vendors such as **Rick's Americaine Cafe** sell vegetables, meat, and other foods, snacks and regular meals, and there are a large variety of crafts. Open from 7:00 a.m. to 7:00 p.m. daily, one of the best features of the market is that it's open Sundays, too, when little else is open in Auckland.

As an alternative to your own walking tour, the Auckland City Council offers a series of free guided walks that take about 1½ hours each. **Albert Park** with its woods, daffodils, tropical glass house, cricket grounds, and the remains of Albert Barracks, built in the 1840s against Maori attacks, is located in the Auckland University grounds behind the main library.

The **Museum of Transport and Technology**, commonly referred to as MOTAT, on Great North Road in the Western Springs District contains an interesting collection of everything that buzzes, spins, calculates, and moves, from music boxes and vintage motor cars to steam locomotives. A whole building of early flying machines features the remarkable inventions of Richard Pearse, whose aircraft first flew in 1902—shades of the Wright Brothers. The site's old buildings have been restored as a pioneer village. An electric tram runs regularly between MOTAT and the Auckland Zoo. Open weekdays from 9:00 a.m. to 5:00 p.m., weekends 10:00 a.m. to 5:00 p.m. Admission NZ$8 adults, NZ$4 children. Allow about three hours. If you're not driving, take bus 145 from Custom Street East.

For insatiable flying buffs, nearby **Keith Park Memorial Airfield** houses a large collection of yesteryear's aircraft. **Auckland Zoological Park**, next to MOTAT, offers a chance to see kiwi birds (in a special nocturnal house) and the tuatara (the only remaining link with the dinosaur), in addition to a selection of over 1,500 mammals, birds, reptiles, and fish. The zoo is mostly outdoors in spacious enclosures set in 45 acres of parklike gardens, with a children's zoo. Open daily from 9:30 a.m. to 5:30 p.m., last admission 4:15 p.m. Admission, NZ$8 adults, NZ$4 children ages 5-15. A family ticket for NZ$22 admits two adults and up to four children. Allow about two hours. You can take buses 043, 044, or 045, which leave every 10 minutes from Customs Street East.

Hauraki Gulf Touring

A one-hour ferry ride (NZ$15 adults, NZ$7.50 children) to Waiheke Island, Hauraki Gulf's largest and most central island, from Half Moon Bay offers sample views of this maritime playground by day and dusk. Flying (10 minutes, NZ$50 per person round-trip) from Ardmore and Mechanics Bay "saves" over 1½ hours, substituting flightseeing for the experience of a leisurely Gulf boat ride. Waiheke's towns and beautiful white sand beaches are an easy walk apart, so there really is no need for a car. The Royal Forest and Bird Society's reserve at Onetangi, a bus ride from the wharf, contains over two miles of bush walks.

The **Auckland Harbour Cruise Co.**'s (734-557) *Pride of Auckland*, a 60-foot catamaran carrying 80 passengers, provides year-round two-hour morning (10:00 a.m., NZ$28) and afternoon (3:00 p.m., NZ$28) cruises, a lunch cruise (12:30 p.m., NZ$40), and a dinner cruise (6:00-9:00 p.m., NZ$66) around the harbor. They also have 3- and 7-day Hauraki Gulf cruises. The *Manu* luxury motor launch, with morning, luncheon, and afternoon cruises, also has a 5-hour cruise to Rangitoto Island with a winding, bumpy 9-mile ride up to its 850-foot summit on "the Magic Bus," followed by a so-so buffet lunch back on board. About four miles wide and full of walking trails, Rangitoto's summit view of the Gulf is worth the trip. The *Manu* occupies the same pier sales office as Fuller's Capt. Cook Cruises (see below), opposite the Downtown Airline Terminal and the Travelodge.

The Capt. Cook Cruises, also known as the **Blue Line Boats**, tel. 34-479, serve Rangitoto Island, Motutapu, Motuihe, and Rakino. The daily service departs Launchman's Steps Monday to Friday at 9:30 a.m., on Wednesday at 7:30 a.m. and 4:30 p.m., on Friday at 6:00 p.m., and on weekends at 9:30 a.m. and 12:30 p.m. The ferries return Monday to Sunday at 3:00 p.m., on Wednesday at 10:30 a.m. and 6:15 p.m., and weekends also at 5:45 p.m. Round-trip cost: NZ$12 adults, NZ$6 children. For solitude and lonely beaches, bush walks, and a free campground, your only access to Great Barrier Island, 55 miles out, is by amphibian (**Sea Bee Air**, tel. 774-406) for NZ$45 round-trip or a 10-minute joyride over the Gulf Island for NZ$35 per adult. **Great Barrier Airlines** (275-9120) has three flights daily out of Auckland's airport to Claris on **Great Barrier Island** with a free shuttle bus to scenic **Port Fitzroy**. Stay overnight at **Tipi and Bob's Holiday Home**, a B&B with great breakfasts, brunches, and dinners in Tryphen. Several other airlines fly to the islands and offer flightseeing excursions.

Region Surrounding Auckland
Kiwi recreational life in Auckland revolves around water sports. They're either in or on the water. Most people seem to have boats or easy access to them. Little wonder with over 100 beaches within an hour's drive, dozens of offshore islands and their hundreds of sandy coves, and a midwinter average temperature of 57 degrees and an average temperature for eight months of the year in the high 60s and low 70s.

On the suburban shore north of Takapuna, see a chain of lovely beaches that runs from Castor Bay northward to Long Bay. The Wenderholm and Mahurangi heads are special reserves with natural beauty and uncrowded shores. Starting at the city's downtown waterfront, the seven-mile scenic Tamaki Drive follows the south shore of Waitemata Harbour to St. Heliers Bay. Tamaki Drive, from Mission Beach, only 15 minutes from the downtown's waterfront, is a scenic road and bicycle route that passes through a series of beachfront suburban "villages," each with its own quiet character. Combine a trip down Tamaki Drive with a visit to either the **Bay Restaurant**, in Mission Bay, tel. 581-879, or **Lizzie's**, tel. 583-930, just down the street. Both have surprisingly sophisticated fare for a little eastern hamlet, such as superb seafood and salmon mousse, and charge accordingly. Both offer nice views of the bay and Rangitoto Island and pleasant decor.

DAY 3
TOUR OF WAITAKERE RANGE AND NORTH SHORE

Spend the morning exploring the surf beaches, rain forests, tracks, and vistas of the Waitakere Range and the black sand beach at Piha along the Tasman Sea. Then drive to the Henderson Valley's vineyards for lunch and wine-tasting. In the afternoon follow the North Shore's lovely beaches and bays to the Waiwera thermal hot springs for a dip before a farewell-to-Auckland dinner at one of Ponsonby Road's many excellent restaurants.

Suggested Schedule

7:30 a.m.	After breakfast, rent a car.
9:00 a.m.	Waitakere Range Scenic Drive.
11:00 a.m.	Piha or other black sand beaches.
1:00 p.m.	Henderson Valley vineyards for lunch at Penfolds.
3:00 p.m.	Sightsee along North Shore beaches and bays.
4:30 p.m.	Enjoy Waiwera natural hot springs.
7:00 p.m.	Clean up and change for dinner.
8:30 p.m.	Dinner.

Driving to the Waitakere Range and Henderson Valley

From the downtown area, take Symonds Street over the Route 1 Motorway to Dominion Road (Route 4) southwest to Hillsborough Road (Route 15, which changes its name several times), then westward to Titirangi Road (Route 24), which becomes the Waitakere Scenic Drive. The Information Centre is about three miles from the intersection of Routes 15 and 24 on your left. About three miles past the Information Centre is the turnoff (Piha Road) to Piha Beach. As you drive down this secondary road, you'll see several tracks heading into the bush to your right (north). This winding road covers about nine

Auckland Region

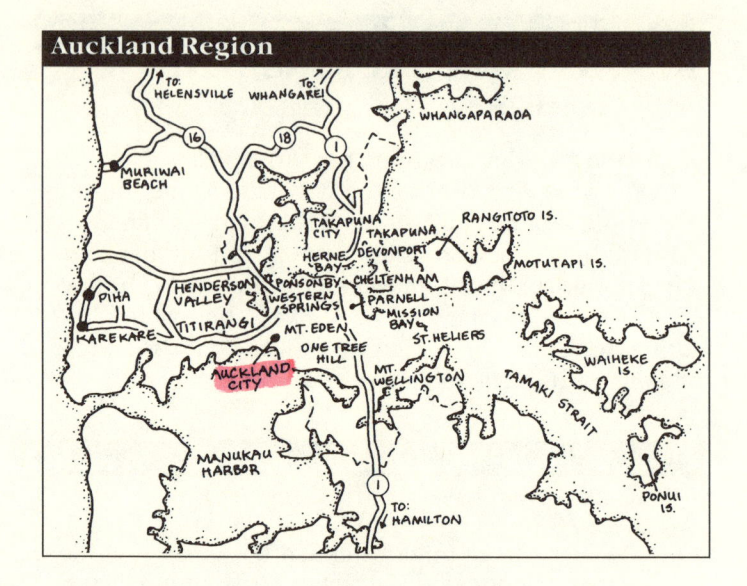

miles and takes half an hour to Piha Beach, a long black sand beach well known locally for its surf (dangerous currents and rips), with good walking tracks off the beach.

From the intersection of Piha Road and Scenic Drive, continue north on Scenic Drive for about another six miles to the intersection with Mountain Road on your right. Mountain Road will take you into Henderson Valley to the vineyards.

Driving from Henderson Valley to the North Shore, take Henderson Valley Road to Henderson. Turn right on Great North Road (Route 16) and then left on Te Atatu to Motorway 16 east through the downtown to Motorway 1, which crosses Waitemata Harbour to the North Shore. Exit at Takapuna-Devonport on Esmond Road (Route 26), turning left on the coastal road, which heads north past the East Coast bays (Milford, Castor Bay, Campbells Bay, and others). At Long Bay, turn west briefly to the Old East Coast Road, which merges with Motorway 1 North just before Silverdale. Take Motorway 1 to Waiwera. Return to Auckland later on Motorway 1.

Sightseeing Highlights
▲▲▲**Waitakere Range Scenic Drive** within the Centennial Memorial Regional Park offers several spectacular views of Auckland and the Gulf, especially Pakinson's Lookout, Pukematekeo Lookout, and View Road up to the summit of Mt. Atkinson. The Scenic Drive, a paved road running from Titirangi to Swanson via the Summit Ridge, passes through fine forests, with outlook views over the city and harbor. Stands of huge, ancient kauri trees remain along the walking tracks that thread through the thick bush. Fine specimens of kauri trees and regeneration can be found at Titirangi and Piha Valley. The forest-covered hills of the Waitakere Ranges are threaded with walking tracks through bush thick enough to get lost in. ARA publishes a map of the Waitakere Ranges covering 135 walking tracks in the area. Public buses do not run to the Waitakere. For those not driving, catch a bus to Titirangi and be prepared to walk or hitchhike. The Aratakai Information Centre, tel. Turangi/TGN 7134, is on the Scenic Drive a couple of miles from Titirangi. It doesn't open until 1:00 p.m. on weekdays, 10:00 a.m. on weekends. The black sand beaches of Muriwau, a lovely seaside area, Piha, Karekare, and the Tasman west coast are wild and treacherous favorites of surfers and gutsy swimmers. The Waitakere Ranges rise between the city and these west coast beaches. The beaches are accessible from trails winding down to the sand from the rim of the mountains. Only swim in the rough surf near "lifesavers" patrolling the beaches.

▲▲**Henderson Valley's** vineyards, on the lower slopes of the Waitakere Range in the western suburbs, produce some first-rate wines that can be tasted in pleasant outdoor restaurants. Almost a dozen wineries were established in Henderson, Waimauku, and Kumeu, four miles farther northwest, by Dalmatian settlers who came from Yugoslavia in the early 1900s to work in Northland's kauri gum fields. In Henderson visit **Corban's Wines** on Great North Road and both **Penfolds and Collard Wines** on Lincoln Road. You can also start the Waitakere Scenic

Drive in Henderson, driving up to Swanson, left up Panorama Heights to the **Cascades** and **Kauri Park**. From Henderson to Auckland along Great North Road is 12 miles.

▲▲ **North Shore** beaches and bays stretch from Takapuna and Castor Bay to Long Bay, with East Coast Bays Cliff Walks providing wonderful views of the Hauraki Gulf islands.

▲**The Waiwera Hot Pools Leisure Resort**, tel. 42-65-369, about 30 miles north of Auckland adjoining the Waiwera Hotel, has public and private hot mineral pools with varying temperatures, private saunas, suntan beds and sun lounges, and water slides for children. The beach down the road is very pretty. Open every day until late evening. Within walking distance of Waiwera, Wenderholm Regional Park offers an excellent day trip combination of bush walking, hot pools, and ocean swimming.

Itinerary Options

A wilder and more unspoiled beach to visit than Piha is **Bethells Beach**. About 6 miles after Waiatarua, turn left (toward the Tasman) on gravel Bethells Road for 6 miles.

If you have an afternoon to spare, contact **Bush & Beach Ltd.** (P.O. Box 4, Greenhithe, Auckland, tel. 779-029) for an excellent small-group tour (1:00-5:00 p.m.) of the beaches, headlands, and rain forests of the Waitakere Range (NZ$45).

On **Waiheke Island**, there are Youth Hostel cabins (and a hotel and motel in Onetangi and a motel in Ostend) if you decide to stay overnight.

DAY 4
AUCKLAND TO THE BAY OF ISLANDS

The drive from Auckland to Russell in the Bay of Islands includes side trips to Kawau Island and scenic coastal areas south and north of Whangarei. Take the Opua car ferry to Russell. The day ends in Russell, first capital of New Zealand and known as the hellhole of the Pacific in the early 1800s. Today, historic Russell is an ideal touring base for the Bay of Islands Maritime and Historic Park and its 150 islands.

Suggested Schedule

7:00 a.m.	Breakfast, check out and departure from Auckland.
10:30 a.m.	Ferry from Sandspit to Kawau Island.
2:30 p.m.	Return to Sandspit and continue north to Mangawhai Heads and Tutukaka Coast.
5:30 p.m.	Opua car ferry to Russell.
6:00 p.m.	Arrive in Russell. Check in and head for the public bar at the Duke of Marlborough Hotel for refreshment and relaxation. If you're energetic, climb to the summit of Maki Hill for a great sunset view of the town and surroundings.
8:00 p.m.	Dine on the latest seafood catch at a restaurant on Russell's Strand. Sleep well in the Russell area.

Orientation

Auckland to Paihia and Russell in the Bay of Islands is 150 miles following Highway 1 via Whangerei. With detours and side trips to the coast to see Kawau Island, Mangawhai Heads, and to Russell via Whangaruru North, the driving distance today is about 175 miles.

For touring purposes the Northland region can be divided into four areas: the coast east of Highway 1 to the Bay of Islands; the Bay of Islands northward to Doubtless

Bay; Kaitaia and Cape Reinga; and the west coast from Aupori at the base of 90 Mile Beach to Kaipara Harbour. The Northland Peninsula stretches 280 miles from Auckland to the tip of Cape Reinga. Including lunch and rest stops, without side trips, it's a ten-hour drive one way. Russell, in the Bay of Islands, is not less than a five-hour drive. With only three days in the Northland, concentrate your sightseeing in the Bay of Islands region and on the west coast.

The Bay of Islands is the birthplace of modern New Zealand's history. The Treaty of Waitangi, establishing British rule, was signed there on February 6, 1840. Fascinating links to the country's past will be found in Russell, on Waitangi Peninsula, and in Kerikeri. Visit sites of conflict, struggle, and habitation of Maoris, whalers, British soldiers and civil government, missionaries and early settlers, now embedded in tranquillity and natural beauty.

The Bay of Islands consists of three resort areas: Paihia, the commercial, accommodations, and excursions center; Russell, historic and fishing charter center; and Kerikeri, a scenic citrus-growing and historic center. Except for Paihia, a very popular Kiwi holiday resort area especially during Christmas and the January school holiday period, the region is not commercial and is protected by the Bay of Islands Maritime and Historic Park.

The Bay of Islands Maritime and Historic Park Headquarters (tel. 37-685) on the Strand in Russell should be the first stop, especially for anyone planning to cruise, sail, fish, hike, or camp in the park. Open daily from 8:30 a.m. to 5:00 p.m. Upon arrival in Paihia, stop at the Bay of Islands Information Centre (P.O. Box 70, Paihia, tel. 0885/27-426) on the waterfront. With no booking fee, the Centre's staff will arrange accommodations of all sorts, sightseeing and other activities in the Bay of Islands area.

On the Way to Russell and the Bay of Islands

Highway 1 up the east side of the peninsula is the fastest route to the Bay of Islands. It passes through rolling hill

Day 4 59

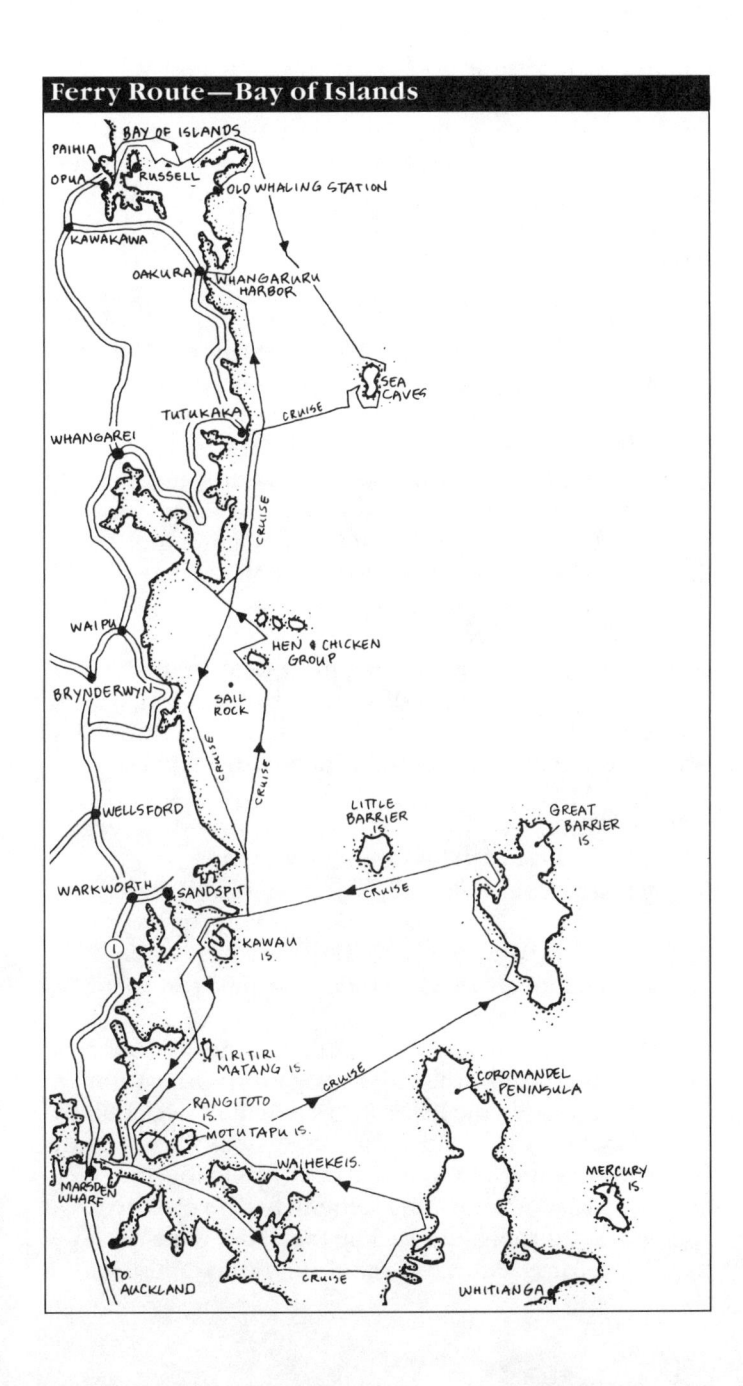

Ferry Route—Bay of Islands

country with pastoral pockets of green flat land. At one time the entire region was covered by kauri, which has disappeared to be replaced by sheep and dairy livestock grazing. Virtually every town you'll see began as a timber town for cutting, milling, or shipping kauri or for the digging of kauri gum. From 1853 to 1910, kauri gum was the second most valuable export from the region—after kauri timber.

The east coast is a constant variety of forms. The sandy crescents of Pakiri and Bream Bay are small safe harbors tucked into small bays between major peninsulas like Whangaparoa and Whangarei heads, and the large deepwater inlet at Whangarei. On the drive north you'll pass Wenderholm Regional Park, where beautiful groves of trees on rolling hills are a backdrop to the beach. Pick up some fresh fruit at the fruit stalls of family orchards on the road to Warkworth before turning off to Sandspit for the ferry to Kawau Island.

Lovers of superb coastal scenery should follow the suggested schedule and take one or more detours: to Kawau Island from Sandspit (east of Warkworth); to Mangawhai Heads and the Mangawhai Walkway, and north through Waipu Cove (about 60 miles); through Whangarei to Whangarei Heads and Ocean Beach (about 22 miles); or along the Tutukaka Coast (about 48 miles), with access to great diving around the Poor Knights Islands.

The coastal road to Russell is more beautiful than the route of Highway 1. At Whakapara, turn off Highway 1 toward Helena Bay, driving about 10 miles of winding roads, sealed for a while and then gravel the rest of the way to Russell. At Helena Bay the road follows coastal hills with short detours to delightful beaches at Oakura Bay, Whangaruru South, and Whangaruru. Drive through the Ngaiotonga Scenic Reserve to a height of over 1,000 feet, descending to Waikare Inlet to Russell. Whanharauru Peninsula has several accessible side trips to lovely beaches and remote historic settlements. If you drive Highway 1, quicker and avoiding the gravel roads, at Kawakawa leave Highway 1 and turn toward Opua and

Russell. From Opua harbor, take the ferry to Okiato, 7 miles from Russell.

Transportation
The Northland is small enough to be covered by car in a few days, though for sailors, divers, and deep-sea fishing and hiking enthusiasts it deserves at least a week. I prefer driving to the Northland for several reasons. It enables you to take several coastal side trips south and north of Whangarei. Bus service from the Bay of Islands to the west coast is infrequent, and without a car it is difficult to schedule visits to the Waipoua State Forest, Trounson Kauri Park, Kai-Iwi Lakes, and Matakohe's museum. Bus transportation to the Coromandel Peninsula from Auckland runs infrequently and is difficult to time with the departure from Northland, although you could stay overnight in Auckland on Day 6 and head for Thames the next morning.

On the other hand, you really don't need a car in the Bay of Islands. Motor coaches and buses connect Auckland with all major Northland attractions and the Bay of Islands with Dargaville. **Clarkes Northerner Coachlines** runs daily coaches from Auckland which depart at 8:30 a.m. Monday through Friday through Whangarei (noon arrival) to Paihia at 1:40 p.m. The fare is NZ$32 one way.

Paihia, Russell, Waitangi, and Kerikeri should be seen on foot. Minibuses can take you from Paihia to anywhere in the area. If you wind up on the wrong side of the water at night, it's an expensive mistake (how expensive depends on the number of people, time of night, and season) but not fatal. Just call **Bay Water Taxi** (tel. 27-221) or **Think Pink Water Taxi Service** (tel. 27-161). A 15-minute ferry runs regularly between Paihia and Russell (NZ$6.50 adult round-trip). Three miles south of Paihia, at Opua, a boat charter harbor, an inexpensive car ferry (car and two people one way NZ$6.50) crosses the channel to Okiato Point, five miles from Russell. The last car ferry from Opua to Russell departs at 7:00 p.m. most nights except Friday, and later in the summer months.

Besides Russell's charm, Waitangi's historic sites, views, and golf course, and picturesque Kerikeri, enjoying the other sightseeing attractions in the Bay of Islands requires a launch cruise, boat charter or, as a last expensive resort, hiring a water taxi.

Sightseeing Highlights

▲▲**Kawau Island**, part of the Hauraki Gulf Maritime Park, is reached by ferry from Sandspit. Fuller's Kawau Island Ferries (tel. 084/68-006) depart (in summer) at 7:45 a.m., 9:30 a.m., 10:00 a.m., 10:30 a.m., 11:30 a.m., 12:30 p.m., 2:00 p.m., and 4:30 p.m., taking 50 minutes to get to the island. Fares are NZ$20 for adults and NZ$10 for children, round-trip. Kawau Island was purchased (1862) and transformed into a subtropical delight of imported trees, plants, and animals, including wallabies and kookaburras, by Sir George Grey, one of New Zealand's mid-nineteenth-century governors. The governor's restored Mansion House (1844 and enlarged in 1867) and gardens are open daily from 9:30 a.m. to 3:30 p.m. Also see cottages and mineshafts (copper and manganese) dating from the 1830s.

▲**Mangawhai Cliffs Track**, a three-mile walkway near Mangawhai Heads, requires strong shoes for the rocky coast. The walk leads along clifftops with magnificent seascape on one side and vistas of green hills on the other.

▲**Whangarei Falls** drop 75 feet into a green pool surrounded by luxuriant bush. With walkways above and below, it's a photographer's paradise. Visit the falls on the way to Tutukaka, taking Ngunguru Road.

▲▲▲**Bay of Islands Maritime and Historic Park** extends from Whangaroa Harbour to the north to Whangauru Harbour in the south, including 54 reserves, 15 of which are offshore islands.

▲▲▲**Russell**, a wild whaling port (Kororareka) in the early 1800s, later a British settlement and scene of British-Maori conflict, today is a charming historic town. One of the first stops should be the Bay of Islands Maritime and Historic Park Headquarters on the waterfront, the Strand, for free information and informative audiovisual displays. The park ranger can tell you everything you want to know about hiking, fishing, and camping and also issues camping permits. Along the waterfront, the Duke of Marlborough Hotel was one of Kororareka's most popular drinking spots and now holds New Zealand's customs house. At the southern end of the Strand stands the impressive Pompellier House, named after a bishop (who didn't actually live there), open 10:00 a.m. to 12:30 p.m. and 1:30 p.m. to 4:30 p.m., NZ$2.75 adults and NZ$.70 children (tel. 37-861). The oldest surviving church in New Zealand, Christ Church, is nearby. The Captain Cook Memorial Museum, York Street (tel. 37-701), displays many relics of early town life and a 21-foot replica of Captain Cook's *Endeavor*. The museum is open daily from 10:00 a.m. to 4:00 p.m., NZ$1.65 adults and NZ$.20 children.

Right from the boat ramp end of the Strand, it's a 30-minute climb up historic Maki Hill (also known as Flagstaff Hill) for a panoramic view of the town and the Bay of Islands.

Where to Stay
Paihia
Motor Camps: Less than two miles out of Paihia, with the old Twin Pines Tavern and Restaurant (see Where to Eat, below) on site and spectacular Haruru Falls as a backdrop, for two decades the friendly and helpful Putt family's **Twin Pines Motor Camp** has set high standards for quality accommodations at low prices: 8 six-berth chalet-style cabins, 9 on-site caravans, and a 25-bed lodge at NZ$13.20 for adults (children half price); a 12-bed lodge for a few NZ dollars less; and 2 four-berth tourist flats, NZ$39.60 double (all incl. GST). Kitchen, dining room, laundry, and other useful facilities are on the premises. If Twin Pines is booked, the Hodern's **Falls Motor Inn** (P.O. Box 14, Haruru Falls, Paihia, tel. 0885/27-816) next door and the **Lily Pond Holiday**

Park (tel. 0885/27-646), also on Puketona Road, between Paihia and Puketona Junction, are comparable alternatives.

Also on Puketona Road, on the way from Paihia to the Treaty House, at the Kerikeri turnoff, the **Mayfair Lodge** (7 Puketona Rd., Paihia, tel. 0885/27-471) supplies sheets and blankets for dormitory accommodations at NZ$12 pp and has a few double rooms at NZ$13 pp.

Motels: Sited for privacy, spacious one-bedroom cottages with full kitchen and bath are available at the **Bay of Islands Motel** (6 Tohitapu Rd., Te Haumi Bay, P.O. Box 131, Paihia, tel. 0885/27-348). Rates are NZ$55 single to NZ$63.80 double. Beneath red-tiled roofs and Spanish-style design in Paihia's **Casa-Bella Motel** (McMurray Rd., Paihia, tel. 0885/27-387) are well-furnished units with kitchen facilities. On nicely landscaped grounds, these units fit moderate budgets at NZ$59-$79 single or double, with NZ$10 for each additional person.

Russell

Motel Flats: On the Russell side, about a mile from the Opua car ferry, Jan and Boerop's **Wairoro Park** (P.O. Box 53, Russell, tel. 0885/37-255) occupies a one-of-a-kind setting on the shores of a cove, with its own beach, and a dingy, motorboat, and 12-foot catamaran for guests. Three fully equipped, two-story A-frame chalets on this beautiful 160-acre site rent for NZ$66 double, NZ$12 per additional adult, and a self-contained cabin for two rents for NZ$45 (incl. GST).

In Russell or the Bay of Islands, you can't do much better for inexpensive, comfortable accommodations, with marvelous views of the bay, than the very pleasant four units in Linley and Bill Shatwell's **Arcadia Lodge** (Florence Ave., Russell, tel. 0885/37-756). Units handle 4 to 6 people comfortably at NZ$20 single and NZ$35-$60 double (plus GST) with a charge for extra adults.

Fishing, sailing, or hiking enthusiasts will find hospitable Carole and Jim Hotchkiss's **Motel Russell** (Matuwhi

Bay Rd., P.O. Box 54, Russell, tel. 0885/37-854) the perfect base for gathering advice and making plans for these activities throughout the bay. Thirteen units with one or two bedrooms and three cabin units rent for a minimum of NZ$55 single or double (with Best Western discounts).

Licensed Hotels: The **Duke of Marlborough Hotel** (The Strand, Russell, tel. 0885/37-829), New Zealand's first hotel and still one of the coziest, is surprisingly affordable for rooms with patios and wicker furniture. Single rooms are NZ$50 to $60, doubles NZ$90 (incl. GST). Even a splurge at the **THC Waitangi Resort Hotel** (Private Bag, Paihia, tel. 0885/27-411) on the superb Waitangi National Trust property is about the same rate at NZ$84.40 for a standard room, single or double (plus GST).

Kerikeri
Budget travelers to the Bay of Islands should make advance bookings at the **Kerikeri Youth Hostel** (Main Rd., P.O. Box 62, Kerikeri, tel. 0887/79-391). Seniors NZ$11.50 and juniors half price. The river, Stones Store and other historic sites, and everything else in Kerikeri are within easy walking distance. But excellent alternatives are plentiful in this area (see, for example, Twin Pines Motor Camp, above).

Where to Eat
There are enough inexpensive places with tasty food like the **Pantry Coffee House** on Selwyn Road and the **Waltons Carvery** in the Paihia Mall or the **Traders Cafe** in Russell to satisfy your appetite three meals a day for under NZ$5-$10 per meal. The **Stone Store Tearoom**'s bistro in Kerikeri still serves some of the best food in the bay area Friday, Saturday, and Sunday nights for NZ$10. But otherwise, the bay area has become the delight of people who love seafood and other traditional New Zealand meat dishes and can afford to spend NZ$20-$25.

Paihia and Waitangi

Have a hearty breakfast any time of day (starting at 7:00 a.m.) at the **Blue Marlin** cafe/diner on Paihia's waterfront, across from the Information Centre. In part you pay for the lovely decor upstairs at the Selwyn Road Shopping Center but otherwise for **La Scala**'s (tel. 27-031) superb seafood, with prices ranging up to NZ$30. Near the Opua ferry terminal, **Ferryman's Licensed Restaurant** has a bistro (BYO) that is open noon to 2:30 p.m. and a restaurant open 6:00 to 9:00 p.m.

Reserve a table at the **Bella Vista** (on the waterfront at Waitangi Bay, tel. 27-451) in the elegant upstairs for lobster or steak dinners, fresh bread, and salad, which can run up to NZ$25. Reserve lunch on Sunday at the **THC Waitangi Hotel** (tel. 24-411) for the all-you-can-eat (steak, lamb, salads, etc.) menu for NZ$17 or dinner on Sunday evening at the hotel's ample, more-than-you-can-eat carvery buffet from soup to desserts for NZ$24. **Jane's Restaurant** has a cozy Old English feel, an extensive menu, excellent food, for lunch (noon-2 p.m.) from NZ$8 or dinner from NZ$18 (6:30-10:30 p.m.).

Russell

On the Strand, **The Quarterdeck** (tel. 37-761) is everyone's favorite for catch of the day, a seafood and salad bar, and other light meals. Expect to spend NZ$8-$10 for lunches and NZ$15 or more for dinners. The **Reef Bar Bistro** in the **Duke Tavern** (tel. 37-831) behind the Duke of Marlborough has lunch or dinner, also with excellent fresh fish, at essentially the same prices as the Quarterdeck. The favorite local splurge restaurant, **The Gables** (tel. 37-618), on the waterfront, has an expensive à la carte menu with main courses of fish, game, lamb, and beef that cost up to NZ$25 (minimum bill per person is NZ$18.50). BYO or enjoy their extensive wine list or licensed bar. Try a smoked marlin with avocado dinner preceded by creamy oyster or mussel chowder topped off for dessert with chocolate mocha mousse.

Itinerary Options

The Clapham Clock Museum (tel. 71-384) on Water Street in Whangarei contains about 1,000 varieties of clocks and watches. Open Monday through Friday 10:00 a.m. to 4:00 p.m., 3:00 p.m. on weekends.

Tutukaka Coast is a favorite deep-sea fishing base. For all information, check at the Whangarei Deep Sea Anglers Club at the marina. The eight miles of coastline between Ngunguru and Sandy Bay are especially good for surfing. A short trail through the woods reaches splendid Whale Bay.

Poor Knights Islands, off the Tutukaka Coast, are world famous for diving and underwater photography. The subtropical waters in this area offer a rich haven for colorful underwater life, with many school fish, large reef fish, and steep drop-offs covered in brilliantly colored anemones and sponges. The best time for scuba diving is January through May. From October through December, the visibility is poor. All necessary information, equipment, and charters can be arranged with the Tutukaka Dive Shop or the Whangarei Deep Sea Anglers Club. From Tutukaka's marina, take a skin-diving or underwater photography trip to the Poor Knights Islands.

In the Bay of Islands area, some of the best diving places are Cathedral Cove almost splitting Piercy Island; between Howe Point and Cape Wiwiki on the Purera Peninsula east of Kerikeri; around Dog Island; Bird Rock and Twins Rock; Hope Reef in the Albert Channel off Unupukapuka; Paramena Reef in Te Uenga Bay; Whale Rock northwest of Okahu Island; Waewaetorea; Takarota Rock between Motutakapu and Nakataunga; and Tokananohia Reef. A seven-hour dive trip with **Paihia Dive, Hire and Charters Ltd.** on Williams Road (tel. 27-551), including all equipment, costs about NZ$125 per person.

Cruising or yachting, perhaps combined with diving or game or light-tackle fishing, is the best way to experience the Bay of Islands for those with the time and budget. **Rainbow Yacht Charters** (Auckland, tel. 790-457; Opua, tel. 0885-27-821; USA, 800-722-2288/Cal., 800-277-5317) offers the most complete skippered or bareboat sailing holiday packages on a wide variety of yachts and motor cruisers. Rainbow has 21 sailing yachts (20 to 38 feet accommodating 6 to 8 people, rates from NZ$260 to $420 per day), three 36-foot motor launches for bareboating, and three luxury boats for skippered cruising. For a Cruise and Learn course, you pay an additional NZ$320 for instruction before you're certified to take the boat out without a skipper. Cruising and sailing instruction is required for those without sufficient experience. The **Northland Charter Boat Association** in Russell and the **Game Fishing Charter Association** in the Paihia Marine Building offer fully equipped single or shared charters, picking up people in Paihia, Russell, or Waitangi at around 8:00 a.m., returning before 6:00 p.m.

Big-game and sport fishing are world class in the Bay of Islands. Zane Grey made them famous back in the 1920s. The main game fish are striped marlin, black and Pacific blue marlin, broadbill, mako, thresher, hammerhead and blue sharks, yellowfin tuna (New Zealand holds every world record), and yellowtail or king fish. In December, striped marlin arrive and dozens of charter and private boats await with tackle and backup photography, and smoking and trophy mounting services. If you can join a group (maximum four) and share the NZ$700-$800 cost for ten hours of fishing, the price comes within the range of possibility. The Bay of Islands International Billfish Tournament in early March and the Duke of Marlborough South Pacific Tournament in early May add festivities and fun to angling activities.

DAY 5
RUSSELL—BAY OF ISLANDS—WAITANGI—KERIKERI

Take a leisurely cruise from Russell to islands in the Bay of Islands Maritime and Historic Park. In the afternoon, leave Russell the same way you came, by the Opua ferry, then drive through Paihia to historic Waitangi Peninsula. Visit the Treaty House and the nearby Maori meeting house and kauri war canoe. Drive to beautiful Haruru Falls on the way to Kerikeri. Explore Kerikeri Inlet until the sunset is gone and it's time for dinner at the Stone Store Restaurant.

Suggested Schedule

8:00 a.m.	Breakfast, local sightseeing, and check-out.
10:00 a.m.	Depart Russell on the Cream Trip.
12:00 noon	Picnic lunch at Otehei Bay on Urupukapuka Island.
1:30 p.m.	Return to Russell.
2:00 p.m.	Depart from Russell via the Opua car ferry and then drive through Paihia to the Waitangi Peninsula. Visit the Treaty House and other historic sites.
4:00 p.m.	Depart Waitangi and pass Haruru Falls on the way to Kerikeri. Check in on arrival.
6:00 p.m.	Explore Kerikeri Inlet until sunset.
8:00 p.m.	Dinner at the Stone Store Restaurant, quiet relaxation and overnight in Kerikeri.

Sightseeing Highlights
▲▲▲**The Cream Trip** is one of the best ways, short of having your own cruiser or yacht, to see the Bay of Islands. It's named for a coastal launch route of the 1920s that collected cream and delivered mail and supplies to dairy farms. Fullers Cruises (tel. 27-421) operates the boat from Paihia (9:45 a.m. daily) and from Russell (10:00 a.m.

Bay of Islands

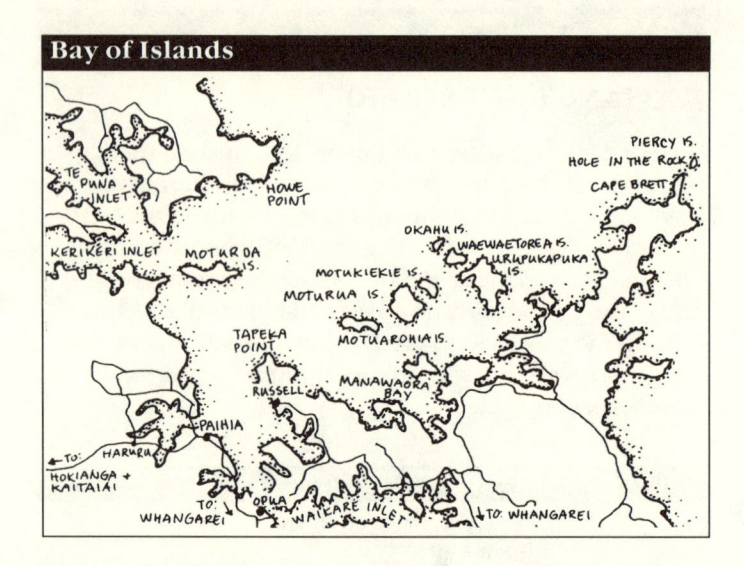

[Map showing the Bay of Islands region with locations including Te Puna Inlet, Kerikeri Inlet, Howe Point, Moturoa Is., Okahu Is., Motukiekie Is., Moturua Is., Waewaetorea Is., Urupukapuka Is., Piercy Is., Hole in the Rock, Cape Brett, Tapeka Point, Motuarohia Is., Russell, Manawaora Bay, Paihia, Haruru, Opua, Waikare Inlet, with directions to Hokianga & Kaitaia, Whangarei.]

daily) to many islands, delivering mail and groceries to farmers and caretakers on Monday, Wednesday, and Friday. The four-hour trip includes a lunch stop at Otehei Bay on Urupukapuka Island. Lunch and the cruise cost NZ$40. (Note: you can camp free almost anywhere on Urupukapuka Island and use the Cream Trip as your transportation to the island. Get the "Urupukapuka Island Campers" brochure at the park headquarters in Russell.) Fullers also has several other cruises including the 3-hour cruise to Cape Brett and Piercy Island's "Hole in the Rock," costing NZ$39 for adults and NZ$15 for children, with three departures a day starting at 9:30 a.m., including two in the afternoon.

▲**Paihia** is jammed with motels and hotels, but the town center at the waterfront and wharf still has the character of a deep-sea fishing hub for dozens of local game-fishing boats. Look for crowds around the wharf as a sign that a magnificent game fish is being weighed in. The Fullers and Mt. Cook cruises, as well as most other sightseeing cruises and charters, leave from Paihia's wharf.

▲▲▲**The Waitangi National Reserve** on Waitangi

Peninsula, only a mile from Paihia, is one of the most historic places in New Zealand. On February 6, 1840, the Treaty of Waitangi was signed on the lawn in front of the home of the first British resident, James Busby. Local Maori chiefs, fearful of takeover of their land by France or other foreign countries, had asked for British protection. Over 2,000 Maoris assembled there to meet Captain Hobson, who informed them that Queen Victoria would offer such protection under a treaty in return for ceding sovereignty to the crown. With much opposition, which persists to this day, the treaty was signed, and, on February 8, the British Colony of New Zealand was proclaimed. Nearby is the Waitangi Meeting House, a gift from the Maoris to New Zealand at the 1940 centennial, with wall carvings from many North Island tribes. Also nearby is a 118-foot Maori war canoe carved from kauri. The 18-hole Waitangi golf course is one of the finest and most scenic in New Zealand. Drive the road that climbs nearly to the top of Mt. Bledisloe for the best panoramic views of the Bay of Islands.

On the way to Waitangi, stop off at the **Museum of Shipwrecks**, a three-masted barque moored near the Waitangi-Paihia bridge which holds a collection of diver Kelley Tarlton's salvage from local shipwrecks. Open 9 a.m. to 5 p.m. daily, admission NZ$4 adults, NZ$2 children. Afterward, walk or drive to **Haruru Falls**, a beautiful waterfall in a very lovely setting, for a swim in the estuary of the Waitangi River surrounded by native trees. The falls, which are floodlit at night, can be reached by a 3.6-mile walking track through the Waitangi National Reserve or by driving less than two miles inland along the road to Puketona. While in the vicinity of the falls, consider having a snack lunch at the Dewdrop Bar or dining upstairs at Goffes Restaurant on the upper floor of Twin Pines Tavern (tel. 27-195).

▲▲**Kerikeri**, founded in 1819 as a mission station, today is known for its citrus fruit groves, large numbers of artists and craftsmen, and two historic buildings in lovely Kerikeri Basin—the Stone Store and Museum (1833), the oldest stone building in New Zealand, and Kemp House (1822), probably the oldest wooden building in the country. On the drive from Paihia to Kerikeri, the road is lined with orchards. On Highway 10, be sure to stop at the **Origin Art & Craft Cooperative** to see and shop for the best weaving, knitwear, leatherwork, stained glass, woodwork, and other fine craft products from the area (open 10:00 a.m. to 5:00 p.m. daily, tel. 79-065).

Approaching Kerikeri Basin, the red roof and white face of the Kemp House, set above the stolid Stone House on the shoreline, are a reminder that the "Fruitbowl of the North" is also a cradle of New Zealand's colonization. Nearby is Rewi's Village, an accurate full-scale reconstruction of a Maori *kainga* (unfortified village). A walking track follows the river from the Ranger Station to spectacular **Rainbow Falls**, about 90 feet high. For fun try the **Orchard Railway**, about half a mile of narrow track with a small train running through gum trees and subtropical orchards, ending at a restored country station.

Itinerary Options

Mt. Cook's Tiger Lily Cruises, tel. 27-099, to Cape Brett Hole in the Rock departs Paihia at 9:30 a.m. and 1:00 p.m., returning at 12:30 and 4:00 p.m., and costs NZ$31 adults. The four-hour Super Cruise departs Paihia at 10:00 a.m. and returns at 2:00 p.m. The cruise visits Cape Brett, Piercy Island, Cathedral Cave, and the Hole in the Rock at Cape Brett.

Join a skippered charter in Kerikeri for a day trip along the Kerikeri Inlet into the Bay of Islands and up the coast to the Cavalli Islands and Whangaroa.

Golfers, check out the Kerikeri Golf Club, a championship course, with facilities available to visitors.

Scenic flightseeing charters are available at the Kerikeri Airport off Highway 10. The Bay of Islands Aero Club operates high-wing aircraft for good visibility and photography. Flights generally last from twenty minutes to two hours.

DAY 6
WEST OF THE BAY OF ISLANDS—SOUTH TO COROMANDEL PENINSULA

Leave the Bay of Islands heading for the west coast of Northland, then south to visit the Waipoua Kauri Sanctuary on the way to Dargaville. Visit two exceptional regional museums, in Dargaville and Matakoke, before continuing south past Auckland to Thames on Coromandel Peninsula.

Suggested Schedule

7:00 a.m.	Breakfast in Kerikeri.
8:00 a.m.	Depart for west coast.
10:30 a.m.	Waipoua Kauri Sanctuary.
12:30 p.m.	Picnic lunch on the West Coast Beach adjoining Dargaville.
1:30 p.m.	Visit Dargaville regional museum.
3:00 p.m.	Otamatea Kauri and Pioneer Museum in Matakoke.
4:00 p.m.	Leave for final leg of trip to Coromandel Peninsula.
6:00 p.m.	Dinner in or near Auckland.
9:00 p.m.	Arrive in Thames, Coromandel Peninsula.
9:30 p.m.	Waterfront stroll before retiring.

Driving to the West Coast, Auckland, and Coromandel Peninsula (Thames)

From the Bay of Islands it's about 50 miles on Highway 1 to Kaitaia at the base of the Aupori Peninsula and another 60 miles up to Cape Reinga, then 260 miles back to Auckland on Highways 1, 12, 14, and 1 again, without any other detours. Following the suggested eastern coastal route through Whangaroa, Manganui, and Doubtless Bay adds about another 25 miles. If you select the itinerary option to Cape Reinga, that's about 245 extra miles, certainly an extra day. From the Bay of Islands across the North Island to the Waipoua Kauri Forest and back to

Auckland covers 228 miles, then another 90 miles to Thames on Coromandel Peninsula, also a very full day of driving.

Head west from Kerikeri on Highway 12 to Opononi via Rawene (about 1½ hours drive). From there, continuing on Highway 12 through the Waipoua Kauri Forest and by Trouson Kauri Park to Dargaville is less than a two-hour drive without stops. Follow Highway 12 through Matakoke to Highway 1 south. Dargaville to Highway 1 also is less than two hours; allow about half an hour at the Dargaville Museum and about 45 minutes at the museum in Matakoke. From Wellsford on Highway 1, it's 1½ hours to Auckland. You should pass by Auckland at about 6:00 p.m. It's about an hour on Highway 1 from Auckland to just before Pokeno, where you turn east for another hour on Highway 2 to Kopu, a few miles south of Thames. Turn north on Route 26 to Thames.

Sightseeing Highlights

▲▲▲**The Waipoua Kauri Forest** contains some of the best specimens of the North Island's once vast forests of giant kauri trees. The Northland's early history was very much shaped by the presence of these aged giants, first cut at a frenzied pace for local use and export as ship's masts and building material. Then the resinous kauri gum was dug from the ground by thousands of Yugoslavian diggers for export to the United States and Europe to make varnish. In just a few decades of the early nineteenth century, kauri forests were reduced to small scattered stands except for some 9,000 acres of these awesome trees within the 22,500-acre Waipoua Kauri Forest. Be sure to climb the **Fire Lookout** for a spectacular view of the kauri domain. Rivaling California redwoods in height (170 ft.), girth (50 ft.), and age (some as old as 2,000 years), kauris can be seen in two forests east of Highway 12 north of Dargaville: Waipoua Forest Sanctuary and Trounson Kauri Park, located about nine miles south of Waipoua (where there are a few campsites). Prepare to drive 43 miles of gravel-surfaced road in the Waipoua Forest and bring a picnic lunch along to have in the preserve or later on the West Coast Beach. The Waipoua Forestry Headquarters (tel. Donnellys Crossing 605) is on Highway 12 on the southern end of the forest. Other kauri preserves can be seen in the Omahuta Kauri Forest in the Ngaiotonga Scenic Reserve east of Russell, the Puketi Forest northwest of Kerikeri, the Waitakere Ranges, and on Coromandel Peninsula.

▲▲ **Regional museums** at Dargaville and Matakoke, as well as Russell and Kaitaia, contain extensive material on the "Kauri era." The Otamatea Kauri and Pioneer Museum (tel. 37-417) in Matakoke has a unique kauri gum collection and the kauri gum story is told with photographs, models, early furniture, industrial tools and more. Open daily 9:00 a.m. to 5:00 p.m. Dargaville, a thriving port during the kauri timber and gum era, has the Northern Wairoa Maori, Maritime, and Pioneer Museum housing pre-European Maori, kauri, and maritime sections. Open daily, except Saturday, 2:00 to 4:00 p.m. only, admission NZ$2.50 adults, NZ$.50 children. West of Dargaville, stretching from Kaipara Head north to Maunganui Bluffs, is the Northland's longest ocean beach (68 miles), the West Coast Beach, with black iron sand typical of Tasman Sea beaches.

Where to Stay
Coromandel Peninsula
Only 10 minutes from the hot springs of Mt. Te Aroha, for NZ$9 you can stay at one of the North Island's nicest **YHA hostels** (P.O. Box 72, Te Aroha, tel. 0843/48-739). Use this hostel as a base for trips into the Kauaeranga Valley to the Coromandel State Forest Park Walk, almost 15 miles from Thames. The park's headquarters (tel. 0843/86-381) will provide walking guide and camping information.

Within 9 miles north of Thames, three motor camps should take care of all campers, hikers, and no-frills travelers looking for places to kick back for a few days. In a lush, beautiful setting, less than 2 miles north of

Thames, **Dickson Holiday Park** (Victoria St., Tarau, tel. 0843/87-308) has tent sites at NZ$6 pp; caravan sites, NZ$7 pp; bunks (your linen), NZ$9 per pp; cabins (with refrigerators and hot plates) and on-site vans, NZ$24-$30 double; and comfortable flats with private bathrooms and kitchens, NZ$50 double.

Essentially the same type of accommodations and rates are available in Te Puru, 7 miles north of Thames at the **Boomerang Motor Camp** (tel. 0843/78-879), and, with the addition of a swimming pool, spa, and tennis courts, at the **Waiomu Bay Holiday Park** (Hwy 25, 9 miles north of Thames, tel. Te Puru 0843/78-777).

Tent sites (NZ$8 pp), caravan sites (NZ$10.50), and cabins (NZ$20-$30 double accommodations) with communal bathroom, kitchen and laundry facilities are available May through October at **Coromandel Motel & Caravan Park** (tel. 0843/58-760).

About 10 miles north of Coromandel, at a beachfront on Amodero Bay, Joan and Alistair Thompson's **Angler's Lodge and Motor Camp** (tel. 0843/58-584), offers a very pleasant and comfortable base for bush walks and side trips around the peninsula. One- and two-bedroom units are NZ$61 singles and NZ$75 doubles.

On the peninsula's east coast, next to two of New Zealand's best beaches—Waihi and Ocean—if you don't mind summer tourist crowds, stay at the **Waihi Beach Holiday Motor Camp** (tel. 5-5044) where tent and caravan sites are NZ$8 pp and cabins are NZ$30-35 double (plus GST).

More than 125 years old, Barbara Doyle's lovely two-story colonial **Brian Boru Hotel** (Pollen and Richmond sts., Thames, tel. 0843/86-523) is a must visit on the North Island for a combination of the old-fashioned atmosphere, marvelous dining room (all meals) for seafood and other meals (see Where to Eat, below), and bar. A wide range of rooms, from small to spacious, with private or shared bathrooms, are available, and rates are NZ$35-$55 singles and NZ$55-$75 doubles, without a private shower and toilet, and NZ$55 and NZ$75, respectively, with them (plus GST). Twice a month, on "Agatha Christie Weekends," guests and local actors join in a "whodunit." The packaged caper costs NZ$350 per person with rooms and meals (reservations necessary).

The **Salutation Hotel** (400 Mary St., 0843/86-488), the **Imperial** (Pollen St., tel. 0843/86-200), and the **Junction Hotel** (Pollen and Pahau sts., tel. 0843/86-008) are less expensive second choices, all with meals optional, at rates ranging from NZ$25 singles to NZ$55 doubles.

Motel Rendezvous, 3 miles south of Thames on Highway 25 at Kopu (tel. 0843/88-536) is for people who want self-contained units. Prices are comparable to the Brian Boru, NZ$48 single, NZ$55 double, and NZ$11 (plus GST) additional adults (up to six in a room). The Rendezvous is near the Totara Valley Vineyards, in Totara (tel. 0843/86-798), with some of the best kiwi-fruit liqueur in New Zealand.

Follow the Coromandel Road for about 7 miles north of Thames to the **Te Puru Park Motel** (West Crescent and Main Rd., Puru Bay, P.O. Box 384, Thames, tel. 0843/78-686). Six motel flats accommodate up to four people. Rates are NZ$40 singles and NZ$50 doubles (plus GST). In case Te Puru is full, about two miles farther toward Coromandel, near Waiomu Bay, the **Seaspray Motel** (P.O. Box 203, Thames, tel. 0843/78-863) costs NZ$10 more (plus GST) per person for about the same accommodations. Both motels have self-service laundries.

Where to Eat
Coromandel Peninsula
The place to eat any of three meals in Thames is the **Brian Boru Hotel**, from bistro lunches to seafood dinners and Sunday night smörgasbord. The **Hotel Imperial** serves budget counter lunches at the bar and a good salad bar in the **Pan & Handle Lounge and Bistro Bar**. Down Pollen Street (702 Pollen), the **Pizza Cabin** serves reasonably priced food, including steaks

and excellent Bluff oysters. Open only 5:00 to 9:00 p.m., Monday through Sunday.

In Coromandel, the **Coromandel Hotel**, Kaponga Road (another overnight option at NZ$25-$50, tel. 0843/58-760), serves good dinners in its bistro from 6:00 to 10:00 p.m. and in its dining room from 6:00 to 9:00 p.m. Next to the Brian Boru, the peninsula's main culinary attraction continues to be the bread, pies, and pizza at the **Bakehouse** (Wharf Rd., tel. 0843/58-554), open seven days a week, 7:30 a.m. to 5:00 p.m. (9:00 p.m. in summer).

Itinerary Options
Waimate North, only 4 miles west of Puketona, is a tiny village with an English atmosphere which is the site of the **Waimate Mission House** (1831-1832), one of the oldest buildings in New Zealand.

Cape Reinga and 90 Mile Beach: If you're driving, head for Highway 10, turn off to **Whangaroa** and follow the harbor, take Highway 1, turn inland to **Mangonui Harbour** and Coopers Beach, follow the road through Cable Bay and Taipa, or head out **Karikari Peninsula** along a gravel road for beautiful beaches (especially Matai Bay); from Awanui head north along the **Aupori Peninsula** (see below for sightseeing).

A bus trip on **Fuller Tours** (NZ$45, tel. 0885) to Cape Reinga takes the entire day, leaving Paihia at about 7:30 a.m. and returning at about 6:00 p.m. Reservations are necessary because of the trip's popularity. Be prepared for many stops: Whangaroa Harbor, Doubtless Bay, tea and lunch, Houhora for the Wagener Historical Museum next to an early Polish home, the Subritizky Homestead, containing extensive displays of Maori and local artifacts (and odds and ends); the tour arrives in the early afternoon at the Lighthouse at the end of the rocky peninsula, where the Tasman Sea and Pacific Ocean meet. According to legend, the spirits of departed Maori journey back to their homeland ("Hawaiki") from the pohutakawa bush below the lighthouse. Fabulous views extend over steep cliffs to Cape Maria van Diemen.

Day 6

At the southern end of the Peninsula, Kaitaia to Opononi is 60 miles, and Opononi to Dargaville (both of which have youth hostels) is 54 miles. An interesting place along the way is Kohukohu, with its craftspeople. The main destination is Waipoua Kauri Forest.

The main attraction for bus tours to the cape is **90 Mile Beach**. Concrete-hard below the high-tide line and bordered by sand dunes miles wide (and in some places 90 feet high), misnamed 90 Mile Beach (64 miles long) is a unique dunescape environment for New Zealand. The **Cape Reinga Walkway** within the **Te Paki Coastal Park** down the beach takes four to seven days from Ahipara but encounters lots of buses and cars until the Te Paki Stream where they enter and leave. At The Bluff, 12 miles farther south, a gravel road leads through planted pine plantations to Te Kao where you can rejoin the main road. On the return to Paihia, bus tours pass through Kaitaia, Mangamuka Scenic Reserve, and Waimate North Mission House, the last of three mission station homes in the region (see above).

Kai-Iwi Lakes—three relatively unspoiled lakes about 19 miles north of Dargaville—deserve a side trip on the way south to Dargaville for trout fishing, swimming, and tramping. From Highway 12 at Maropui, turn west on Omamari Road to the end, then right onto Kai-Iwi Lakes Road, then right on Domain Road to Taharoa Domain. The white sand beach on this beautiful lake is a perfect stop for swimming or fishing before continuing to Auckland and Coromandel. Taharoa Domain also offers lakeside camping.

DAY 7
COROMANDEL PENINSULA—ROTORUA

Make a partial circuit of the west and east Coromandel Peninsula coastlines, then follow the Bay of Plenty through Tauranga and Mt. Maunganui before turning south to Lake Rotorua and the thermal region.

Suggested Schedule

8:00 a.m.	After breakfast, head north to Coromandel.
10:00 a.m.	Visit Coromandel.
11:00 a.m.	Take Highway 309 to the east coast for a picnic lunch on Hot Water Beach.
1:00 p.m.	Head south to Tauranga on the Bay of Plenty.
4:00 p.m.	Arrival in Tauranga and possible side trip to Mt. Maunganui.
7:30 p.m.	Arrive in Rotorua, check in, and enjoy a thermal bath before a late dinner.

Driving from Coromandel to Rotorua

From the town of Coromandel across the peninsula to Whitianga is 29 miles, about 40 miles with suggested side trips. From Whitianga on Highway 25 to Whangamata and Highway 2 to Tauranga is 105 miles. It's another 55 miles to Rotorua on Highway 33. This makes at least a 200-mile day with any short detours.

Just 75 miles southeast of Auckland, the Coromandel Peninsula's volcanic mountains and rugged coastal scenery jut out between the Hauraki Gulf and the Bay of Plenty. A car is necessary on the peninsula. The Auckland Railways Road Service's coaches travel between Auckland and Thames, but otherwise bus service is limited to Thames, Coromandel, and Whitianga on the Bay of Plenty.

Leaving Auckland on Highway 1 and then 2, the drive along connecting Highway 25 is lush and scenic. The route passes through rolling green farmland with few settlements. Just a few miles past Mangatawhiri, the road branches to the left toward the extensive vineyards of Mangatangi. The pine forest south of Highway 2, planted by the New Zealand government, can be used for recreation. Route 25 from Thames to Coromandel is paved and from north of Coromandel to Fletcher Bay is gravel, turning to a hiking trail between Fletcher Bay and Stony Bay, then back to gravel to Port Charles and on to Whitianga. Route 25A, the most recently constructed of four roads across the Coromandel Range, from Thames through Kopu across the peninsula to Hikuai, is paved and so is Route 25 from Whitianga south to the Bay of Plenty.

From Whitianga, head to the stone wharf at Ferry Landing, Cooks Beach Road, the gravel road three miles to Hahei beach and then, a few miles farther on, a four-mile gravel road to Hot Water Beach. Back on Highway 25 to Tairua, with a possible detour to Pauanui resort, continue to Whangamata (with a suggested detour to Opoutere) where the beach is beautiful and the sealed road starts. Toward Paeroa, from Waihi, the road parallels Karangahake Gorge (and 3-mile Karangahake Gorge Historic Walkway along the river and old mining reminders). Drive on Highway 2 through a fruit-growing region to Tauranga and Mt. Maunganui across the harbor, a major port and crowded holiday town in season, which now can be reached by bridge.

Here you have two driving choices: the adventuresome one (get out your map), mostly on gravel, from Tauranga to Pyes Pa, Ngawero and Lake Rotorua at Ngongotaha; or the simple way, head on Highway 2 for kiwi-fruit country to Te Puke, possibly with a side trip to Maketu (according to Maori legend, the landing place of the Arawa canoe), then south on Highway 33 to Rotorua.

After a beach stop, continue south on Highway 25 to Waihi where it connects with Highway 2 south to Tauranga, Mt. Maunganui, and the turnoff to Highway 33 to Rotorua which is a few miles past Te Puke. Highway 33 merges with Highway 30 into Rotorua.

Sightseeing Highlights

▲ **Coromandel's Courthouse**, built in 1873 for the gold warden twenty years after discovery in Coromandel of the first gold in New Zealand, now serves as the local Council Chambers.

▲▲ **Highway 309**, a narrow and winding unpaved "shortcut" across the peninsula from Coromandel Harbour to Kaimarama, has stunning scenery.

▲▲ **Mercury Bay to Waihi Beach** displays spectacular headland and beach scenery, though it can be very crowded during vacation and holiday periods. In this coastal stretch, stop off at Hahei Beach, Hot Water Beach, Pauanui, and Mt. Paka. At Opou, a turnoff to the left south of Hikuai, the Opoutere Youth Hostel (tel. Whangamata 59-072) puts you within a short walk of Opoutere Beach.

▲▲ **Hahei Beach** (pink sand) and **Hot Water Beach** are both beautiful and quite different from one another. Within a few hours of low tide, just dig a hole on Hot Water Beach between the cliff and large rock offshore to soak in your own natural hot pool bath seeping through the sand. The fabulous headland scenery, two pa (Maori village) sites, nearby blowholes (seawater forced through holes in coastal rocks) at the southern end of Hahei's pink sands, and the huge cavern at Cathedral Cove Reserve on the northern end make this an unsurpassed beach getaway. Tent sites are available at Hahei Tourist Park, in case you just can't leave.

▲ **Pauanui**, a holiday town, nestles in the pines along a golden beach.

▲ **Twin-peaked Mt. Paka**, across the Tairua Harbour from Pauanui, is the site of an old pa, where still-visible earthworks rise up over 500 feet from the sea.

▲▲ **The Bay of Plenty** has a mild climate, fine broad beaches, clear water, excellent game-fishing or diving near Mayor Island, and great bush walks on the island, Tauranga's beautiful parks, and the new Tauranga Historic Village, a restored colonial village, gold mining area, Maori pa, and restored locomotive. "The Mount" has

Coromandel Peninsula

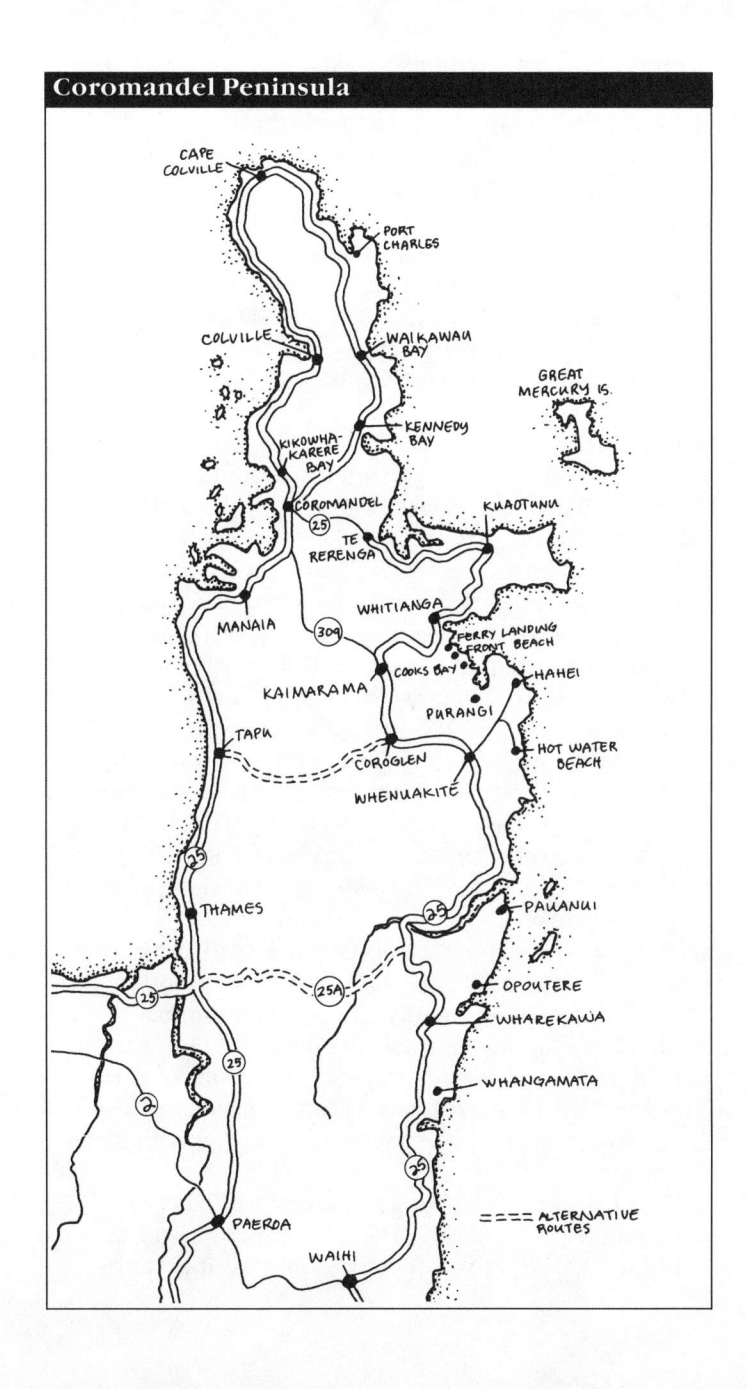

magnificent views, natural hot saltwater pools, a surf beach, launch trips to Motiti Island, excellent white-water rafting, and golf courses.

▲ **Mount Maunganui**—This beach resort, reached by ferry, is on the eastern shore of Tauranga's harbor and has a 760-foot wooded peak that is worth the climb for outstanding views of the ocean, Matakana Island, Tauranga City and Harbour, and marvelous Ocean Beach, the surf beach stretching for 12 miles south to Maketu's headland. Maketu is the site of the Awhi-o-te-rangi meeting house, an outstanding example of Maori carving.

Where to Stay
Hostels/Motor Camps: Centrally located at the corner of Eruera and Hinemanu streets in Rotorua, the YHA Hostel, the **Colonial Inn** (tel. 073/476-810), stays bright and cheerful winter and summer. The 18 rooms, kitchens, steam ovens, laundry facilities, and even a thermal plunge pool offer one of the best deals in town at NZ$14 pp, accommodating up to 70 people. Doors close at 11:00 p.m. The **Ivanhoe Tourist Lodge** (off Turanekai St. at 54 Haupapa St., tel. 073/486-985) offers carpeted single cabins, twin/double cabins, and serviced rooms (supply or rent your linen), a big communal kitchen and dining area, and a thermal pool for NZ$14-$20.50 pp (incl. GST); and **Waiteti Holiday Park** (14 Okona Crescent, Ngongotaha, Rotorua, tel. 073/74-749), has tent sites (NZ$6.50 pp), caravan sites (NZ$16), and on-site caravans (NZ$25 double), a 48-person bunkhouse (NZ$9 pp), cabins (NZ$25 double), tourist flats (NZ$38 double) and motel flats (NZ$45 double), a fully equipped communal kitchen, and an indoor pool (all plus GST). One advantage of these hostel-type/motor camp accommodations over the YHA Hostel is that you can come and go as you like. Rent mountain bikes for NZ$12 per day or regular 10-speeds for NZ$6.

Near Lake Rotorua, **Cosy Cottage** (Whittaker Rd. off Lake Rd., tel. 073/483-793) has plenty of tent and caravan sites for NZ$15 double, spartan to fully equipped, thermally heated cabins for NZ$22-$35 double, and two-bedroom flats with private bathrooms for NZ$45 double. Stay near the Whakarewarewa at the **Rotorua Thermal Motor Camp** (60 Tarewa Rd., tel. 073/470-931) for slightly higher rates per person and basically the same facilities.

Motels: Close to the city's center but still quiet, the **Acacia Lodge Best Western**'s 18 units have kitchens and just about every other amenity for NZ$57 single and NZ$67 double (plus GST, and with offsetting Best Western discounts).

B&Bs: Only a block from the city's center, Leon and Doreen Maitland's comfy **Tresco Guest House** (3 Toko St., tel. 073/498-611) has available attractive rooms for NZ$36 single, NZ$55 double, and NZ$66 triple with a full breakfast, mineral plunge pool, and guest laundry. You have to pay NZ$5 extra for a full cooked breakfast, instead of a continental breakfast, down the street (20 Toko St., tel. 073/488-511) at Kerry Lee's **Morihana Guest House**, but otherwise the rates are about the same. Across the street (23 Toko St., tel. 073/487-089), the **Fernleaf Motel** provides all comforts and facilities for the same rates as the Acacia above.

Hotel Splurge: If you get the special rate of two nights and two cooked breakfasts for NZ$99 pp (plus GST) at the **THC Rotorua International**, remember that this is slightly more than the lowest standard rate for a double without the breakfasts. For one person, it's worth the splurge; for two people with the money, it's worth considering. Otherwise, stay anywhere in the city that's comfortable and definitely attend the Maori hangi and concert one night at the THC or at the Geyserland Motor Hotel.

Where to Eat
First priority for dining (or should I say feasting) in Rotorua goes to a traditional Maori hangi. The carefully timed and controlled steam oven cooking of lamb, pork, seafood, vegetables, pumpkin, and pudding has been

perfected by large hotels like the **Rotorua International**, tel. 481-174, the **Rotorua Travelodge**, tel. 481-174, the **Tudor Towers Restaurant**, tel. 481-285, in Government Gardens, and **Geyserland Motor Hotel**, tel. 482-039. Prices range from NZ$27 to $38.50.

Start your quest for good food, light meals, grills, or counter service on Arawa Street with fish and steaks at the upstairs **Palace Tavern and Friar Tuck**, tel. 481-492, in Ye Olde English Tavern atmosphere; and, for pancake fans, the **Pancake Parlour Restaurant**, Tutanekai Street, has a few local and tourist favorites; for game dishes, try the enormous portions at **Karl's Dining Room**, tel. 480-231; a combination of roast beef, lamb, seafood, wild game, and other main and side dishes at **The Bushman's Hut**, tel. 483-285, will cost as much as NZ$20.

Cobb & Co., tel. 482-089, in the Grand Establishment on Hinemoa Street, is reliable, from decor to relatively inexpensive and satisfying food, seven-day-a-week service from 7:00 a.m. to 10:00 p.m.

Overlooking the lake and Ohinemutu Village, **Lake View Restaurant** (Lake Rd., tel. 485-585) should be one of your local mainstays with its variety of good food, from vegetarian dishes to steak, and especially reasonable prices ranging from NZ$8 to $14, including vegetables and salad. Standard lunch and dinner hours. When visiting the Agrodome, don't miss the **Agrodome Farmhouse Tearooms** for a savory lunch and excellent desserts. Open daily 9:00 a.m. to 4:00 p.m. It turns into a steakhouse at night.

Splurges: The **Gazebo** (45 Pukuatua Street, tel. 481-911) has casual and pleasant decor but elegant continental menu items like baby salmon in lemon cream. Open Tuesday through Friday from noon to 2:00 p.m. and Monday and Saturday from 6:00 to 10:00 p.m. Lunches and dinners will cost from NZ$10 to NZ$22.
Aorangi Peak Restaurant, tel. 486-957, is over 1,000 feet up Mt. Ngongotaha. If the view and venison medallions don't leave you breathless, the bill will (NZ$25-$40

minimum). Elegant continental food (and BYO), seafood, game, and other delicious dishes at small, modern, **Rumours** (81 Pukuatua St., tel. 477-277) will cost NZ$35-$40. Hours are 6:00 to 10:00 p.m. Tuesday through Saturday. In the high season, you may have to make reservations at any of these three restaurants and for a hangi before leaving Auckland or Coromandel Peninsula to head south.

Itinerary Options
Around Coromandel Peninsula
You can drive on gravel road to Fletcher Bay, but then you have to turn around or hike the Coromandel Walkway. North of Coromandel the road is fringed by pohutakawas, rocky coves, and sandy beaches, mostly hugging the coast. At Amadeo Bay north of Coromandel, the seal ends as the road winds through Colville and Port Jackson (just a beach) along more scenic, rugged, rocky coast until it disappears in the hills near Fletcher Bay. At this point, the sometimes steep and narrow **Coromandel Walkway** twists around the coastal hills for about 4 miles to Stony Bay. From Stony Bay, the road is gravel to Sandy Bay and Port Charles (which, of course, you can only reach up the east coast unless you walk or ride and push a mountain bike over the Walkway). Coromandel to Whitianga via Kuaotunu also is mostly gravel—beautiful but dirt for 24 jarring miles (and definitely not suited to motor homes), with magnificent views over the east coast from the summit above Whangapoua Harbour, Matarangi Beach, and Kuaotunu. About 2 miles south of Kuaotunu, before turning to Whitianga, be sure to take a short detour to beautiful **Waitaia Beach.**

Northland to Rotorua via Waitomo
From the Bay of Islands to **Waitomo's Glowworm Grotto** is a full day of driving (with a lunch break). It's 125 miles from Auckland, through Hamilton, a city of lovely gardens and parks but not much otherwise for sightseeing. About 10 miles before Waitomo, stop at the

Otorohanga Nocturnal Kiwi House off Kakamutu Road (NZ$5 adults, NZ$1.50 children, 10:00 a.m. to 5:00 p.m. in summer) to see the walk-through aviary and one of the nocturnal kiwis that the Otorohanga Zoological Society staff somehow keeps awake for visitors.

If you decide to stay overnight in the area, make reservations at the **Waitomo Country Lodge** (Waitomo Caves Rd. and Hwy. 3, P. O. Box 343, tel. 08133/8109) in Otorohanga, a first-rate Best Western Motel (NZ$48 single, NZ$60 double, incl. GST). For dinner, the **Otorohanga Royal Hotel's Rangatira Room** (Te Kanawa and Maniapoto sts., tel. 8129) provides Victorian atmosphere and good food at moderate prices.

You'll arrive at Waitomo around 5:00 p.m, which is too late for tours March through September (9:00 a.m. to 4:30 p.m.) but perfect for after-the-crowds tours at 5:30 and 6:30 p.m. October through February or even 8:30 p.m. January through February (tel. Kuiti 948). Forty-five-minute guided tours in all three caves (**Waitomo** and, 2½ miles away, **Aranui** and **Ruakuri**) can be purchased in a combined ticket for NZ$15. One cave costs NZ$9.60 (half price children), or NZ$30 for a family of two adults and two children. Before seeing the caves, visit **The Waitomo Caves Museum and Interpretation Centre**, down the hill from the still-charming **THC Waitomo Hotel** (1911), which explains the caves' formation, how insect life evolves in the caves, and the caves' ecosystems, and displays fossils from the area. See all three caves if possible. Ruakuri's cave labyrinth is filled with sounds of an underground waterfall and roaring river, and Aranui's limestone formations are especially delicate and lovely. Bring a sweater and good walking shoes.

Your guide will tell you the whole fascinating life-and-death- cycle story of the glowworm and what makes the glowworm glow. In short: an egg hatches into a grub that covers itself in a mucous tube-nest attached to the grotto roof with tiny threads made luminous with an eerie and beautiful blue-green light produced by the larva's light organs; for about six months the sticky lighted threads attract and "catch" midges, which are paralyzed by acid in the threads and eaten, until the lava pupates into a cocoon suspended in luminous threads; attracted males free the female fly to lay her eggs, in only four days, before she falls into the sticky lines of new larvae to be eaten herself. It's an unforgettable combination: the amazing story of nature's wonders and the incredible boat ride, necessarily in absolute silence, down the 100-foot-long, 40-foot-high, 50-foot-wide underground river of the Glowworm Grotto surrounded by thousands of twinkly blue-green lights.

Even novices can join **guided caving tour** parties, with equipment provided, that take you into some of the limestone caves honeycombing the area. Get information at the Waitomo Caves ticket office.

On the branch road from Highway 3 into Waitomo are: **Merrowvale**, a model of a New Zealand village on 3 acres surrounded by farms and pine forests, with a scale-model railway operating through the town; and **Ohaki Maori Village**, a replica of a pre-European Maori village, with Maoris working at crafts that are for sale and demonstrating weaving, flax-making, and other handicrafts.

From Waitomo it's about a three-hour drive to Rotorua. En route, about six miles south of the Waitomo turn-off on Highway 3, is the **Te Tokanganui-a-Noho Meeting House** (1878) on the main route through **Te Kuiti**, the center of violent conflict in "King Country" between tribes making their last stand against the New Zealand government and settlers taking over their land (1850-1885). You need permission to enter, and my suggestion is to be satisfied with a look at the splendid porch carvings and the exterior of one of the finest Maori meeting houses outside of museums.

New Plymouth-Egmont Option

For travelers who have not been through the beautiful **Taranaki** region and have at least three days, take the road west from Waitomo to the **Marokopa Falls**, a series of falls on the Marokopa River ending in a 100-foot drop;

south through Awakino where you can see the spectacular gorge up the **Awakino River** and join a jet boat trip up the scenic **Mokau River**; past very picturesque fishing settlements like Tongaporutu, start of the **Whitecliffs Walkway to Pukearuhe** (following the Kapuni natural gas pipeline for about 6 miles) with dramatic bush and coastal scenery; on through Waitera, center of New Zealand's energy industry to **New Plymouth**. Located 18 miles from New Plymouth on Upper Carrington Road, azaleas and rhododendrons flourish in the gorgeous **Pukeiti Rhododendron Trust** (best seen from September-November), also a bird sanctuary in a beautiful bush setting between the Kaitake and Pouakai ranges. Also don't miss one of the loveliest parks in the world, **Pukekura Park**, its gardens, artificial lakes, and landscaping designed for day or floodlit nighttime enjoyment; adjoining **Brooksland Park** is especially active during the **January-February performing arts festival**.

New Zealand's most beautiful mountain—**Mt. Egmont**—stands like Mt. Fuji in isolated splendor, in the midst of dense bush and dairyland. Stop at the Department of Lands and Survey or PRO in New Plymouth, the **North Egmont visitors' center** (14 miles from New Plymouth), the **Stratford Mountain House** (9 miles west of Stratford), or the **Dawson Falls Tourist Lodge** (18 miles north of Manaia) for information on the relatively easy climb to Egmont's summit, a variety of scenic local bushwalks, skiing on the mountain, and the 110-mile road around Egmont.

DAY 8
ROTORUA—LAKE TAUPO

The region between Rotorua and Lake Taupo is crammed with so many things to see and do that visiting the best of it takes a full day and is worth every minute of it. The day starts early with stops at trout springs just outside of Rotorua and thermal, Maori, and other attractions in Rotorua. Move south after lunch through Waikato Valley sightseeing to Lake Taupo. Before the day is over you'll have seen hot water springs, eerie boiling mud pools, steaming silica terraces, the blue-green lake of Waimangu Cauldron, smoldering rocks, steaming bush, and cliffs with hot water gurgling out of rock crevices.

Suggested Schedule

7:00 a.m.	Rise early for a full day.
8:00 a.m.	Breakfast and checkout.
9:00 a.m.	Rainbow and Fairy Springs.
10:30 a.m.	Whakarewarewa and the Maori Arts and Crafts Institute.
12:00 noon	Snack lunch at the Agrodome.
1:00 p.m.	Waimangu Thermal Valley.
3:30 p.m.	Huka Falls, Aratiatia Rapids and the Wairakei Geothermal Steam Power Station.
6:00 p.m.	Check in at Taupo accommodations and fish for trout in Lake Taupo while there's still light.
8:00 p.m.	Dinner followed by a lakefront stroll.

Orientation

Ancestors of the Maoris landed on the shores of the Bay of Plenty around A.D. 1340 and pushed inland to Lake Rotorua, the center of a giant (150 miles long and 20 miles wide) thermal region. The natural wonders confirmed the phenomenal activities of the gods. The many lakes and the thermal activity supplied food and warmth. The

Rotorua—Lake Taupo Region

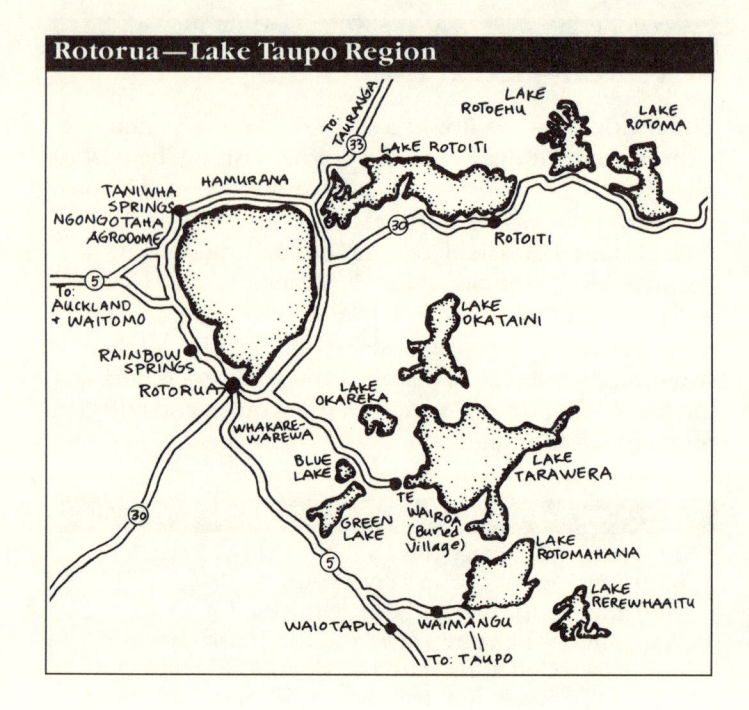

result today is New Zealand's largest concentration of Maori culture, arts, and crafts, in the midst of an extraordinary assortment of thermal sites, volcanic mountains, and the world's best trout fishing.

To the south of Rotorua, the beautiful Waikato River flows placidly northward, with a brief intermission at Huka Falls. To the east of Rotorua is a collection of magnificent bush-fringed lakes and the Bay of Plenty, which is about the same distance from Rotorua as Lake Taupo to the south. The Bay of Plenty's waters teem with yellow fin and mako shark. Fine beaches abound.

Rotorua to Taupo is only 50 miles. The sightseeing route adds another 15 miles, still a light driving day.

Sightseeing Highlights

▲▲▲ Rotorua is "Spa City," with over 600,000 visitors annually. The resort hugs the southwestern shore of Lake

Rotorua. The city's three primary attractions are Whakarewarewa Thermal Reserve, Maori Arts and Crafts Institute, and Government Gardens. Stop at the NZTP office at 67 Fenton Street on the corner of Haupapa (tel. 073/485-179), 8:30 a.m. to 5:00 p.m., to pick up information and accommodations and transportation booking assistance. InterCity coaches and trains and most sightseeing tours arrive and depart at the Travel Centre on Amohau Street (tel. 481-039).

▲▲▲**Whakarewarewa Thermal Reserve** is the best location in New Zealand to see many of the elements of living Maori culture. Walk around the traditional village site, Whakarewarewa, where carved meeting houses (*maraes*) and huts are located among boiling pools and geysers. The local Maoris still use thermal energy for cooking, washing, and heating. The Whakarewarewa thermal area is entered through an ornately carved gateway into a replica of a fortified Maori village (pa). Steaming cracks, boiling mud, silica terraces, and small geysers lead to Pohutu Geyser, New Zealand's highest (100 ft.), with erratic bursts of boiling water and steam clouds. Open daily from 8:30 a.m. to 5:00 p.m. Admission NZ$6.80 adults and NZ$3 children.

▲▲▲**The New Zealand Maori Arts and Crafts Institute**, outside the main entrance to the Whakarewarewa, is the training center for Maori wood carvers. Maori flax weaving techniques are demonstrated there as well. Open 8:30 a.m. to 5:00 p.m.

▲▲**Government Gardens** and its Elizabethan-style Tudor Towers, built as a bath house in 1906-07 and restored by the city, houses the Rotorua Museum and Art Gallery (admission free to both), the Fleur International Orchid Gardens, the Rotorua Cricket Club, the Sportsdrome (a new sports center), Polynesian Pools, and thermal waters of varying mineral content and temperature. Pool hours are 9:00 a.m. to 10:00 p.m., NZ$6 per person.

▲▲**Rainbow and Fairy Springs** (tel. 81-887) combine beautiful bush growth, pools full of rainbow and brown trout viewed from above and below water, and a variety of other attractions. Open 8:00 a.m. to 5:00 p.m., admission NZ$6 adults and NZ$2 children. To see more trout pools in equally beautiful settings, continue north on Highway 5 to Taniwha Springs and Hamurana Springs.

▲**The Agrodome** (tel. 74-350), 7 miles from Rotorua, offers three shows daily (9:15 a.m., 11:00 a.m. and 2:30 p.m.) with a 60-minute demonstration of sheep shearing and the use of sheepdogs. Admission NZ$4.84 adults and NZ$2.20 children. Combine the show with lunch at the Agrodome Tea Room.

▲▲**Ohinemutu** is an unusual Maori village with both the Tamatekapua Meeting House and Tudor-style Maori Anglican St. Faith's Church (with Maori carvings). The two structures have faced each other for generations next to Lake Rotorua. There are Maori concerts every night in summer at the Ohinemutu meeting house (8:00 p.m., tel. 82-269).

▲▲**Ngongotaha**, 3 miles west on Highway 5, has natural pools filled with thousands of rainbow, brown, and brook trout amidst 30 acres of natural growth, including Rainbow and Fairy Springs, a bird aviary, nocturnal kiwis, and a deer farm. Drive up Mt. Ngongotaha to the Aorangi Peak Restaurant for a breathtaking panorama or take the new **Skyline Skyride** up 2,700 feet in a glass-enclosed gondola for NZ$5 adults and NZ$1.50 children.

▲▲▲**Maori hangi**, a feast traditionally steam cooked in an underground pit includes chicken, pork, seafood, fish and other basics and delicacies and, after dinner, a Maori concert. Hangis are put on at several hotels around town for about NZ$18 per person. The THC International Hotel traditionally has had the best one.

En Route to Taupo
Driving Directions: Rotorua to Waimangu
From Whakarewarewa on the southern end of Rotorua, drive on Fenton Street, Sala, Te Ngae Road, and Highway 33 to Ngapuna/Tarawera Road, to **Blue and Green Lakes**. On the isthmus between the lakes, head west on the gravel road to a sealed road, turn left on Highway 5

for 4 miles to the Waimangu intersection, then another 4 miles down Waimangu Road to the **Waimangu Thermal Valley**.

Taupo is a 1½-hour (50-mile) drive from Rotorua on Highway 1. About 12 miles from Taupo, shortly before Wairakei, is the turnoff to Aratiatia Rapids and Huka Falls. Wakirakei means "Waters of Adorning," an apt name for this geothermal area. Huka means "foaming," which also describes the sight of the blue-green Waikato River plunging through a narrow cleft of rock.

▲▲ **Huka Falls** is not high, but the Waikato River funneling powerfully through a narrow gorge near Taupo catapults the water over the ledge into the calm pool below.

▲▲ **Aratiatia Rapids** are about 2 miles from Highway 5, just north of its intersection with Highway 1. The rapids flow through a deep, rocky ravine to a small spillway and hydroelectric power station at the head of the rapids on the Waikato River downstream from Lake Taupo. Millions of native plants have been planted in the area around the rapids. Water is released over the dam from 10:00 to 11:30 a.m. and 2:30 to 4:00 p.m. daily.

▲▲▲ **Waimangu Thermal Valley** (see Itinerary Options, below) contains Waimangu Cauldron, one of the world's largest boiling lakes. Walk past the bubbling crater lake to the shores of Lake Rotomahana, where a launch takes you to the Steaming Cliffs and site of the former Pink and White Terraces. The devastating eruption of Mt. Tarawara, on June 10, 1886, is said to have been foretold by the appearance of a phantom war canoe paddling across Lake Tarawara ten days before the eruption. Several villages were completely destroyed, including Te Wairoa, a busy center for trips to the world-famous Pink and White Terraces of Lake Rotomahana. The three truncated peaks of Mt. Tarawara, across Lake Tarawara, a short distance from Te Wairoa, are still devoid of vegetation, an ominous reminder of the disaster that occurred only a moment ago in geological time.

Visit the buried village of Te Wairoa, Blue and Green lakes, and the Waiotapu thermal area containing the Lady

Knox Geyser that erupts daily at 10:15 a.m. to a height of 60 feet. See the Bridal Veil Falls cascade over tinted silica terraces changing colors from white through deep red and lemon to emerald green. Admission to **Waiotapu Thermal Wonderland**, almost 3 miles past Waimangu, is NZ$5.50 adults and NZ$2.50 children, with an extra charge of NZ$5 (NZ$3/child) for the launch ride.

▲**The Wairakei Geothermal Steam Power Station**, 50 miles south of Rotorua between Huka Falls and the Aratiatia Rapids, generates billows of clouds over an interesting energy project. Take the walkway from Huka Falls to Aratiatia through wildflowers in season.

▲▲ **Lake Taupo** fills a gigantic (238-square-mile) crater. One of the biggest volcanic eruptions in history, greater than Krakatoa and Mt. St. Helens combined, devastated the region 1,800 years ago. Today Lake Taupo is the trout fishing capital of the world. About 100 years ago, trout eggs were brought from California to what turned out to be perfect breeding grounds at Lake Taupo. Fishing in the sparkling clear lake waters, at the mouths of streams flowing into the lake from the Kaimanawa Mountains, or in the trout pools of the famed glacier-fed Tongariro River yields legendary rainbow (3-6 lbs.) and brown trout (5 lbs. and over) from April to August during spawning runs. Lake Taupo also offers superb waterskiing, pleasure boating, and swimming.

Where to Stay
Taupo Cabins (50 Tonga St., P.O. Box 795, Taupo, tel. 074/84-346) consists of cabins furnished with bunks (NZ$12 to NZ$20 per person, incl. GST), "flatettes" and tourist flats with cooking facilities (NZ$41 double, NZ$8.50 each additional person, incl. GST), a community kitchen, shower, and laundry, with linen, blankets, crockery, cutlery, and cooking utensils for rent with the units as needed. On the road to Acacia Bay, Davie and Martha Hyland's **Acacia Holiday Park** (Acacia Bay Road, P.O. Box 171, Taupo, tel. 074/85-159) rents tent and caravan sites on grassy grounds for NZ$15 for two persons,

cabins (NZ$24 double), on-site caravans (NZ$33 double), and tourist flats for NZ$42 for two persons (incl. GST). Linens and cooking utensils are extra. The site along the lake also has a hot spa pool.

One of Best Western's gems, Fay and Gordon Clark's **Adelphi Motel** (Kaimanawa and Heu Heu sts., P.O. Box 1091, Taupo, tel. 074/87-594) offers one- and two-bedroom units, sleeping up to six people, equipped with kitchens. A laundry is on the premises and guests enjoy two spa pools. Rates are NZ$58 single and NZ$70 double (plus GST, with offsetting Best Western discounts). Around the corner at 140 Heu Heu Street, Peter and Virginia Webb's **Dunrovin Motel** (P.O. Box 647, tel. 074/87-384) has one- and two-bedroom units sleeping up to eight, with complete kitchens. Rates are NZ$47 single and NZ$60 double (incl. GST). Both Adelphi and Dunrovin provide breakfasts for a small charge.

Next door to the Dunrovin is the very attractive, cozy **Bradshaw's Guest House** (130 Heu Heu St., Taupo, tel. 074/88-288), with 12 bedrooms, including a few singles and units with private baths. The rates in this homey B&B are one of the best deals in town: with private bathrooms, NZ$35 single, NZ$55 double (incl. GST, NZ$5 less without private bath). Dinner is available starting at NZ$12. All of these accommodations are near the center of town with views of the lake. Other motel and B&B choices will cost at least NZ$50 single and NZ$65 double (plus GST).

DeBrett's Thermal Motor Camp (Taupo-Napier Hwy, 074/88-559) is clean, well run, and nicely landscaped, on a hill overlooking the lake and volcanic mountains, with its own wonderful hot spring spa for only NZ$1 extra. Tent sites NZ$6.50 pp, caravan sites NZ$7.50 pp, cabins at NZ$24 double, and self-contained units NZ$42 double (plus GST).

Where to Eat
El Toreador Coffee Lounge on Horomatangi Street has lunches for about NZ$7. Across the street is the similar **Alpine Coffee Lounge**. Near the waterfront, **Echo**

Cliff, at 5 Tongariro Street, tel. 88-539, offers lunches for about NZ$10. Indonesian and continental dinner fare is somewhat more expensive—three courses for about NZ$25-$30.

Located on Huka Falls Road (near Hwy 1 north), **Huka Homestead Restaurant** (tel. 82-245; open 10:00 a.m. to 4:00 p.m., 7 days a week) offers lunches for about NZ$12-$15, or just have tea. The lunch or tea ticket will save you the Huka Village admission. **Brookes**, 22 Tuwharetoa Street, tel. 85-919, opens for dinner at 6:00 p.m. daily and offers excellent value for the dollar with a range of menu items from seafood to steak dishes for about NZ$20.

Splurges: Consider splurging at the **Huka Lodge**, tel. 85-791, on the banks of the Waikato, where you'll fantasize about spending a week rather than merely having dinner. Conviviality, elegance, and exquisite decor meld perfectly with predinner and dinner drinks, food and wine selections, for as much as NZ$150 pp (and overnight rates of NZ$500 single and NZ$374 pp double). A delicious smorgasbord lunch costs NZ$23 at the **THC Wairakei Hotel** (Hwy 1, Wairakei, tel. 48-021). The beautifully decorated **Edgewater** (Lake Terrace, tel. 074/85-110) at the elegant and expensive lakeside Manuels Motor Inn offers superb three-course meals starting at NZ$40.

Itinerary Options from Rotorua

A full-day round-trip tour of **Waimangu Valley** (Waimangu Thermal Tours Ltd., tel. 073-89-137) leaves from the NZTP Office (67 Fenton St.) at 8:00 a.m. and returns by 5:00 p.m. for NZ$18.50. InterCity's Thermal Wonderland Safari (tel. 04/725-599) costs NZ$54 for adults and NZ$26 for children. Bring lunch or buy it from the bus operator for NZ$6.

Mokoia Island in the middle of Lake Rotorua is reached by a two-hour launch cruise (Rotorua Launch Service, tel. 479-852) for a dip in Hinemoa's hot pool, NZ$20 adults, NZ$8 children. Lake Okataina, the most unspoiled of the lakes surrounding Rotorua, is reached by a scenic drive along Lakes Rotoiti, Rotoehu, and Rotomo. The Eastern

Walkway (six hours round-trip) starts at the northern end of the lake at Tauranganui Bay and finishes four miles later at Humphries Bay on Lake Tarawara. Hell's Gate, ten miles east of Rotorua on Highway 30, consists of ten acres of volcanic activity highlighted by the Kakahi hot waterfall.

Orakei Korako, 12 miles off the Rotorua-Taupo Highway, is one of the finest thermal areas. Board a jet boat to cross Lake Ohakuri, formed by a hydroelectric dam that submerged three-fourths of the silica deposits. The remaining terraces colored by sinter and algae are well worth seeing. Nearby is Alladins Cave with its mirrorlike pool of jade green water. Flightseeing excursions (Floatplane Air Services, tel. 84-069) land on a strip at Mt. Tarawara's summit for a great view of the crater and surrounding region, NZ$60 per person.

Huka Village on Huka Falls Road, a little over a mile from Taupo, is an authentic reconstruction of a New Zealand pioneer village. Open daily 10:00 a.m. to 5:00 p.m., NZ$3.50 adults, children free.

If you have plenty of time, there are several intriguing possibilities for further explorations from Rotorua.

Lake Waikaremoana: Follow Highway 38 south of Rotorua to Wairoa on coastal Highway 2, then on to the unspoiled wilderness of Urewera National Park and the park's gem, Lake Waikaremoana. Driving is most convenient, but a bus from Rotorua to and through the park runs twice a week. On a summer afternoon, take the two-hour Huiarau launch trip around the lake from Home Bay. Visit the park and you'll find incredible vegetation and waterfalls—as well as fog, mist, and chronically wet conditions. The drive takes four to five hours, much of it on unpaved road. The Wairoa bus goes there twice a week, on Tuesdays and Thursdays. Stop at park headquarters at Aniwaniwa for trail information, fishing permits, and so on. In addition to many short walking trails, from November through March consider a five-day trek from Ruatahuna down the Whakatane Valley or three to four days on the Waikaremoana Track, starting at Onepoto, for vast panoramas and beautiful views of the lake. This track can get crowded between mid-December and the end of January. Especially for this period, book long in advance at the Waikaremoana Motor Camp (Home Bay, tel. 826 Tuai) at the shore on the eastern arm of the lake, at the center of a park trail system. Tent sites are NZ$5; caravan sites are NZ$6; cabins are NZ$24 double; and motel and chalet units are NZ$44-$50 double. There's a store, but bring in your own nonperishable food.

East Cape: Another alternative is to head northeastward on Highway 30 around Lake Rotorua to the Titikere thermal area (Hell's Gate), Lakes Rotoiti, Rotoehu, and Rotomo to Whakatane (57 miles) on the "Sunrise Coast," and then 37 miles on Highway 2 to Opitiki, circling East Cape to Gisborne, 205 miles (2 days) of isolated splendor, idyllic golden beaches and picnic spots with lots of sunshine, camping on deserted sandy bays, ancient and beautiful pohutukawa trees, rugged mountains creating major rivers (Waiapu, Waipaoa, and remote Motu) with outstanding white water rafting and canoeing challenges, superb cycling, and visits to elegantly carved Maori meeting houses. The coastal route to Te Kaha and beyond it to Whanarua Bay, Waihau Bay, and Whangaparaoa is beautiful. Break the trip with a stop at Hicks Bay and see the Tuwhakairiora meeting house (1872). Along the way, there are two beautiful walkways: Anaura Bay Walkway (two hours) through the Anaura Scenic Reserve and the Cooks Cove Walkway at the end of Tolaga Bay, each less than six miles round-trip. When you finally arive in Gisborne, the treat awaiting is the Bread and Roses Restaurant (tel. 486-697) for excellent crepes, quiches, vegetarian dishes, and fresh bread.

Several excellent motor camps with tent sites, caravan sites, cabins, bunks, and tourist flats are located around East Cape, near beaches, good fishing, and hiking, in **Tolaga Bay** (tel. 716), between **Hicks Bay** and **Te Araroa** (tel. 873), and near **Te Kaha** (tel. 894).

Next to beautiful **Waikanae Beach** (safe for swimming), near an Olympic-size pool, and within half a mile of downtown **Gisborne, Waikanae Beach Motor**

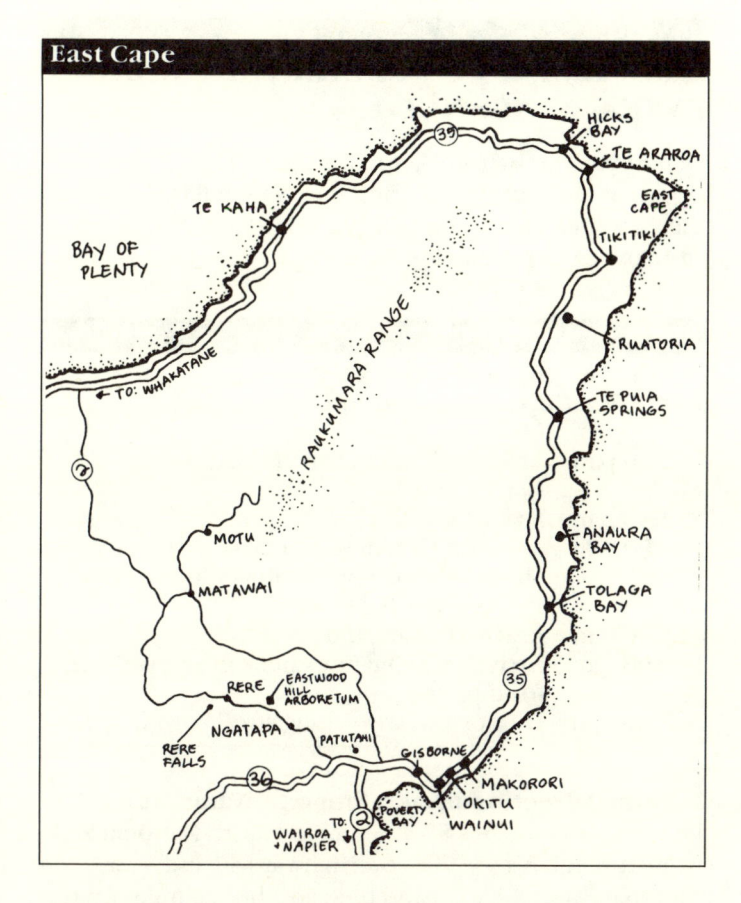

Camp (Grey St., tel. 079/75-634) has tent sites (NZ$10 for two), power sites (NZ$12 for two), ranch house cabins (NZ$20 single or double), and tourist cabins with private bathrooms (NZ$43, all plus GST).

For obvious reasons, guests keep coming back to Hilton and Elizabeth Croskery's charming old **Greengables Travel Hotel** (31 Rawiri St., Gisborne, tel. 079/75-872), which offers nine spacious and nicely furnished rooms sharing four showers and an excellent full breakfast for NZ$40 single and NZ$65 double (incl. GST).

DAY 9
LAKE TAUPO—TONGARIRO NATIONAL PARK—WANGANUI

Depart very early from Taupo for sightseeing on the slopes of Mt. Ruapehu in Tongariro National Park. From the park, head for Wanganui, the "Garden City" on the Tasman Sea, for a relaxing evening.

Suggested Schedule

8:00 a.m.	Breakfast and check out.
11:00 a.m.	Explore Taupo and have an early lunch.
1:00 p.m.	Leave Taupo for Turangi.
2:00 p.m.	Arrive in Turangi and visit the Trout Hatchery.
2:30 p.m.	Leave for Ohakune.
4:00 p.m.	Arrive in Ohakune and drive up Ohakune Mountain Road on Mt. Ruapehu. See the sunset from Turoa ski lift.
5:30 p.m.	Leave for Wanganui.
8:00 p.m.	Arrive in Wanganui, check in and prepare for dinner.
8:30 p.m.	Dinner and an evening stroll before bed.

Driving Directions: Lake Taupo to Wanganui
From Lake Taupo, it's 58 miles to Tongariro National Park; from Turangi, it's 55 miles on Highways 47 and 4 past National Park to Raetihi and then another 20 miles on the Wanganyui River Road to Pipiriki, and 48 miles along the river to Wanganui, unless you decide to stay all the way on sealed Highway 4 to Wanganui, 56 miles from Raetihi. At most, today's drive should be 140 to 160 miles, including a visit to Tongariro National Park.

Take Highway 1 from Taupo to Turangi; Highway 47 toward National Park and the Chateau up the Te Ponanga Saddle for great views of Lake Rotoaira and Mt. Tongariro; drive up Mt. Ruapehu to the Chateau and Tongariro National Park Headquarters, and then back down to the highway and the town of National Park; turn on Highway

4 and take a left on Highway 49A to Ohakune on Mt. Ruapehu's southwestern flank or continue straight to Raetihi, the decision point for taking either the Wanganui River (gravel) or Mangawhero River (Highway 4, sealed) route to Wanganui. Both are scenic.

Although travel through the area between Taupo and Wanganui is much more scenic by car or bicycle, canoe or boat, the main Auckland-Wellington railway line runs through the western part of the region, stopping at National Park, Ohakune, and Taumarunui.

Sightseeing Highlights

▲▲**Tongariro Trout Hatchery** tells about the history of trout fishing in the area. In the underwater viewing chamber downstairs, you can observe trout of all sizes and watch the spawning process.

▲▲▲**Tongariro National Park**, New Zealand's first, consists of three volcanoes: Tongariro (6,458 feet), Ngauruhoe (7,515 feet), and Ruapehu (9,175 feet). All three have erupted within memory, showering forest and scrub with hot ash; the most recent was Mt. Ruapehu in 1975. Rings of mud flows surround the mountain below the snow line. Crater Lake at its summit is warm and acidic, a shallow liquid lid for its smoldering volcanic depths. It is actually dangerous to descend the steep cliffs surrounding Crater Lake, and conditions around the lake vary with volcanic activity.

The Te Maari Crater on the north side of Tongariro, a truncated multiple volcano, shows signs of recent activity and lava flows. The Te Maari Crater and the Red Crater on Tongariro, past the Emerald Lakes, are steaming and sulfurous. The perfectly symmetrical cone of Mount Ngauruhoe is the most active of the three volcanoes. For information and interesting displays covering the park's geology, volcanic activity, flora and fauna, hiking trails and walking tours, stop at the Tongariro National Park Headquarters in Whakapapa Village (tel. 23-729) or the Ohakune Ranger Station and Park Information Centre at the start of Ohakune Road (tel. 58-578) from 8:00 a.m. to 5:00 p.m.

▲ **Ohakune** is the start-off point for many rafting, fishing, hiking, and canoeing trips, as well as the winter base for skiers in the national park and the Kaimanawa State Forest Park. From Ohakune drive up Ruapehu's southwestern flank traversing the park's various climatic zones. Weather in the park is very unpredictable, turning very bad (rain or snow) quickly on the western slopes. There's rain almost 200 days a year at Whakapapa Village. Bring rain gear and warm clothing. From mid-December to January 31, book ahead for accommodations in Turangi and Whakapapa Village.

Where to Stay
Tongariro National Park
Expect accommodations in the park to be scarce. Book well in advance. Campers have some additional choices. Ask at the Whakapapa Information Centre about the nine **huts** with bunks in the mountains (NZ$8 pp) and tent sites (NZ$4) for rent. **Mahuia Campground** located on Highway 47 about 3 miles from National Park, near the Mangahuia Stream, has free tent and caravan sites with toilets and fireplaces. Also check out **Mangawhero campground** on Ohakune Mountain Road. On the west side of Ohakune, near the post office, the modern **Ohakune YHA Hostel** (Clyde St., tel. 58-724) even has some private rooms with your own key for NZ$12. Book well in advance.

Surrounded by lush bush, **Whakapapa Motor Camp** (c/o Department of Conservation, Private Bag, Mount Ruapehu, tel. 0812/22-3897) offers tent (NZ$6) and caravan sites (NZ$8) with privacy, bunk rooms (NZ$10 pp), four- and six-berth cabins (NZ$9 pp/NZ$28 min.), and tourist flats (NZ$12 pp, NZ$38 min.), communal toilets, showers, laundry facilities, and a small camp store.

At the junction of Highways 4 and 47 in National Park, the Marshall Gebbie's **Buttercup Alpine Resort** (tel. 0812/22-702) has a variety of lodge units with shared and private bathrooms for singles, couples, and up to four people. With breakfast and dinner (in the Butternut Farm-

Day 9 105

Wanganui

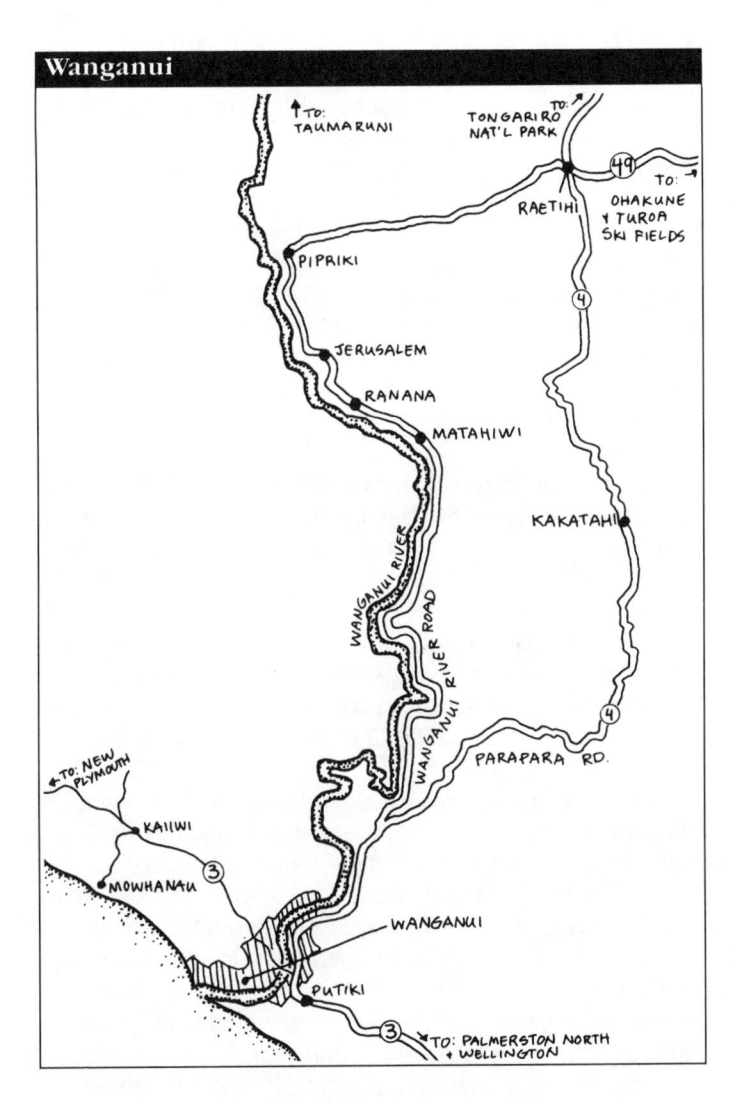

house Restaurant, see Where to Eat, below), rates are NZ$60 pp adults and NZ$40 children under 13.

Located in Whakapapa Village, with spectacular valley and Ngauruhoe views, the **Ruapehu Skotel** (c/o Mt. Ruapehu Post Office, tel. 0812-Mt. Ruapehu 819) in summer has lodge rooms accommodating up to four with shared bathrooms (NZ$36-$48 single or twin) and private bathrooms (NZ$65-$85 double) and chalets with fully equipped kitchens and private bathrooms (NZ$82), with a guest kitchen, washer-dryers, glass-enclosed hot spa and sauna, gym, Pinnacles Restaurant (see Where to Eat, below), and bar. Remember, rates almost double in winter. Ask about the low-budget rooms with a handbasin and heater for NZ$17 pp.

THC Chateau Tongariro (Mt. Ruapehu, Tongariro National Park, tel. 0812-23/809) has elegant rooms for NZ$83 single or double (in summer), with a heated pool and sauna, which is a very good value.

Wanganui

Centrally located, the **Wanganui YH Hostel** (43 Campbell St., tel. 064/56-780) has small and large rooms for NZ$12 pp. The homey **YWCA** (232 Wicksteed St, tel. 064/57-480) is even less expensive (NZ$9 pp), and its nine single rooms are no less comfortable than the hostel.

Four miles from Wanganui and near Castlecliff Beach (near a city bus line), the hospitable Fiddes' **Alwyn Motor Court and Motel Flats** (65 Karaka St., Castlecliff, Wanganui, tel. 064/44-500) has 30 fully equipped cabins, most with bunk beds and communal showers (NZ$22 double, NZ$7 for extra adults), and three with shower, toilet, and stove for NZ$30 double (incl. GST). Four very nice, self-contained two-bedroom motel flats rent for NZ$46 double, NZ$11 for extra adults (incl. GST). **Castlecliff Camp** (corner of Karaka and Rangiora sts., Castlecliff, tel. 064/42-227) has inexpensive tent sites, caravan sites, on-site caravans, and one cabin next to the beach.

On the city-side bank of the river, out east on Somme Parade, **Aramoho Motor Camp** (Camp Manager, 460 Somme Parade, Wanganui, tel. 064/38-402) has tent sites (NZ$8 double), caravan sites (NZ$15 double), bunk spaces (NZ$10 pp), cabins (NZ$23-$35), and tourist flats (NZ$40-$50 single/double), all incl. GST.

Just a short walk from the center of town, the almost 100-year-old but carefully renovated **Riverside Inn** (2

Plymouth St., tel. 064/32-529) has ten comfortable, old-fashioned rooms (only one with a private shower) that rent for NZ$32 single and NZ$43.50 double with a continental breakfast (incl. GST). Lunches and dinners are available on request. Also close to the city center and on a city bus line, Alison and Graham Shaw's **Avro Motel** (36 Alma Rd., tel. 064/55-279) offers both motel units (NZ$60-$70 single/double (incl. GST) and unusual caravan hookups that each also have little cabins with a shower, toilet, and washroom/dressing room (NZ$20 double, incl. GST). A large swimming pool and spa pools are on the premises.

You'll confuse **Acacia Park Motel** (140 Anzac Parade, Wanganui East, tel. 064/39-093) with a lovely tree-filled park along the river. It's about a mile from the center of the city, but you can get up in the morning and just cross the street to Wanganui River Jet Boat Tours. In two parkland acres, there is no better value in the area than Acacia's eight fully self-contained units (NZ$50-$65 single/double, plus GST), spa pool, and other facilities.

Also just a mile from the center of town (near a city bus line), across from sheep grazing in pretty Peat Park Deer Reserve, **River City Motel** (59 Halswell St., tel. 064/39-107) has eight fully equipped two-bedroom units that are ideal for families and, like the Acacia, good value (NZ$56-$77 single/double, incl. GST).

Where to Eat
Tongariro National Park
For sit-down meals in Whakapapa, the bistro meal at Skotel's **Pinnacle Restaurant** for lunch or dinner will cost NZ$12-$20. In Ohakune, where the choices are much greater and the food less expensive, sit-down or take-out pizza, fish, salads, and other fare from the **Cafe Stutz** (Clyde St., tel. 58-563) is as good as any for less than NZ$8. Out on Highway 4, the **Butternut Farmhouse Restaurant** has excellent, moderately priced lunches and dinners.

Wanganui

On the riverbank, for less than NZ$12 the **Garden Bistro Restaurant** (33 Somme Parade, tel. 38-800) serves generous portions of fish, beef, salad or whatever you order at lunch or dinner (5:30-9:00 p.m.) Next door, at **The Riverside Cellars and Deli**, pick up a variety of excellent deli items for a picnic excursion. Monday through Friday, 8:00 a.m. to 4:30 p.m., relax and enjoy light lunch or tea at **Dr. Johnson's Coffee Lounge** at a patio table under the skylight in the Tudor Court Arcade on Victoria Avenue. **Capers** in the Victoria Mall also is a local favorite for coffee, tea, and snacks.

Overlooking beautiful Virginia Lake and the winter gardens, have a light lunch at **Shangri-La Restaurant** (BYO) on Great North Road. This is one of Wanganui's and New Zealand's most pleasant dining or afternoon tea experiences.

Itinerary Options

Lake Taupo—Turangi: Try the easy three-hour walk along the river from Taupo to Aratiatia or vice versa. Turangi, at the southern end of Lake Taupo on the banks of the Tongariro River, is the self-proclaimed "Heart of the Great New Zealand Outdoors" and "Trout Fishing Capital of the World." There you can be outfitted, licensed, and pumped full of valuable information for fishing in the best places for brown trout in March and April and rainbow trout May through September. Local fishing guides are available.

Four hours of rafting on the Tongariro or Mohaka rivers (contact Tongariro River Rafting, tel. 073/80-233) costs NZ$65 per person.

Fly-fish on Lake Tarawera, where 9- to 10-pound rainbow trout can be netted during the May-June spawning season.

Tongariro National Park: For "trampers," the Ketetahi Track from Highway 47 near Lake Rotaira to the Mangatepopo trail hut offers great views over hundreds of square miles to the north, including all of Lake Taupo. As an alternative to this two- to three-day hike, Venture Treks, a local guide service, offers a five-day guided trek, the Mt. Ruapehu Alpine Walk, around the mountain to Ruapehu's crater lake. In summer, a walk from Whakapapa Village to the summit of Mt. Tongariro offers breathtaking views across Tongariro National Park to Lake Taupo, the Kaimanawas, and Mt. Egmont. In winter, Whakapapa is an enormous ski field, mostly for intermediate and advanced skiers, with an uphill capacity of 13,500 skiers an hour. Combine excellent spring skiing with incredible trout fishing or local white-water rafting in the Tongariro or Rangitikei rivers. National Park Headquarters in Whakapapa will supply all needed information, maps, hunting licenses, and suggested guide services. Just 11 miles from Ohakune and an hour's drive from Whakapapa on the southern slopes of Mt. Ruapehu, the Turoa skifield offers plenty of slopes for all levels of skiers.

Pick up maps and detailed information at Park Headquarters about two longer treks: the Round-the-Mountain Track, a 4- to 5-day walk around Mt. Ruapehu or 4 days around Mt. Ngauruhoe, starting in Whakapapa Village, and the 5-day walk across Tongariro National Park starting near Ohakune (called the "Tongariro Traverse").

Wanganui River Road: At Pipiriki, 18 miles west of Raetihi, center of the new Whanganui National Park, see the reconstructed riverboat *Ongarue*. This is the northern starting point of the **Wanganui River route**, 30 scenic miles of narrow, winding, tortuous, mostly gravel (about half unsealed, between Koriniti and six miles west of Raetihi) along the banks of the Wanganui River, with numerous one-lane bridges, offering marvelous views at a price. Village settlements along the river are mostly Maori, and you'll see various churches, mission houses, a carved meeting house, and other historic buildings. Above Pipiriki, to Taumaruni, the river and its 239 rapids are navigable only by jet boats or canoes. An all-day trip from Wanganui takes you 18 miles beyond Pipiriki for

NZ$95. Contact **Pipiriki Jet Boat Tours** (tel. Raetihi 54-633) for information.

Napier from Taupo: Napier is about 85 miles southeast of Taupo (146 miles south of Gisborne and about 180 miles northeast of Wellington), but the drive from Taupo to Napier through very varied landscape takes much longer than you would normally expect—about 5 hours on Highway 5 through some rugged mountain areas. Napier is the largest city on **Hawke's Bay**, in a fertile fruit-growing region. Destroyed by an earthquake in 1931, the city was rebuilt into perhaps the world's foremost example of Art Deco-style buildings with many unusual attractions.

After watching the 20-minute audiovisual about the 1931 earthquake at the **Hawke's Bay Art Gallery and Museum**, take the 45-minute self-guided tour of this unique city. Most important is the **Marine Parade**, lined with towering Norfolk pines, that south to north includes the three-story **Hawke's Bay Aquarium** with a huge oceanarium of tropical and freshwater fish (open 9:00 a.m. to 5:00 p.m. daily, admission NZ$4.50 adults and NZ$1.50 children under 15); the 45-minute **Marineland** show, like Seaworld in the United States but without killer whales (open 9:00 a.m. to 5:30 p.m., admission NZ$4.50 adults and NZ$1.75 children under 15); and the **Nocturnal Wildlife Centre** with kiwi, kiore, cave weta, bush gecko, and other native and exotic wildlife (open 9:00 a.m. to 4:30 p.m., admission NZ$2.20 adults and NZ$.82 children).

Other special attractions in the area include the view of Hawke's Bay from **Bluff Hill**, a visit to wineries, especially **Vidals**, in the vicinity of pretty **Hastings**, about 12 miles away, and the drive up **Te Mata Peak** for spectacular views over the region from 1,300 feet up.

Nature lovers shouldn't miss **Cape Kidnappers Gannet Sanctuary**, the world's only mainland gannet colony. From Clifton Domain, 12 miles southeast of Napier, the two-hour trip to the sanctuary along 4 miles of sandy beach can only be made at low tide (timed carefully with the tides). Join the **"Gannet Safari"** from **Summerlee Station**, a high-country farm with thousands of ewes and hundreds of breeding cows, which will take you to within a few yards of the gannets' breeding ritual on the cape.

For travelers electing to head southeast to Wellington via Napier, rather than southwest to Wanganui, continue past Hastings on Route 2, with a stop at the **Mt. Bruce National Wildlife Centre**, 18 miles north of Masterton, on the slopes of Mt. Bruce. New Zealand's common and rare birds inhabit this beautifully natural environment, including the takahe, a flightless relative of the pukeko, and the black stilt, both very rare bird species from South Island habitats. Open 10:00 a.m. to 4:00 p.m. daily.

DAY 10
WANGANUI—WELLINGTON

Take a relaxing break from driving. Stroll in Wanganui's lovely parks, travel by riverboat up the tranquil Wanganui for a wine-tasting tour, and visit a regional museum before driving on very good roads down the scenic west ("Kapiti") coast to Wellington.

Suggested Schedule

8:30 a.m.	Breakfast.
9:30 a.m.	Drurie Hill vistas.
10:30 a.m.	Visit your choice of parks or museum.
12:30 p.m.	Lunch and check out.
2:00 p.m.	Tour the Holly Lodge Estate Winery along the Wanganui River.
4:30 p.m.	Return to Wanganui and depart for Wellington.
6:30 p.m.	Dinner near Levin on the west coast.
9:00 p.m.	Arrive in Wellington and check in.

Driving Directions: Wanganui to Wellington
Wanganui to Wellington is a 125-mile drive. The quick way is on Highways 3 and 1 through Bulls and Levin. Driving at night you'll miss very little. Past Levin you can leave Highway 1 at historic Otaki to see the impressive Rangiatea Maori church (1850). From Waikananae you can drive down the Akatarawa Valley to Highway 2 in Upper Hutt, then continue through Lower Hutt and Petone to Wellington. The enjoyable part of this trip is the coastal beaches, especially shell collecting at Paekakariki.

Sightseeing Highlights
▲▲**Wanganui**'s tree-lined riverfront, green hills, and many lovely parks make it one of New Zealand's more picturesque cities. Visit the "Garden City's" Cook's Gardens, Queen's Park, the Aramoho Park, Moutoa Gardens, Victoria Park, Peat Park, and especially beautiful Virgina Lake. Also see Bushy Park, 15 miles northwest of Wanganui, a fine old home with spacious gardens and a

bush park, open Wednesday through Sunday, 10:00 a.m. to 5:00 p.m., NZ$2 adults, NZ$1 children. Drop by the Hospitality Wanganui Information Centre at 100 Guyton Street (tel. 064/53-286) for maps, brochures, and even a personalized tour guide (free).

▲▲**The Wanganui River** offers a pleasant riverboat (or jet boat) ride. For information on the historic *MV Waireka* riverboat trip to Hipango Park with a stop at the Holly Lodge Estate (Papaiti Road, Upper Aramoho) call 39-344. NZ$20 adults, NZ$10 children. For jet boat information, contact **Wanganui River Jet Tours**, tel. 36-346.

▲▲**Wanganui Regional Museum** in Queen's Park houses a large and exceptional Maori collection, including a 75-foot war canoe. Open weekdays from 9:30 a.m. to 4:30 p.m., weekends 1:00 to 4:30 p.m., NZ$1.76.

▲▲**Durie Hill** (216 feet) at the south end of the Wanganui Bridge provides a splendid view of the region. Take the elevator to a platform at the summit. For an even better view, ascend the Durie Hill War Memorial Tower.

Where to Stay
Hostels: Wellington YHA Hostel (40 Tinakori Rd., tel. 04/736-271) couldn't be more central, just up the hill from the Parliament, railway station, and Picton ferry terminal, or the other way, to the Botanical Garden and cable car. This big, rambling house has room for 48 overnighters (seniors NZ$14 and juniors half, incl. GST).

Somewhere on Mt. Victoria, no-frills travelers will find a place to stay. The renovated **Ivanhoe Inn** (52 Ellice St., Mt Victoria, tel. 04/842-264) nestled among colonial houses on Mt. Victoria's southeast flank is very nice. Spacious single, twin, and double rooms rent from NZ$22-$29 single/double and NZ$14 for a dormitory bed (with your own sleeping bag). If the dormitories in nearby **Beethoven House** (89 Brougham St., tel. 04/842-264) are not jammed, travelers without reservations anywhere may appreciate a bed and other facilities here at NZ$13 pp including breakfast (and GST). No reservations accepted. Otherwise, just down the street, **Rowena Budget Travel Hotel** (115 Brougham St., tel. 04/857-872) has singles, doubles, and triples (NZ$16.50 pp, incl. GST) as well as dormitory space at NZ$13.20, with full or continental breakfast at a small charge (NZ$2-$3). There is off-street parking, and plenty of bus routes pass by. The **Richmond Guest House** (116 Brougham St., tel. 04/858-529) has B&B rooms for NZ$30 pp (incl. GST).

Motor Camps/Cabins: There are plenty of tent sites (NZ$12-$16, single/double) and caravan sites (NZ$18, incl. GST) on the 92 acres of the **Hutt Park Motor Camp** (95 Hutt Park Rd., Moera, Lower Hutt, 04/685-913), but 58 two-berth and other cabins, cottages, and tourist flats (NZ$22-$42) go fast, especially now that the place has improved so much, so book them while driving south from Wanganui or before leaving Wellington (only a 15-minute drive).

Motel Flats: "Budget" in 1990 among Wellington's motels means rates less than NZ$70 single or double plus GST. The spacious and attractively furnished five units at the **Wellington Luxury Motel** (14 Hobson St., tel. 04/726-825) probably are the only quality units that qualify. If you're prepared to pay for extra measures of comfort and central location, head for the **Apollo Lodge** (49 Majoribanks St., tel. 04/851-849) for one of 33 units, including separate bedrooms, full kitchens or serviced units (NZ$88 single or double incl. GST); or the 14 one- and two-bedroom apartments in the **Majoribanks Apartments** (38 Majoribanks St., tel. 04/857-305) across the street, with off-street parking, also NZ$88 single or double (incl. GST).

Licensed Hotels: The relatively new (1985) **West Plaza Hotel** (110-116 Wakefield St., P.O. Box 11648, Wellington, tel. 04/731-440) may still be a surprising "budget-splurge," especially for two or three people. This beautifully designed hotel in the center of Wellington near the new Michael Fowler Centre (contemporary auditorium added to Wellington's old Town Hall) was only NZ$176 (plus GST) for certain rooms for up to three people or better still on a weekend rate, which makes even the **THC James Cook** (The Terrace, tel. 04/725-865) a worthwhile budget-splurge.

Where to Eat
If you rent a place on Brougham Street, almost inevitably you'll be tempted to try soup, salad, and a variety of dishes for lunch at the **Victoria Cafe** (59 Brougham St.). Lunch is NZ$10 or less, but dinner can be pricey (NZ$20 or over). On the main shopping street, attractive, small **Glossops** (149 Willis, tel. 849-091) has a variety of tasty lunch and dinner menu items from salads and sandwiches to gourmet main courses from NZ$10-$13.

Soups, salads, and muffins at **The Great New Zealand Soup Kitchen** (32 Waring Taylor St.) are among the best in town. And vegetarians flock for lunches and dinners to **That's Natural** (88 Manners St. Mall, tel. 736-681) or **Amrita Vegetarian Restaurant**, 127 Cuba Mall.

Before leaving the North Island, try the great charcoaled steaks at **Beefeater**, 105 The Terrace, tel. 738-195. **Il Casino**, 108 Tory Street, tel. 857-496, is the best North Italian restaurant in New Zealand for decor and fine pasta, seafood, gnocchi, and other tasty dishes. If you prefer just darn good hamburgers and sundaes, stop at **Rockefellers**, 132 Oriental Parade, tel. 846-975.

Around Country Place, you'll find: rarified atmosphere and prices at the **Bacchus**, 8 Courtney Place, tel. 846-592, where you can order anything confidently; BYO French lunch or dinner at **Chez Nigel**, 29A Courtney Place, tel. 844-535; **Java**, 99 Courtney Place, tel. 857-620, for one of the most interesting dining experiences in Wellington; and delicious venison dishes at **Marcel's**, 104 Courtney Place, tel. 842-159.

Itinerary Option
John Hammond's River Road Tours (tel. 54-635) offers a complete river tour by minibus with a stop in the picturesque Maori village of Jerusalem for tea and to meet residents. Hammond drops off mail and picks up locals all along the way, which adds to the casual fun.

DAY 11
WELLINGTON

Enjoy leisurely sightseeing on Marine Drive, overlooking the harbor from many different view points, followed by a cable car ride to the Kelburn Terminal area to choose a restaurant for dinner and views of the city. In between, tour the city's most interesting architectural, historical, and cultural attractions. All the while, enjoy no fog, no smog, and no pollution in "Windy Wellington."

Suggested Schedule

8:30 a.m.	Breakfast.
9:30 a.m.	Depart for Marine Drive.
12:00 noon	Picnic lunch along Marine Drive at Lyall Bay.
1:30 p.m.	Drop off your car, then tour Parliament buildings.
2:30 p.m.	National Museum and Art Gallery.
4:00 p.m.	Cable car to Kelburn and the Botanic Gardens.
7:00 p.m.	Dinner and possibly entertainment at the Michael Fowler Centre.

Transportation
The Wellington City Corporation bus system mainly operates south of the city. Trains are used to the north. Eastern, western, and southern bus routes start at the railroad station on Waterloo Quay or at Courtenay Place. Pick up timetables from newsstands. Four commuter trains run to Upper and Lower Hutt and other northern destinations. InterCity buses run up the peninsula's west coast and center (tel. 725-399 for bus and rail information). Newmans Coach Tours operate east coast intercity services from 260 Taranki Street. Mt. Cook Landlines runs between Wellington and Auckland (11 hours). Day (Silver Fern) and night (Northerner) trains to Auckland and intermediate points leave Monday through Saturday from the New Zealand Railways Terminal.

You can't beat local buses for inexpensive touring. The **Downtowner** provides five trips for NZ$2.20 (including off-peak rides on the cable car) and the **Daytripper** gives one adult and two children rides all day for NZ$5.50. (Leave your car parked and travel to Lyall Bay this way.) Take the **East by West ferry** (tel. 499-1273), which provides an inexpensive (NZ$5 adults one-way) harbor tour while crossing between Queen's Wharf and Days Bay. (Take a stroll to Eastbourne, then return.)

Inter-Island ferries leave Wellington at 8:00 a.m. (except Mondays and Tuesdays), 10:00 a.m., 4:00 p.m., and 6:40 p.m. (except Sundays) for Picton. The crossing takes three hours.

Orientation

Approach Wellington along the "Gold Coast," actually an elongated suburb on the western edge of the southern peninsula. The rugged mountain forests of the Rimutakas and Tararua ranges separate the Wairapa Plain to the east from the western coastal area.

New Zealand's capital city at the tip of this peninsula is set in a green amphitheater on a sparkling harbor. On a sunny and windy day, Wellington becomes a very beautiful city. It can be best appreciated from the Cook Strait ferry heading through the harbor; from atop Mt. Victoria; or at various points on the 24-mile Marine Drive, especially from the north side of Miramar Peninsula. The winds funneling through Wellington from Cook Strait allow crisp, clear views of the surrounding forested peninsulas, the pastel wooden buildings climbing the hills above Oriental Bay, and the conglomeration of government and office buildings rimming the waterfront.

On weekends the government and corporate population disappears and, unlike in Auckland, it's a good time to visit and bargain for reduced hotel rates. Otherwise book in advance. Good city bus service from the railway station will take care of your transportation needs. For bookings and other information, use the Information Office at the railway center or the Government Tourist Bureau.

Wellington—Marine Drive

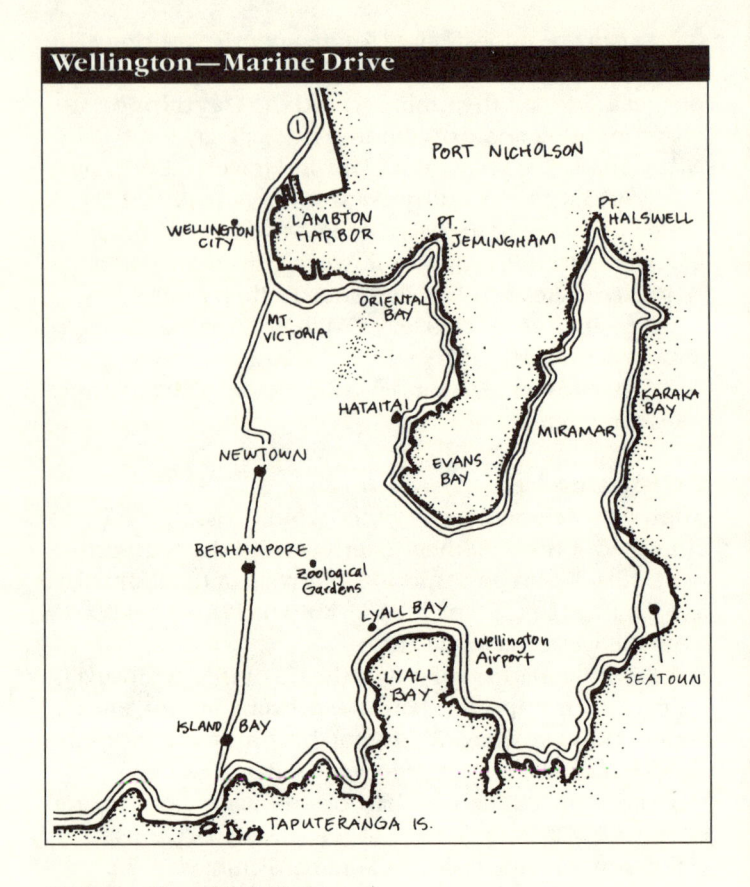

Sightseeing Highlights

▲▲ **Marine Drive** hugs the harbor shore for 24 miles, skirting Oriental and Evans bays, looping around Miramar Peninsula, where there are fine views of the harbor at the Massey Memorial. Several soft sandy swimming beaches, including Scorching, Karaka, and Worser Bays in the inner harbor and Lyall and Island Bays in the outer harbor, offer inviting places to stop and see spectacular bush-covered hills around the bright blue bay waters.

▲The circular domed **Parliament**, the "Beehive," houses the government's executive offices. Free tours are conducted hourly from 9:00 a.m. to 3:30 p.m.

▲**The Old Government Building** at the northern end of Lambton Quay is one of the largest all-wooden buildings in the world. In a city where old edifices are rapidly being replaced by modern office structures, this wooden Italianate civic building is all the rarer and more precious.

▲▲**The National Museum** has excellent Maori and Pacific Island collections (10:00 a.m. to 4:45 p.m. daily). Also see the adjoining National Art Gallery, with New Zealand and international art.

▲**City Council**'s 2½-hour afternoon bus tour, costing NZ$10 adults, is an inexpensive and easy way to see all of Wellington's sightseeing highlights. The Public Relations Office (PRO) Visitor's Centre at 2 Mercer Street (and Victoria St., tel. 735-063) offers a more extensive 2½-hour tour for NZ$17 adults, NZ$8 children.

▲▲▲**Cable cars** climb for about four minutes up to the Kelburn terminal from Cable Car Lane off Lambton Quay in the heart of the shopping district. The cost is NZ$.80 adults, NZ$.40 children, one way. From there, walk down through the Botanic Gardens and the Lady Norwood Rose Gardens, to Thorndon, where some of the city's older wooden cottages (dating from the 1870s) cluster on Ascot Street.

DAY 12
WELLINGTON TO CHRISTCHURCH

Over a thousand years ago, the original Polynesian settlers in the Marlborough Sounds region started hunting moa, the giant flightless relative of the ostrich, until its inevitable extinction. Four hundred Maoris watched in astonishment as Capt. James Cook's *HMS Endeavor* sailed past in 1770. Abel Tasman had been the first European arrival, 128 years before the *Endeavor* dropped anchor, but Tasman stayed only a few days before sailing north. After claiming the land for the king and naming the sound for Queen Charlotte, Cook circumnavigated the South Island, returned to the sound for reprovision, and sailed back to England, revisiting the sound four more times for a total of 15 weeks between 1770 and 1777. The bush-covered hillsides of Queen Charlotte Sound, which you pass aboard the Inter-Island Ferry from Wellington to Picton, were heavily forested in Cook's time. Today you'll still have no difficulty understanding why it was one of his favorite anchorages.

Suggested Schedule

8:00 a.m.	Breakfast and check out.
10:00 a.m.	Inter-Island Ferry across Cook Strait to Picton. Lunch on board.
2:00 p.m.	Train, bus, or car to Christchurch.
8:00 p.m.	Arrive Christchurch and check in.
9:00 p.m.	Late dinner and stroll along the Avon.

As in the Bay of Islands, which is closer to the equator but actually less sunny and warm than the north coast of the South Island, you can charter yachts and cruisers, rent fishing boats of all kinds in the Marlborough Sounds area, and find a remote island, bay, or cove with white sand beaches for a getaway day or week, or join a variety of cruises almost any time of day. There are over 600 miles of coastline to choose from. Behind the sounds are warm hills and valleys with fruit orchards and vineyards, national parks with trout-filled lakes and rivers, and even mountains for skiing.

From Wellington's Aotea Quay, board the Cook Strait ferry in the morning for Picton on the South Island, leaving the marvelous views of Wellington's harbor and sailing through beautiful Marlborough Sound to the head of Queen Charlotte Sound. Nearby Blenheim, Nelson, and the entire north coast and its national parks and lakes offer sufficient temptations to spend at least a week instead of immediately departing for Christchurch. Travel south along the scenic Kaikoura coast to Christchurch.

Transportation
Turn in your rented car in Wellington (without penalty or one-way charge) and pick up another car in Christchurch from the same rental company, continuing your weekly rental agreement, or pick up another car in Picton if you prefer not to take the train or bus.

Between Wellington and Picton on the South Island there are four ferry services daily each way (with exceptions noted above, Day 11) for NZ$30 adults and NZ$15 children (plus GST, without car). A car is NZ$75-$100 depending on the season and the car. The crossing in daylight and in good weather is a scenic, fun trip.

The train, more quaint than comfortable, leaves the Picton station near the ferry landing at 2:10 p.m. and arrives in Christchurch at 8:05 p.m., NZ$43 one way.

If you decide to drive, book ferry space for the car or camper van as far in advance as possible (months ahead, for travel during Australian holidays). The wharf terminal buildings at Wellington are off Aotea Quay. The turnoff is clearly marked by road signs. Report one hour before sailing time. Driver and passengers must have passenger tickets.

Picton is 210 miles from Christchurch not counting worthwhile short side trips such as a 12-mile round-trip up Kaikaura Peninsula for splendid views from the Lookout. From Picton, train and bus travelers as well as drivers will follow Highway 1 south through Blenheim, along the seaward Kaikaura range and its narrow, wild coastline. In Kaikaura, motorists can take a break in the six-hour trip to walk along the shoreline and have refreshments.

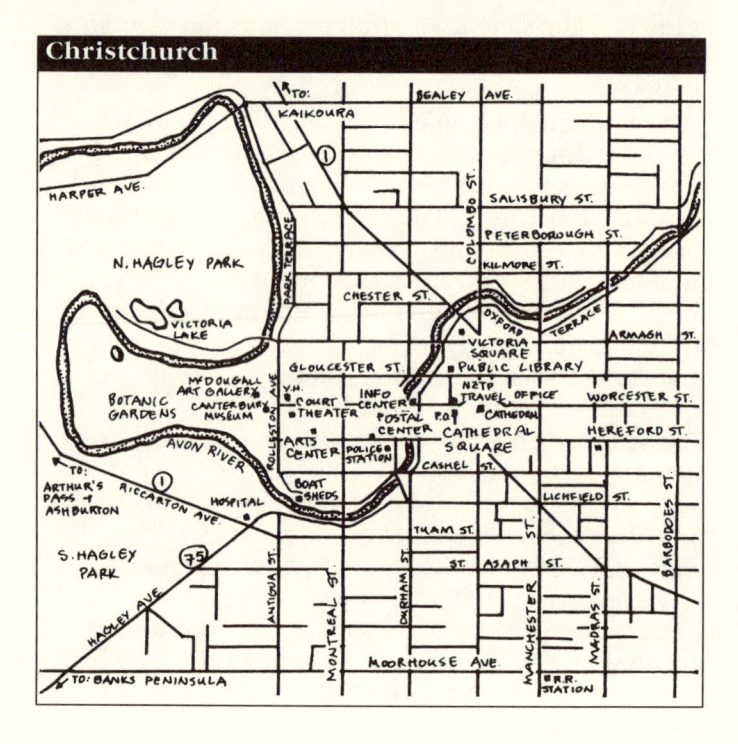

Sightseeing Highlights
▲▲▲ **Marlborough Sounds Maritime Park** region contains a marvelous variety of outdoor recreation. From Picton, Havelock, and Motueka, rent charter yachts, line-fishing boats, and game-fishing boats, or cruise to sandy bays, coves, islands and their virtually untouched beaches in the region's deep inlets. The rangers' offices in Blenheim and Havelock, as well as local Visitors' Information offices, have all the necessary maps, guides, and other information.

Where to Stay

Hostels: A wonderful old mansion almost two miles from Cathedral Square, the **Cora Wilding Youth Hostel** (9 Evelyn Couzins Ave., Avebury Park, Richmond, Christchurch, tel. 03/899-199), accommodates 40 people in 7 cheerful sleeping rooms at NZ$12 (incl. GST) for seniors, juniors half price. Much closer to Cathedral Square and just a few blocks from the river, **Rolleston House YHA Hostel** (5 Worcester St., tel. 03/666-564) accommodates 47 in 11 pleasant sleeping rooms at NZ$14 seniors (incl. GST), juniors half price. Both places have a friendly, comfortable atmosphere that is a pleasure to come home to.

Motor Camps: About three miles from the city's center, **Meadow Park Motor Camp** (39 Meadow St., off Hwy 1, tel. 03/529-176) has tent sites (NZ$14 double), caravan sites (NZ$15 double), cabins, and other units from NZ$27 to $38 (incl. GST). About six miles from the city's center, **Russley Park Motor Camp** (372 Yardhurst Rd., on Hwy. 73, tel. 03/427-021) has tent sites (NZ$14 double), caravan sites (NZ$15 double), on-site caravans (NZ$26-30 double), and small and large chalets from NZ$30 to $45 double (incl. GST).

Private Hotels/B&Bs: Only a few blocks from Cathedral Square, the busy **Hereford Private Hotel**, has a bunk room (NZ$15 pp) and single/double/twin (NZ$22-$32), breakfast extra. **Eliza's Manor House** (82 Bealey Ave., tel. 03/668-584) is in a class by itself, well worth the NZ$60 (plus GST). A beautiful 1860s mansion restored inside and out, 6 of its 10 beautifully furnished bedrooms have private baths. (See Where to Eat, below.)

Nicely renovated and decorated, the 37 rooms of the old brick **Windsor Private Hotel B&B** (52 Armagh St., tel. 03/661-503) seem all the more comfortable because of host Don Evans's gracious hospitality. Including outstanding breakfasts, the rate is NZ$63 double (plus GST). Every one of the 14 rooms in the **Wolseley Lodge** (107 Papanui Rd., tel. 03/556-202) and the lounge have all the comforts of home for only NZ$33 pp (plus GST).

Motel Flats: Just down the street from Eliza's Manor is one of Christchurch's nicer, modern motels, **Southern**

Comfort (53 Bealey Ave., tel. 03/660-383) at NZ$68-$72 (plus GST). However, it's expensive compared to the **Holiday Lodge** (862 Colombo St., tel. 03/666-584), which offers large duplexes (bedroom and glass-enclosed sun porch upstairs) for NZ$45 (plus GST).

Where to Eat

An ample variety of cafes and tearooms are distributed around Christchurch to take care of your breakfast, brunch, and lunch needs. For special dining in the spirit of the town and unique to Christchurch, follow these suggestions.

The **Gardens Restaurant and Tea Kiosk** (tel. 65-076) has a wonderful smorgasbord lunch for NZ$9.80. Another outstanding smorgasbord is at the **Sign of the Takahe** in the beautiful stone buildings on your Summit Road trip, with great views of Lyttelton Harbour estuary and Christchurch. This is a pricey (NZ$25 meal) dress-up restaurant but well worth it.

Eliza's Manor House (82 Bealey Ave., tel. 668-584) serves excellent, moderately priced meals in old paneled, red velvet decor dining rooms that fit the mansion's overall elegance (see Where to Stay, above). If you want to see one of Christchurch's favorites, try the **Dux de Lux Gourmet Vegetarian Restaurant** (Montreal and Hereford Sts. near the Arts Centre, tel. 666-919) for gourmet vegetarian dishes served cafeteria-style in a very pleasant tree-filled courtyard. Main course dishes are about NZ$17. For a fish and salad lunch with delicious desserts, try the **Greenhouse Restaurant** (663A Columbo St., tel. 668-524).

Extra-large appetites will be well rewarded at the **Wagon Wheel Restaurant** (Papanui Rd., tel. 556-159), which includes an all-you-can-eat salad bar. Main courses of chicken, lamb chops, seafood, beef, and more cost about NZ$10. Opposite the library, the **Jail Restaurant** (106 Glouster St., tel, 666-641) has all the same main courses and excellent salads for NZ$10-$20.

Save a splurge favorite, **Grimsby's** (tel. 799-040), for your last dinner in New Zealand (see Day 22).

Itinerary Options
If you have plenty of time, instead of heading directly to Christchurch, tour in the Marlborough Sounds region. Visit Nelson's Botanic Gardens, Matai Valley, and Tahuna Beach. Thirty-five miles to the northwest is Kaiteriteri, the best beach in the area. (Watch out for the katipo, a poisonous spider that lurks in beach driftwood.) See the view of Tasman Bay from Takaka Hill. The Nelson area's high-quality pottery clays have contributed to a thriving pottery craft in Nelson, Hope, Motueka, Brightwater, and Wakefield.

Nelson: About 85 miles west of Picton, Nelson's residents and visitors enjoy more sunshine than most New Zealanders and generally some of New Zealand's balmiest climate. Nelson is very popular among vacationing New Zealanders. The area has a special feeling of peace and plenty with apple orchards to the west and fertile farms of hops, tobacco, and fruits, golden beaches, and genuine hospitaiity. Little wonder that Nelson is very strong in arts and crafts: painters, weavers, glassworks, jewelry, woodcraft, silver- and goldsmiths, and dozens of full-time potters drawn by the area's fine clays. The local PRO (corner of Trafalgar and Halifax Sts., tel. 82-304) can give you a list of artists' studios and *A Guide to Nelson's Wineries*. Sample local crafts and stop for lunch at the restaurant in the Tudoresque **Suter Art Gallery** on Bridge Street adjacent to **Queen's Gardens**; walk up **Botanical Hill** through the lovely **Botanical Reserve** for a wonderful views of the city over to Nelson Haven and across Tasman Bay to the Tasman Mountains.

Sail in beautiful Kenepuru Sound off Pelorus Sound. Pelorus is the most extensive sound (32 miles) with the finest scenery. Fish for cod, terakiki, snapper, garfish, grouper, and kahawai. Surfcast between Kaikoura and Cape Koamaru. Fly fish in the Rai, Pelorus, Wairau, and Opawa rivers and Spring Creek for brown trout. In summer, try salmon fishing in the Wairau River.

Visit vineyards in Redwoods Valley, Ruby Bay, Upper Moutere, and especially Blenheim's Wairau Valley. Ski in

Rainbow Valley, west of Blenheim, and enjoy outstanding views. Wine-tasting tours in the Blenheim area should include **Hunter Wines** in Spring Creek, between Picton and Blenheim (with inside and outside dining); **Riverlands Winery of Montana**, 5 miles south of Blenheim on Highway 1; and **Cellier Le Brun**, near the intersection of Highways 5 and 6.

From Nelson, head west on Highway 60 toward Motueka and Abel Tasman National Park with its golden beaches, rocky headlands, and tidal inlets. Enter the park at Marohau. To return, hire a taxi from Motueka to pick you up in Totaranui, at the north end of the park, or charter a boat in Motueka or Kaiteriteri Beach and Kaka Pa Point, which should not be missed. Alternatives for exploring the beautiful coastlines of Tasman Bay and Golden Bay are hiking and cruising combinations, including guided walks and lodging with John Wilson (Abel Tasman Park Enterprises, Green Tree Rd., Motueka, RD #3, tel. 0524/87-801), such as a four-day launch trip and guided walk, which includes three nights at the Lodge at Torrent Bay. For a full day on a Royal Mail boat picking up and delivering mail, supplies, and people, join Glenmore Cruises from Havelock (P.O. Box 34, Havelock).

Highway 63 from Blenheim joins Highway 6 following the Buller River (from its origin in Lake Rotoiti) in Nelson Lakes National Park. On Lake Rotoroa, a YMCA camp on Gowan Valley Road provides bunks at NZ$9 per night, and the Alpine Lodge Rotoiti at St. Arnaud (tel. 0524/36-869) and Lake Rotoroa Lodge at the other end of the spectrum (NZ$200 single, NZ$250 per person double, tel. Matiri 0524/39-121) provide everything that trout fishermen could want.

In the North-West Nelson State Forest (930,000 acres) is one of New Zealand's best-known tracks, the Heaphy Track, a 42-mile (one-way), five-day hike linking Golden Bay at the Abel Tasman National Park with the west coast. There are seven huts and five shelters, but they can be crowded any time of year so pack your own tent.

DAY 13
CHRISTCHURCH REGION

Stroll along the Avon, people-watch in Cathedral Square, visit the museums and Arts Centre, see Gothic and Victorian architecture, and experience the tranquillity of Christchurch. Leave Christchurch in the afternoon, going over the Port Hills to Lyttelton, then return to the urbane delights of the city's center.

Suggested Schedule

8:00 a.m.	Leisurely breakfast.
9:00 a.m.	Stroll along the Avon and walking tour around city center.
12:00 noon	Picnic lunch on the banks of the Avon.
1:00 p.m.	Port Hills drive.
6:30 p.m.	Dinner.
8:30 p.m.	Attend theater at the Arts Centre.

Orientation

Christchurch was planned by a young English Tory, John Robert Godley, to be an English city, and the magnificent parks and gardens adjoining the serpentine Avon River attest to that vision. In contrast to other New Zealand cities, the city's center is a pleasure for pedestrians. It is a city to be seen by bicycle, on foot, and by boat.

Colonial wooden architecture has fine examples such as the homes along Bealey Avenue and the McLeans Mansion on Manchester Street and distinguished commercial buildings including the Pegasus Press building in Oxford Terrace and the Occidental Hotel in Hereford.

The city's urban amenities balance its regional outdoor recreation and scenic highlights: the inner city with the beautiful Avon, Hagley Park and Botanic Gardens, and Cathedral Square, and the city's perimeter with Summit Road atop Port Hills, the very special Banks Peninsula, and picturesque Canterbury farms. Farther afield are the

Rakaia, Rangitata, and Waimakariri rivers and lakes for fishing or rafting, snow-clad Mt. Hutt, thermal Hamner Springs' hills and exotic forests, and the spectacular Arthur's Pass National Park. The Canterbury Information Centre (75 Worcester St., at the corner of Oxford Terrace, tel. 799-629) and the NZTP Travel Office (Government Life Building, Cathedral Square, tel. 794-900) will take care of most of your needs for information, maps, brochures, bookings, tickets for local attractions, vehicle rentals, and tours. For complete information and advice on outdoor activities and tour operators in the Christchurch region, visit the Outdoor Recreation Centre in the Arts Centre (tel. 799-395).

Sightseeing Highlights
▲▲▲ **Inner Christchurch Walking Tour—Cathedral Square** is the center of the city. Colombo Street runs north and south through it. From the entrance to the cathedral, Worcester Street leads west toward Hagley Park. Christchurch Cathedral (Anglican), the finest Gothic-style church in New Zealand, soars almost 200 feet. Climb the 133 narrow stone steps through the bell chamber to the balconies of the tower 100 feet above the square where you get a great view of the city, plains, and even the Southern Alps on a clear day.

From the square, walk one block north on Colombo Street to Victoria Square, turn through the Square to Victoria Street and the **Avon River**. Gracefully winding its way through the city, its grassy banks dotted with flowerbeds, weeping willows, old oaks, and daffodils in spring, spanned by ornate bridges, this river is the main feature of Christchurch's "English" character and charm. Bicycles and canoes are the best ways to tour the Avon and the historic and modern buildings lining the river.

Cross the Avon to the floral clock artwork in Victoria Street at the corner of Chestnut on the way to the Town Hall on Kilmore Street. In a city of history and fine old buildings, this very modern glass-and-marble structure is a bold contrast. You can stroll through the building weekdays between 9:00 a.m. and 5:00 p.m. or take a guided

Christchurch Region

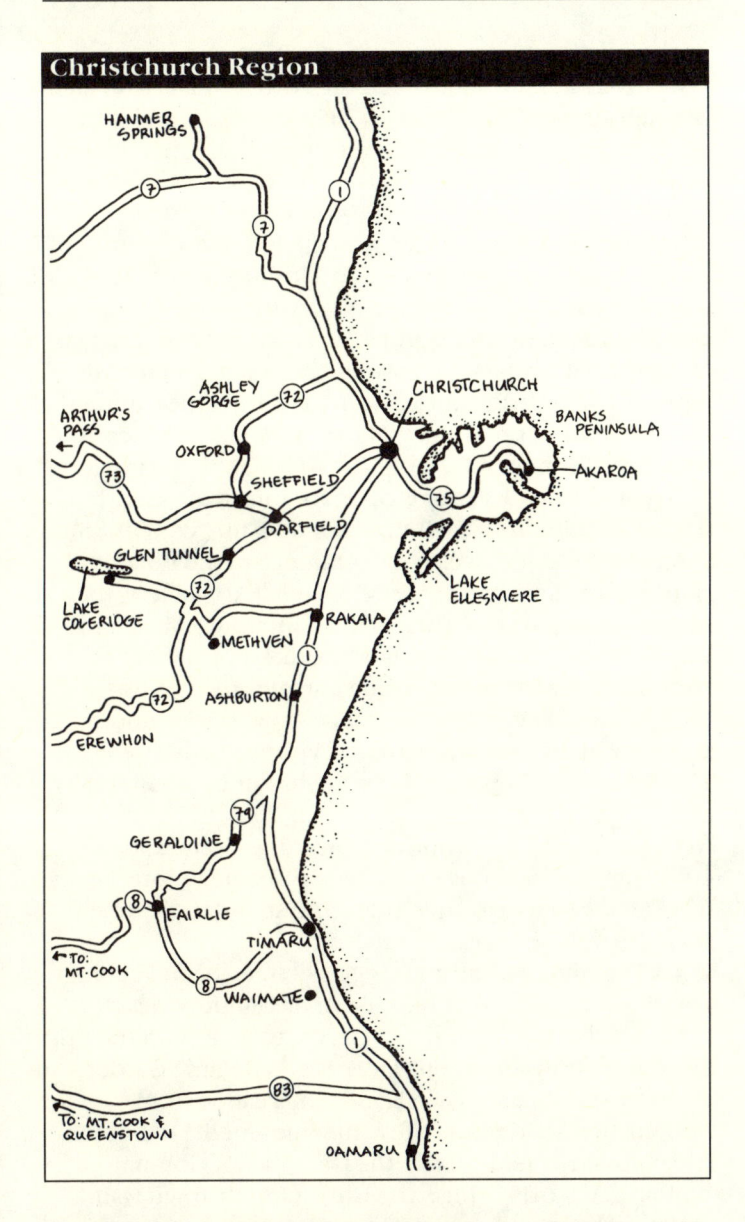

tour between 11:00 a.m. and 3:00 p.m. for NZ$1.50 adults and NZ$.75 children. Outside is the beautiful Ferrier Fountain. Continue along the Avon to the Gothic Provincial Government Buildings on the corner of Durham and Armagh streets, built between 1859 and 1865, and the only remaining provincial government buildings in New Zealand (the system was abolished in 1876). The Stone Chamber is open daily from 9:00 a.m. to 4:00 p.m.

At Worcester Street turn left (west) to the Arts Centre of Christchurch. Housed in the neo-Gothic former University of Canterbury, the Centre is now the home for day and evening performing and visual arts, crafts, dramatic, instrumental, and choral groups, shopping, and restaurants. If you're strolling on Saturday, during the summer, an Arts, Crafts, and Antique Market is held in the Centre from 10:00 a.m. to 3:00 p.m. The Arts Centre Information Office in the clock tower is open for information and bookings daily from 8:30 a.m. to 5:00 p.m. (tel. 60-988).

Across Rolleston Ave., at the entrance to the Botanic Gardens and adjacent to the McDougall Art Gallery, the region's major art museum, is the Canterbury Museum. The museum contains outstanding displays of early Maori culture during the moa hunting era, mounted birds, Oriental art, a reconstruction of colonial Christchurch, and the Hall of Antarctic Discovery. Open daily from 10:00 a.m. to 4:30 p.m. Behind the museum, bounded by a loop of the Avon, is the Botanic Gardens, full of native New Zealand plants, tropical, flowering, alpine and desert plants, orchids, flowering trees and much more. You may decide to return after lunch and spend more time in both the museum and the gardens.

▲▲▲The **Avon River** and its grassy tree-shaded banks winding around Christchurch's inner city provides a superb pathway, on foot, bicycle, or water, to visit the primary attractions between Hadley Park/Botanic Gardens and Victoria Square/Town Hall. Rent a canoe from Antigua Boatsheds and follow the tree-lined Avon downstream past riverside parks, the Chamber of Commerce Building, Victoria Bridge, the Christchurch Town Hall, and nearby floral clock in Victoria Square, passing under many picturesque bridges, notably the Bridge of Remembrance. Enjoy a riverside walk if you have the time.

▲▲**Cathedral Square** is surrounded by gift and souvenir shops. North of the square, New Regent Street, Columbo Street, and a network of arcades are full of boutiques and specialty and antique shops. See the Christchurch Cathedral tower's panoramic view of the city (9:00 a.m. to 4:00 p.m. weekdays and Saturday, 12:30 to 4:30 p.m. on Sunday). Red buses from Cathedral Square leave at 1:30 p.m. for a city and suburb tour.

▲▲**Town Hall** is New Zealand's most striking modern town hall design.

▲**Ferrier Fountain** outside the Christchurch Town Hall and the **Bowler Fountain** in Victoria Square both light up at night with varied patterns of water and color.

The Art Centre Museum and Art Gallery (2 Worchester St., off Rolleston, tel. 660-989) is a focal point for local artists, musicians, craftspeople, and all types of performers, on stage and in many shops, with an open-air market on Saturdays in the summer. Check the current calendar for theater and ballet and other dance recitals and arts and crafts exhibits.

▲▲**The Nga-Hua-E-Wha National Marae**, comprised of a meeting house, arts and crafts center, and the Riki-Rangi Carving Centre in the Arts Centre, is a showcase of local and New Zealand Maori culture.

▲▲**The Canterbury Museum** (Rolleston Avenue, tel. 669-379) at the entrance to the Botanic Gardens and directly across from the Arts Centre, has the finest Antarctic collection in the world as well as fine colonial and Maori sections. Open 10:00 a.m. to 4:30 p.m. weekdays, 2:00 to 4:30 p.m. Sunday.

▲▲**The Botanic Gardens**—75 acres include spectacular displays of exotic and native plants and trees. Open 8:00 a.m. to dusk.

▲The **City Mall Complex** contains the Shades Shopping Precinct, Cashfields, and the National Mutual Arcade. It is linked by an overhead pedestrian walkway to the Canterbury Centre and the Triangle Centre.

Fine old Gothic-style buildings, dating from the 1870s, dot the city center: the Canterbury Provincial Government Buildings, the Arts Centre, Canterbury Museum, and the State Trinity Centre. Also see neo-Gothic or High Victorian church design in wood and stone: Cathedral Church of Christ, St. Michael's, All Angels Church, and Cathedral of the Blessed Sacrament.

▲▲ **Hadley Park**, a 450-acre haven close to the city center, has thousands of daffodils blooming in spring in Daffodil Woodland and azaleas and rhododendrons in Milbrook Reserve off North Hadley Park.

▲▲ **Port Hills** offers magnificent views of Christchurch to the north and Lyttelton and Banks Peninsula to the south. By car or bus, Lyttelton is easily reached via the Lyttelton Tunnel through Port Hills. Today's route, however, is over Port Hills. Take Columbo Street south from Cathedral Square to Dyers Pass Road, past the Sign of the Takahe tearoom and restaurant to the Sign of the Kiwi (refreshments), about 1,000 feet above the city. Turn left on Summit Road, along the high ridge of Port Hills, crossing Bridle Path in about 4 miles, then Evans Pass where you can turn south to Lyttelton or north to Sumner, Ferry Road to High Street back to the city center. Port Hills has walkways with spectacular vistas.

Itinerary Options

Ferrymead Historic Park (269 Bridle Path Rd., Heathcote, tel. 841-708), a 100-acre site next to the Heathcote River, includes train and tram rides through vintage township and museum areas displaying the history of aeronautics, musical instruments, printing, motor- and horse-drawn vehicles, fire-fighting, military and photographic equipment, urban transport, and railways. Open 10:00 a.m. to 4:30 p.m. daily. Admission NZ$6 adults, NZ$3 children.

The Christchurch Transport Board (tel. 794-600) has a three-hour Port Hills and Harbour Tour with a Lyttelton Harbour launch cruise (NZ$15 adult, NZ$7.50 child). Try walking the Bridle Path to Lyttelton Harbour (2 hours) or the Godley Head Walkway across Summit Road (2 hours).

Lyttelton, the South Island's leading port, located on the flanks of a flooded volcanic crater, has a fine collection of nineteenth-century buildings and churches. Regular launches shuttle to the attractive Diamond Harbor on the south side of the harbor (tel. Lyttelton 28-8368).

Waimakariri River Gorges, 85 miles round-trip from Christchurch, is famed for trout and salmon fishing. From the Main West Road through Darfield and Sheffield, cross the Waimakariri River to the gorge. Try a Waimakariri or Rakaia jet boat or a raft tour for a half day, one day, or two days. Rafting tours also operate on the Waiau, Hurunui, and Rangitata rivers. (North of Oxford, follow the turnoff to the Ashley River Gorge, returning to Christchurch via Rangiora and Belfast.)

Salmon fishing in the Rakaia, Rangitata, and Waimakariri rivers is from October 1 to April 30, with the best runs from December through March. October through December is noted for sea-run trout in all local rivers and brown trout throughout the season. Rainbow and brown trout, landlocked salmon, and brook trout are found in Lakes Taylor, Sumner, Coleridge, Lyndon, and Selfe from early November to the end of April. Excellent sea fishing is available around river mouths. Kawhai (Australian salmon) and cod are the main species caught. For the best locations for river, lake, and sea fishing, use the services of one of the many excellent local fishing guides.

Mt. Hutt Ski Area has the longest and most reliable ski season in New Zealand and offers a "snow guarantee." Snow conditions range from powder in early winter to corn in late spring. Seventy-five percent of the skiing terrain of its huge basin is rated "learner-intermediate," but advanced skiing in the back bowls is outstanding. Heli-skiing is some of the best in the world.

Methven, the winter resort serving Mt. Hutt ski field (late May through early December), also operates as a base for mountaineering, deer hunting, and fishing. Within an hour's drive of Methven are three major rivers and numerous lakes. The Rakaia Gorge (100 miles round-trip), 10 miles north of Methven, is a very picturesque canyon. Follow Highway 72 to Darfield via scenic Glentanner, returning to Christchurch via the Main West Road.

DAY 14
CHRISTCHURCH—QUEENSTOWN

Drive from Christchurch through alpine foothills over Burke's Pass to glacial lakes mirroring Mt. Cook National Park's mountains. Pass through the handful of vacation villages in Mackenzie Valley which cater to skiers and sportsmen, then over the winding Lindis Pass road down to magnificent vistas of the Queenstown area.

Suggested Schedule

7:00 a.m.	Breakfast and check out.
7:30 a.m.	Rent a car for the drive around South Island and depart for Mt. Cook.
12:00 noon	Lunch in Mt. Cook Village.
1:00 p.m.	Walk from the village; scenic drive and walk to Blue Lakes (or) flightseeing to Tasman Glacier.
2:30 p.m.	Leave for Lake Ohau.
4:00 p.m.	Refreshments at the Ohau Lodge.
4:30 p.m.	Leave for Lindis Pass and Queenstown.
7:30 p.m.	Arrive in Queenstown and check in.
8:30 p.m.	Dinner and stroll.

Christchurch to Mt. Cook

From Christchurch, it's 205 miles to Mt. Cook and about the same distance from Mt. Cook to Queenstown via Cromwell. A 410-mile drive is a long day, but the scenery is varied and the stop-offs frequent enough to break up the trip. However, a stopover along the way at Mt. Cook still makes sense if you have the time, especially if you want to travel to Geraldine via Ashley and Rakaia gorges (see Itinerary Options), another 60 miles of driving.

The South Canterbury and North Otego provinces are separated by the Waitaki River, paralleled by Highway 83 and, from Kurow, Highway 82 linking Lake Benmore, New Zealand's largest man-made lake, to Oamaru and the east coast. Both provinces in this region look much alike: prosperous farming lands, vivid green in spring and brown at the end of summer.

Driving south across sheep-covered plains from Christchurch to Timaru is a monotonous 2½-hour trip, usually best seen from the air as a pattern of pastures, farmland, rivers, and streams descending the foothills of the Alps. The same is true of the 1½-hour trip from Timaru south to Oamaru. Instead, head for the Rakaia Gorge (and possibly the Ashley Gorge, see below), then south on Highway 72 to Geraldine, switching to Highway 79 through Fairlie, Burke's Pass, and Tekapo, and then 30 miles to beautiful Lake Pukaki, a deep milky blue from glacial minerals. Turn north on Highway 80, from the southern end of Lake Pukaki going along the western side of the lake to Glentanner (20 miles) and Mt. Cook Village (another 20 miles) paralleling Lake Pukaki to Mt. Cook.

Directions: Mt. Cook to Queenstown

There are two main routes from Lake Pukaki to Queenstown. Today you'll take Highway 8 via Cromwell and Kawarau Gorge and, on Day 18, you *may* choose to take the Cardrona route, which has a spectacular leg in and out of Queenstown (7 miles of steep, rutted, gravel road from the 3,300-foot top of the Crown to Kawarau Valley, with fantastic, spine-tingling views).

Sightseeing Highlights

▲▲▲ **Mt. Cook** is the highest mountain in New Zealand (12,349 feet) and is surrounded by 140 peaks over 7,000 feet. Between the mountains are glaciers, including the Tasman Glacier (18 miles long and 2 miles wide), the largest outside of the Himalayas and Antarctica. In winter, Mt. Cook offers excellent skiing: glacier, heli-skiing, alpine, nordic, and ski mountaineering. Walkers, hikers, and climbers will find Mt. Cook National Park to be a feast of scenery and native plants, including beautiful wildflowers from October to January. Stop at the Mt. Cook National Park Headquarters (tel. 818) in Mt. Cook Village for park information.

Even a 10- to 30-minute walk from the village will reveal the park's great natural beauty. For a combination of a scenic drive and a short hike, take Highway 80 to Ball Hut Road, the Tasman Valley Road, a gravel road that follows the Tasman River and glacier to the carpark at Husky Flats. Follow the sign to Blue Lakes and in 15 minutes you have a grand view of the lakes. It's just a few more minutes up the Clacker View Track for tremendous views of Tasman Glacier, Mt. Tasman, and Mt. Cook.

For hikers there are several excellent 2- to 2½-hour walks: Kea Point, Sealy Tarns, and Red Tarns. The Hooker Valley Trail leads over Copeland Pass to Fox Glacier (only for hikers with alpine experience in ice and snow, the right equipment, and a guide). From Mt. Cook, light planes fly over the divide to Fox and Franz Josef glaciers. The Helicopter Line offers a 20-minute cruise around Mt. Cook for NZ$80 (tel. 05621/855). Fifteen minutes to Hooker Glacier costs NZ$68; forty-five minutes buys a snow landing for NZ$125 per person (tel. Mt. Cook 855). A 40-minute Mt. Cook Line ski-plane flight landing on the Tasman Glacier is NZ$165 (tel. 05621-849).

The Hermitage Hotel's travel desk (tel. 05621-809) can book any activities in the area.

Besides shopping for picnic items at the village food store, the two most practical alternatives for eating in the Mt. Cook Village area are light lunches at the **Coffee Shop** in the Hermitage Hotel or plan to have the smorgasbord lunch (NZ$21 pp) at the hotel's **Alpine Room** as your main meal of the day. (For overnight stays, see below.)

▲ **Mackenzie Basin**'s vast tussock-covered expanses can seem barren and monotonous in winter, but the dramatic backdrop of the Southern Alps adds spectacular beauty.

▲▲ **Lakes Tekapo and Pukaki** acquire blue-green and turquoise colors from the fine dust, created by glacial grinding, that feeds into their waters. In summer, Lake Tekapo's shores are covered with bluish purple, pink, and yellow lupines. In winter (July to late October), Lake Tekapo has a large beginners' ski area and a ski school catering to novices. Nordic skiing on the Hooker River and Tasman River flats or on the glaciers and heli-skiing flights to the 6- to 8-mile-long runs of the Tasman Glacier

Day 14 137

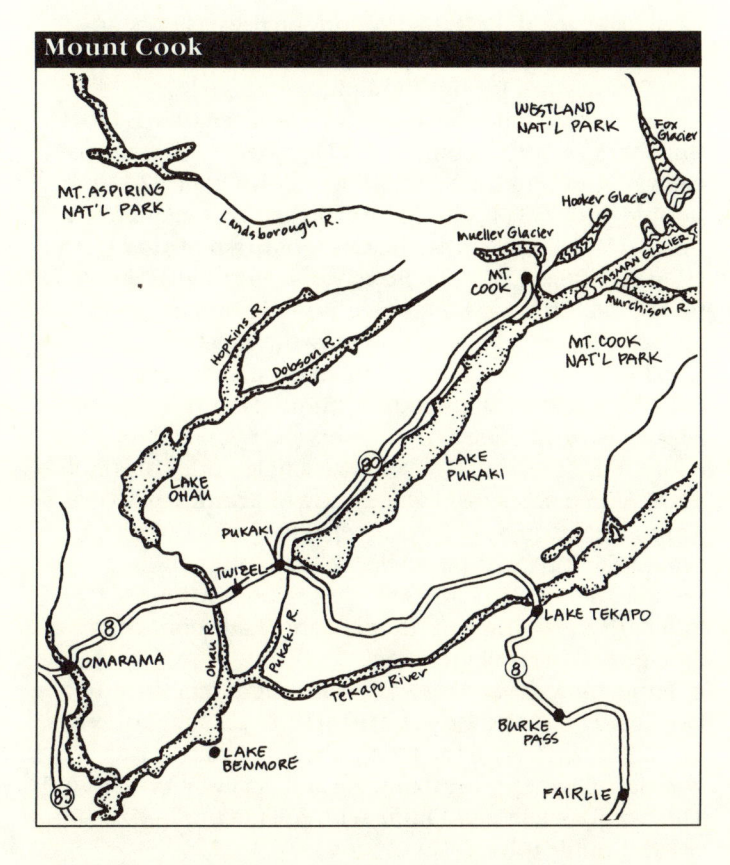

Mount Cook

are available from the local airfield. Contact Alpine Guides (P.O. Box 20, Mt. Cook, tel. 0562/834) or Alpine Recreation Canterbury in Lake Tekapo (tel. 0562/736) for the latest information, costs, and bookings.

▲▲**Lake Ohau** west on Highway 8 between Twizel and Omarama, 1½ hours from Mt. Cook, is a beautiful place for fishing, boating, hiking, and skiing. Nearby Mt. Sutton has superb heli-ski runs. Lake Ohau Lodge provides luxury accommodations at NZ$75 double.

Where to Stay
Lake and mountain views are as good as anywhere in town from the **Queenstown YHA Hostel** (80 Lake

Esplanade, tel. 0294/28-413), and the price is right at NZ$14 pp. With a large capacity for overflow, chances usually are good for finding a place to stay.

About three miles north of town, **Queenstown Holiday Park** (Arthur's Point Rd., tel. 0294/29-306) tent and caravan sites rent for NZ$7.50 pp, cabins from NZ$30 double (incl. GST). With mountain and lake views from nicely wooded grounds, the **Queenstown Motor Park** (Man St. off Lake St., P.O. Box 59, Queenstown, tel. 0294/27-252) is *big* but as nice as you'll find in the area and less than a mile from downtown. They have several hundred campsites (NZ$7), twice that many caravan sites (NZ$7.50), cabins with beds or bunks (NZ$31-$65), tourist lodges with toilets and showers (NZ$42), and fully equipped motel units (NZ$57), all single or double (incl. GST). Three miles from Queenstown, **Frankton Motor Camp** (Stewart St., Frankton, tel. 0294/27-247) has tent sites (NZ$5 pp), caravan sites (NZ$5.50 pp), self-contained flats (NZ$30.80 single or double), tourist lodges (NZ$28 single or double), and a self-contained cottage (NZ$42), all incl. GST.

Three miles from Arrowtown and eight miles from Queenstown, **Lake Hayes Motel** (R.D. 2, Queenstown, tel. 0294/21-705) on the lovely shores of Lake Hayes, is a wonderful base for local touring and yet away from town. The rate for these eight units with full kitchen is NZ$60 single/double (plus GST).

Goldfields Guesthouse B&B (41 Frankton Rd. at Dublin St., Queenstown, tel. 0294/27-211) has six bedrooms in the guest house for NZ$40-$74 single/double (plus GST), four chalet units (NZ$68 double plus NZ$10 per additional person), with family-style breakfast, hostel-type accommodations for NZ$12, and two caravans for NZ$15 (all plus GST).

Within easy walking distance from town, the **Mountain View Lodge** (Frankton Rd., Queenstown, tel. 0294/28-246) is best known for its motel units, some with full kitchens, and all the comforts. With kitchens, these units rent for NZ$75 single or double; without kitchens, NZ$55-$60. At the lodge (on Frankton Road) with bunks and a communal kitchen, you supply sleeping and cooking gear, NZ$36-$52 for two to four persons (all including GST). Tents and caravan sites are on the upper and lower parts of the hill (pick the dryer upper ones) at NZ$6 pp. (See Where to Eat, below.)

The chalets (NZ$85) and the deluxe lakeside suites (NZ$100), all plus GST, at the **Alpine Village Motor Inn** (Frankton Rd., P.O. Box 211, Queenstown, tel. 0294/27) are as much of a splurge as you need to make in the Queenstown area for spectacular views of the lake, wonderfully comfortable units, and unique semi-enclosed heated spa pools (facing the lake). Best Western discount rates apply.

Directions: Christchurch to Rakaia Gorge

From Cathedral Square, head for Highway 73 to Charing Cross and Windwhistle, turn on Lake Coleridge Road into the Rakaia River Valley and Rakaia Gorge. (This same route continues on gravel—Lake Lyndon Road to Lakes Coleridge and Lyndon, 37 miles from Arthurs Pass, to Lake Pearson and the Waimakariri River to Arthurs Pass Township.) An alternate route is north from Christchurch to Kaiapoi and Rangiora, crossing the Ashley River to the north side and heading west to Ashley Gorge, then south to Oxford and Highway 72 to Sheffield, a local road south to Hororato, right on Highway 73 to Windwhistle and then to the Rakaia Gorge (see above). At Rakaia Gorge, take Highway 72 to Geraldine.

Itinerary Options—Overnight in the Mt. Cook Area

White Horse Hill Campground (White Horse Hill Picnic Area) has tent sites (NZ$3 pp) with running water and flush toilets. **Glentanner Park** motor camp on Lake Pukaki and Highway 80 (12 miles south of Mt. Cook Village) has tent sites at NZ$6 pp, caravan sites (NZ$6 pp), on-site caravans (NZ$12 pp/NZ$24 min.), and cabins at NZ$15 pp. With a spectacular view of snow-capped

South Island

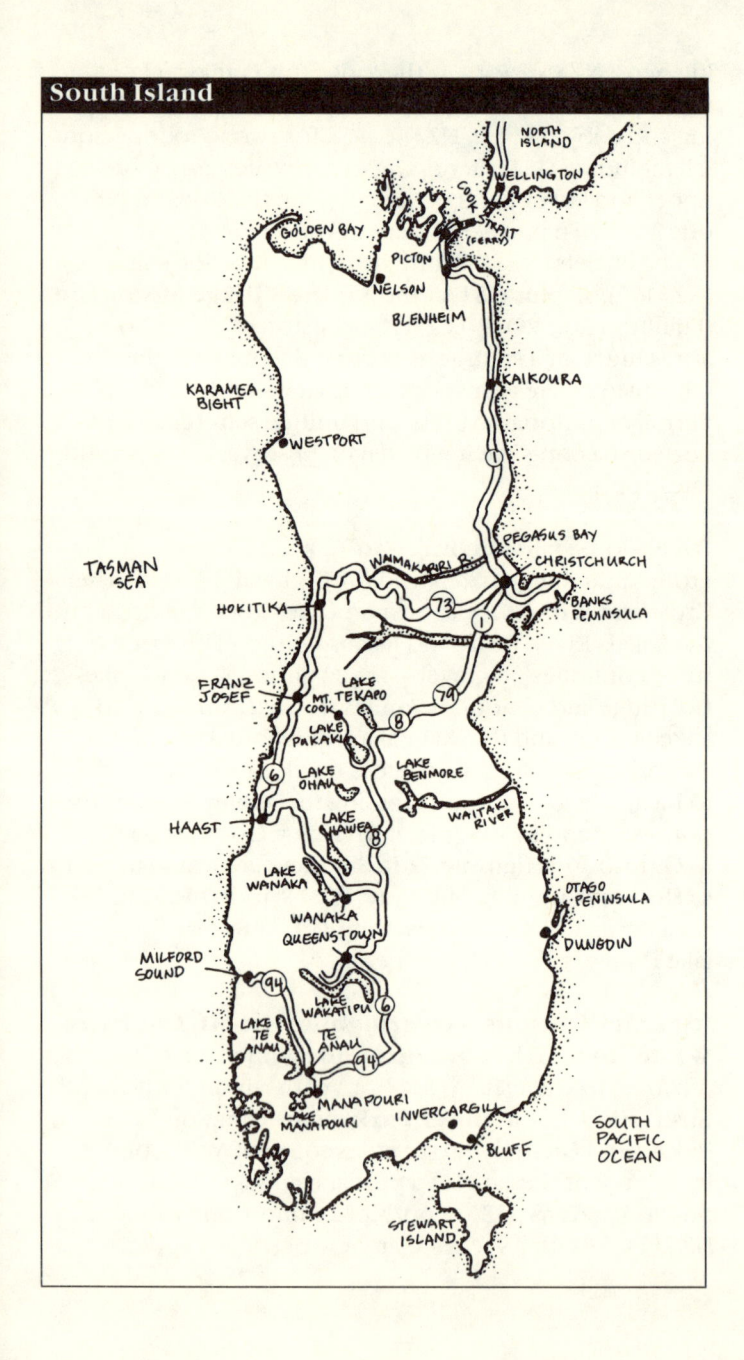

mountains, the **Mt. Cook YHA Hostel** (Bowen and Kitener drives, P.O. Box 26, Mt. Cook 8770, tel. 05621/820) costs NZ$15 for seniors, juniors half price. Otherwise, a **Mt. Cook Chalet** (call The Hermitage, tel. 0562/809) at NZ$82.50 single/double (plus GST) is the least expensive alternative near Mt. Cook Village. The **Glencoe Ski Lodge** (tel. 05621/809) rates are NZ$154, and **THC Hermitage** starts at NZ$204 single/double (plus GST) unless you book as part of a package.

DAY 15
QUEENSTOWN

Board the *S.S. Earnslaw* for a midmorning cruise on Lake Wakatipu to a lakeside working sheep station. After returning to Queenstown, visit Arrowtown for lunch as a leisurely start for a memorably exciting afternoon of jet-boating on the Shotover River and backcountry four-wheeling, or possibly horse trekking, to catch the sunset.

Suggested Schedule

8:00 a.m.	Breakfast in Queenstown Mall. Sightseeing, information gathering, and booking activities in downtown Queenstown.
12:00 noon	Drive or bus to Arrowtown for sightseeing and lunch, with a side trip up Coronet Peak for the view.
2:00 p.m.	*S.S. Earnslaw* cruise to Mt. Nicholas Sheep Station
3:00 p.m.	Shotover jet boat trip.
6:30 p.m.	Gondola trip up Bob's Peak for dinner and entertainment.
10:00 p.m.	Early to bed for an early start tomorrow.

Orientation

Queenstown is the South Island's and New Zealand's (and one of the world's) most outstanding recreational resort. The variety of spectacular year-round lake, mountain, and river recreational attractions in the region, including Queenstown, Te Anau, Fiordland National Park, Wanaka, and Mt. Aspiring National Park, is unsurpassed anywhere. Nestled at the head of a small bay on Lake Wakatipu (52 miles long), surrounded by rugged mountains rising steeply from the shoreline, Queenstown is a compact village easily toured on foot. Using Queenstown as a base, after arriving you can book a seemingly unlimited variety of excursions: white-water rafting, jet boats, cruise trips, hydrofoil rides, four-wheel drive and horseback trips, climbing, hiking, backcountry camping, skiing (mostly

Queenstown Region

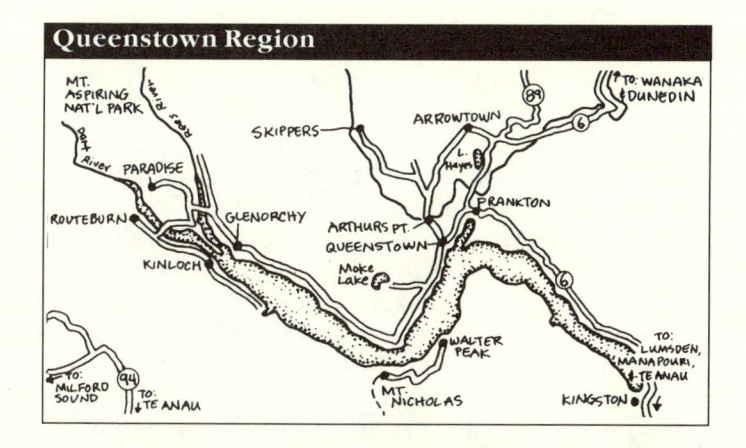

downhill and heli-skiing), fishing, and combinations thereof, with guides and helicopter transport options, from a half-day to a week or more.

The more popular excursions fill rapidly, especially during peak season, so be prepared to make booking decisions as soon as you arrive in town. The NZTP Travel Office (49 Shotover St., tel. 28-238) can fill all your information and booking requirements for lake and river trips, horseback trips, flightseeing excursions to Milford Sound, and accommodations from Te Anau to Wanaka.

Sightseeing Highlights

▲▲**Arrowtown** is a pretty village of old wood and stone cottages nestling beneath sycamore trees, the relic of a gold mining boom that brought thousands of miners to the Arrow and Shotover rivers. The Lake District Centennial Museum in Arrowtown contains one of the country's best gold-mining sections.

▲▲▲**Lake Wakatipu** deserves a leisurely cruise or launch trip for one to three hours. The *S.S. Earnslaw*, a completely renovated coal-burning steam ship, which made her debut on the lake in 1912, sails several times a day: the lunch and dinner cruise is NZ$19 (without lunch and dinner), and the three-hour cruise (starting at 2 p.m., NZ$28 adults, NZ$10 children) takes you to the Mt.

Nicholas Sheep Station for a sheep-shearing demonstration. Cross the lake by launch (NZ$17 adults, NZ$8.50 children) to the Cecil Peak Sheep and Cattle Station (soon to have a major resort development). The hydrofoil *Meteor III* offers a 25-mile cruise to the upper reaches of the lake (NZ$22 adults, NZ$11 children) and a 20-minute mini-cruise (NZ$10 adults, NZ$7.50 children).

▲▲**Coronet Peak**, 12 miles north of Queenstown on the way to Arrowtown, has a chair lift to the summit station for a magnificent panoramic view of Lake Wakatipu and the Southern Alps. In winter, from mid-June to October, Coronet Peak and the Remarkables offer two of the most challenging skiing terrains in the Southern Hemisphere. Even if you don't ski, the views of surrounding mountains and lakes from the Remarkables' access road is worth the trip (put on chains in the winter). Lift fares are NZ$10 adults and NZ$5.50 children, round-trip.

▲▲**Bob's Peak** and its Skyline Restaurant, reached by a 4-minute (1,530-foot) gondola ride (NZ$5.50 adults, NZ$3 children) starting near the town center, is the best and easiest way to see the town and its surroundings on a clear day or night.

Where to Eat
Seven days a week until 10:30 p.m., gather around the fireplace and wait your turn to sit at the long tables with friendly locals and select from a large variety of pizza (under NZ$16 for two) and spaghetti dishes, salads, and soups for under NZ$20, all packed into the small, happy surroundings of the **Cow Pizza and Spaghetti House** (Cow Lane off Beach St.). Its BYO, so stop first at the bottle shop on Cow Lane for wine or beer.

For snacks and light fare, **Rees Cafe** (Rees Arcade) offers very good homemade soups and sandwiches.

There are a surprising number of restaurants in town that serve a delicious three-course meal for around NZ$15. **Westy's** on the Mall (tel. 28-635) is an old standby that creates surprisingly exotic vegetarian dishes or good seafood, with salad and homemade bread.

Avanti (20 the Mall, tel. 28-503) is another one for fresh pasta or breakfast inside or in the courtyard. You might try German cuisine at **Upstairs Downstairs** (66 Shotover St., tel. 28-290) or spicy Mexican dinners at **Saguaro de Pablos** (upstairs, Trust Bank Arcade, Beach St., tel. 28-240) until late (bar stays open until 1:00 a.m.). From early breakfast (one of the few in town) and hamburgers to rack of lamb at very reasonable prices, you'll find cheerful table and counter service at the **Gourmet Express Restaurant and Coffee Shop** (Bay Centre, Shotover St., tel. 29-619).

Roaring Megs (57 Shotover St., tel. 29-676) is a bit more expensive (main course NZ$15-$22), but what can you expect for fresh salmon and other such normally expensive dishes? Like these other local favorites, expect Megs to be crowded. Book ahead.

Not to be missed during your stay in Queenstown, take in the panoramic view and anything from a snack to the evening all-you-can-eat smorgasbord plus live entertainment (NZ$35 pp with a gondola ticket) at the **Skyline Chalet Restaurant** (Brecon St., tel. 27-860).

Both the **Mountain View Lodge** (tel. 28-246) and the **Alpine Village Motor Inn** (tel. 27-795) on Frankton Road have excellent restaurants, menus, and lake views.

Itinerary Options

The Shotover and Kawarau rivers offer the ultimate in white-water rafting and jet boating. Jet boat from Queenstown down the lake to the Kawarau River and then downriver. Shoot incredible white-water rapids through the narrow canyon of the Shotover River and then raft through the Upper Kawarau. Rafting trips range from NZ$55 to NZ$110 pp (contact Danes Shotover Rafts, tel. 0294/27-318, or Kawarau Raft Expeditions, tel. 0294/29-792); jet boat trips cost NZ$30 adults, NZ$15 children.

Skippers Canyon is about four hours round-trip by mini-coach or four-wheel-drive vehicle from Queenstown (NZ$41 adults, NZ$20 children). The narrow, single-lane road that snakes high above the Shotover

River is unforgettable, especially on a winter trip! A three-hour horseback trip up the Shotover and Moonlight valleys leaves at 9:30 a.m. and 2:00 p.m. from **Moonlight Stables**, NZ$37. A three-hour ride through Arrow River Gorge from **Hunters Horse Trekking** leaves at the same times and costs the same.

Skiing in the Southern Alps: The scenery is stunningly beautiful and virtually unmarked by resort or other development. The ski lifts and slopes are comparatively uncrowded. Waiting at lifts is uncommon. You spend most of your time skiing, even on weekends. With a favorable currency exchange rate, lift tickets, equipment rentals, excellent ski instruction, accommodations, and apres-ski activities cost about half as much as in the United States. Returning from the ski mountains, if there's time, you can engage in virtually all of the other year-round activities mentioned above. Sounds too good to be true? Except for very rare lack of snow, in the Queenstown-Wanaka region it's all true.

Close to Queenstown, Coronet Peak has excellent skiing at all levels, especially advanced and intermediate, with one of the best ski schools in New Zealand. Lift tickets are interchangeable with the Remarkables. The Remarkables have more excellent beginner and intermediate trails than Coronet. There are Nordic ski trails above the lifts, and telemark instruction is available.

The Harris Mountains are New Zealand's leading heli-skiing area with over 140 runs from 40 different peaks in three mountain ranges. Experienced and advanced skiers can have 12,000 feet of awe-inspiring runs in the Tyndall Glaciers and Buchanan Range. The cost is about NZ$350 per day or about NZ$16 per 1,000 vertical feet.

Treble Cone, 18 miles from Wanaka, deserves to be much better known for its skiing and scenery. A ski chalet at the top of the double chair lift offers spectacular views. Many of the Harris Mountain heli-skiing trips begin from Treble Cone. Cardrona is the South Island's most promising new ski area. A high base elevation (4,500 feet) and southerly exposure provide ample snow coverage in the June-November season.

DAY 16
QUEENSTOWN—TE ANAU

Te Anau, near the southern end of the largest of the region's lakes, is the gateway and touring base for excursions to Milford and Doubtful sounds and Lake Manapouri. The 120-mile trip from Queenstown on Highways 6 and 94 through Lumsden and sheep and cattle country should take no more than three hours.

Suggested Schedule

6:30 a.m.	Early start and breakfast.
10:00 a.m.	Arrive in Manapouri.
10:30 a.m.	Triple trip to Doubtful Sound.
6:30 p.m.	Check in at Te Anau and have a leisurely dinner.

Driving: Queenstown to Te Anau

There's only one way to drive directly from Queenstown to Te Anau (95 miles). Take Highway 6 though Kingston (30 miles). At Five Rivers (30 miles south of Kingston) turn onto the road to Mossburn (11 miles), and travel 24 miles to Te Anau. From Te Anau, Milford Sound is a 140-mile round-trip excursion. Queenstown to Milford Sound round-trip can be done in one day, and several such tour packages are offered; however, even two days is barely minimum time in this outdoor wonderland.

Sightseeing Highlights

▲▲▲**The trip to Doubtful Sound** is the second reason for coming to Te Anau; the first is Milford Sound. If at all possible, even though it's expensive, you should see both. (Milford should be a full-day round-trip, leaving early tomorrow morning by bus so that you don't have to keep your eyes glued to the road through much of the best scenery.) Fiordland Travel's triple-trip (tel. 02296/602), a seven-hour tour (van to Lake Manapouri, boat across the lake, tour of the underground powerhouse, bus to Deep Cove in Doubtful Sound, and return, adults NZ$85, children NZ$42.50), starts at 10:30 a.m. from Manapouri's riverfront at Pearl Harbour. You can make it if you start very early from Queenstown or drive over to Te Anau the night before instead of staying in Queenstown. If you're satisfied with just seeing the underground power station, it's a four-hour, half-day tour that you can start in the early afternoon.

▲▲▲ **Fiordland National Park**, New Zealand's largest and most remote park, covers over three million acres in the southwest of South Island. Take the main road out of Queenstown to Frankton, then south on Highway 6 along the Remarkables through Kingston to just before Lumsden, where Highway 94 branches west to the towns of Te Anau and Manapouri, just outside the park's boundary, and Fiordland National Park. Gaze in wonderment at the deep glacier-formed fiords, their still waters broken only by seals, dolphins, and penguins. Towering waterfalls tumble from sheer 4,500-foot walls. Mountain peaks reflect in deep blue lakes dotted with forest-covered islands. Crystal clear rivers, powered by seemingly endless days of rain or drizzle, flow from rugged, snow-capped, and often mist-shrouded mountains covered with dense green beech forests that shelter the blue and iridescent green takahe and the nocturnal, flightless kiwi, weka, and kakapo, some of the world's rarest birds. These unique sightseeing experiences are unsurpassed anywhere on earth, even on gloomy, overcast Fiordland days. Winter—June through August—is the best time for clear views and relatively little rain. The road to Milford is open in winter, but the higher elevations are subject to heavy snowfalls. In summer, prepare (with your favorite insect repellent) for the fly in the Fiordland's ointment: tiny ferocious black sandflies that inflict painful, itchy bites, especially around dusk.

▲▲ **Lake Manapouri**, 12 miles south of Te Anau, tends to be overlooked in relation to Lakes Wakatipu and Te Anau and may be New Zealand's most beautiful lake, as well as the deepest (1,500 feet). The lake contains 30 picturesque islets. Stockyard Cove is a lovely spot for picnics. Take a launch tour to the West Arm to visit the hydroelectric powerhouse 700 feet under a mountain. Water from the lake plunges through turbines and then along a six-mile tunnel into Doubtful Sound. From the tunnel a bus travels over the 2,200-foot Wilmot Pass to Deep Cove. Then board a two-hour launch cruise on Doubtful Sound, ten times larger than Milford Sound, with waterfalls cascading hundreds of feet.

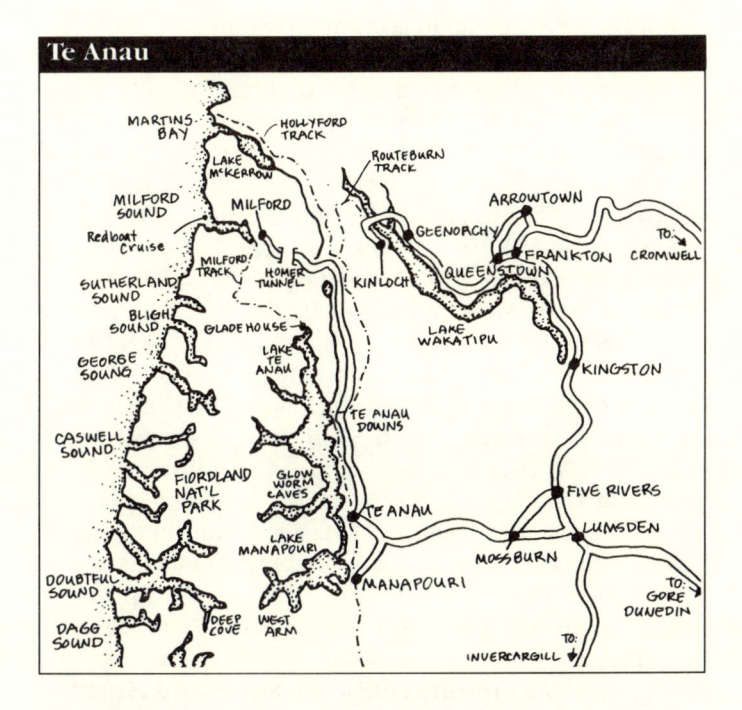

Where to Stay
One of the most attractive and comfortable hostels in New Zealand, about a mile from the lakefront, the **YHA Hostel** (Milford Road, Te Anau, tel. 0229/78-47) has six pine-paneled rooms for 40 guests at NZ$12 seniors and half price juniors (incl. GST). Make this your base for hiking the Milford or other tracks; the YH can provide storage facilities for your gear.

For the next step up in accommodations, definitely check out Marilyn Redfern's homey budget B&B near the center of town, **Matai Lodge** (42 Mokonui St., Te Anau, tel. 0229/73-60), NZ$35-$60 single/double, with hearty breakfasts (incl. GST); and the **XL Motel** (52 Te Anau Terrace, tel. 0229/72-58), across from the lake, still the most inexpensive for this type of accommodation at NZ$60 double (incl. GST).

Near the lake, **Te Anau Mountain View Cabin and Caravan Park** (Mokonui St., tel. 0229/74-62) has tent and caravan sites (NZ$8 pp), cabins (NZ$25 double), on-site caravans, and tourist cabins (NZ$33, plus GST for all rates). In a beautiful tree-covered, lakeside setting, large **Te Anau Motor Park** (Manapouri Hwy., P.O. Box 81, tel. 0229/74-57) has hundreds of tent and caravan sites (NZ$8 pp), bunks (NZ$11 pp), cabins sleeping up to five people, and A-frames (NZ$25-$40, NZ$12 per extra adult, plus GST for all rates), lodge rooms, kitchens, laundries, a sauna, a food shop, and all the assistance and information you need to make the most of this region. Near the start of launch trips to Doubtful Sound and beautiful lake Manapouri, **Manapouri Lakeview Motel and Motor Park** (Te Anau Rd., Manapouri, tel. 0229/66-24) has cabins with and without kitchens, single and shared, from NZ$13-$25, and tourist flats, NZ$45-$50 single/double (plus GST), that are well worth booking for budget-minded travelers.

The only place to stay between Te Anau and Milford Sound, just a 10-minute walk from Lake Gunn and near the start of the Routeburn and Hollyford walks, **Lake Gunn Motor Inn** (Milford Highway, Cascade Creek, Fiordland, Private Bag, Te Anau, tel. 0229/73-35) is an ideal base in this area. The rooms (30) are well worth the NZ$60-$72 single/double rates (plus GST), the lounge and its stone fireplace are delightfully cozy, and anglers will enjoy the trout fishing.

Where to Eat
Pop-in Catering (92 Te Anau Terrace, tel. 78-07) in the Waterfront Merchants Complex overlooking the lake serves light, inexpensive (NZ$3-$16) meals in a delicious home-cooked style from 8:00 a.m. to 5:30 p.m. At **Bailey's Restaurant and Coffee Shop** (Milford Rd., next door to the Luxmore Motor Lodge, which has a licensed restaurant), the menu also runs the gamut from light dishes to hot meals at about the same prices. **Vacation Inn** (The Gallery) has a good salad bar in addition to good, moderately priced food. Fans of roast beef will enjoy the restaurant in **Te Anau Downs Motor Best Western Inn** (tel. 78-11).

Itinerary Options
Hiking in the Southern Alps: Fiordland National Park and Mt. Aspiring National Park contain incredibly beautiful terrain, both tame and wild. The rugged, snow-capped mountain ranges, dense rain forests, alpine lakes and rivers, waterfalls, and majestic fiords offer a marvelous variety of "tramping" experiences of varying difficulty. Accessed from Te Anau and Queenstown, the Milford Track, Routeburn Walk, Hollyford Valley Walk, and Greenstone Valley Walk range from difficult to easy, and none requires more than good physical fitness, comfortable and waterproof gear, and adequate time. Experienced independent "trampers" hike these trails all the time. Track and weather information is supplied by national park offices. Various tour operators in the region provide guides, transportation, meals, camping equipment, and accommodation arrangements for small groups in a competent but delightfully easygoing manner.

The Milford Track, a 35-mile trail, is New Zealand's best-known walk. Highlights of the track are views from MacKinnon Pass, the 1,800-foot Sutherland Falls, the incredible variety of rain forest, and the torrents of water cascading everywhere after rain.

With an early morning departure to Te Anau from Queenstown, the Milford Track round-trip takes five days (including an arrival day in Queenstown). Open from early November to early April, a permit is necessary from the Park Headquarters in Te Anau. For independent hikers, an NZRR bus leaves Te Anau for the 45-minute ride to Te Anau Downs at 1:15 p.m., connecting with the boat to Glade House. Each of the next three days of walking is divided into 10- to 13-mile segments, followed by hot showers and meals at Pompolona Lodge and then Quintin Hut. At the end of the trail, boats leave Sandfly Point for Milford at 2:00 and 4:00 p.m. If you do not plan to catch the 3:00 p.m. bus to Te Anau, know that the next bus leaves at 7:45 a.m.

The Hollyford Valley Walk is a way to combine tramping, river jet-boating, and flightseeing to Milford Sound, the scenic drive from Milford to Te Anau, and fishing for trout and kahawai. From late October to mid-April, tramp along the broad Hollyford Valley to the Tasman Sea at Martin's Bay (four-day trip), departing on a scenic flight to Milford Sound or flightsee over Milford and Routeburn tracks; or a five-day trip alternative including a jet boat on Lake McKerrow. Contact **Hollyford Tourist & Travel Ltd.**, Invercargill, tel. 44-300. The walk in/walk out tour is 24 miles; walk in/fly out is 16 miles. Optional side trips are another 12 miles; and there is a 55-mile jet-boating option.

For a much easier walk than Milford or Hollyford, the 22-mile Greenstone Valley Walk has much to offer. The trail passes beautiful Lakes Howden and McKellar, then follows the Greenstone River to Lake Wakatipu. Greenstone is one of the walks that can be done all year, but October through April is the best time.

Much less well known than the Milford Track, the Routeburn Walk is one of the best rain forest/subalpine trails in the world. Spanning two magnificent national parks, the 25-mile trail starts and finishes about 1,500 feet above sea level, with a great variety of scenery and flora. Highlights of the trip are views from Harris Saddle (4,200 feet) and Key Summit. The higher elevations mostly eliminate the sandfly problem that plagues the Milford Track.

The keen tramper can combine a Hollyford and Routeburn walk. Often the Greenstone Walk is used as the return to Queenstown from Routeburn. At Elfin Bay you can charter a jet boat to Queenstown or walk to Kinloch to meet the bus to Routeburn. One of the very best guided treks in New Zealand is offered by Routeburn Walk Ltd. (P.O. Box 271, Queenstown, tel. 282-09, or the NZTP travel office), four days in November-April for NZ$484 adults and NZ$418 children (supplies, transportation, meals, and comfortable accommodations, including Routeburn Falls and Lake MacKenzie lodges, included).

DAY 17
TE ANAU—MILFORD SOUND

Start very early on a full-day round-trip from Te Anau to fabulous Milford Sound, including a three-hour drive over The Divide and through Homer Tunnel to the end of the road at THC Milford Resort Hotel, then a cruise through Milford Sound to see pyramid-shaped Mitre Peak, Stirling Falls, and several other magnificent waterfalls arching into the sound from high sheer walls and hanging valleys.

Suggested Schedule

7:00 a.m.	Breakfast in Te Anau.
8:30 a.m.	Drive to Milford Sound with sightseeing stops at lakes along the way.
12:00 noon	Lunch Cruise on Milford Sound.
2:30 p.m.	Return to Te Anau.
3:00 p.m.	Te Anau-au Caves Tour.
5:00 p.m.	Return to Te Anau for an early dinner.

Transportation

Te Anau to Milford Sound is a three-hour drive by way of Eglinton and Hollyford valleys and Homer Tunnel. It's 60 miles through beech forests surrounded by high rugged peaks. The high rainfall creates dark green beech forests covering thick fern and shrub, rich carpets of spongy moss and peat, and other plant growth, even on steep rock faces. Start driving early to Milford on Highway 94 (Milford Road) to be ahead of the mountains clouding up or bad weather. A call to Park Headquarters (tel. 7521) at 8:00 a.m. for the weather report would be sensible. Be sure to wear or bring waterproof and warm gear. The first 18 miles of the road skirts the shores of Lake Te Anau, then follows the Eglinton River flanked by beech forests. On the way through Eglinton Valley to The Divide, the 1,500-foot pass over the Southern Alps, Mirror Lakes (about 25 miles), and beautiful Lake Gunn (about 50

Milford Sound Region

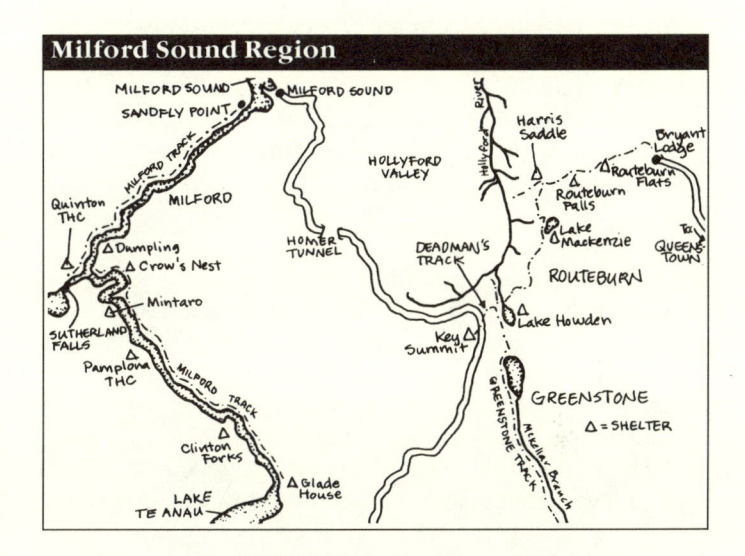

miles) are worthwhile stopping places. Although little more than ponds, Mirror Lakes yield perfect reflections of surrounding peaks. Climb the forested ridge to Cascade Creek, which, in addition to accommodations and refreshments, has views of many waterfalls cascading from bush-covered valley walls. Then drive over The Divide, eight miles before Homer Tunnel, the starting point of the Routeburn and Greenstone tracks to Lake Wakatipo. From Hollyford Road to Homer Tunnel, pass through the beech forest and tussock river flats of Hollyford Valley, some of the best scenery on the trip.

Named after Harry Homer, who discovered the Homer Saddle in 1889, the 3,600-foot-long Homer Tunnel, begun in 1935, wasn't completed until 1953. The eastern entrance to Homer Tunnel is 8,100 feet in elevation, descending through the tunnel to 2,700 feet. At the end of the drive or, better still, bus trip to Milford, is a one- to two-hour Milford Sound launch cruise with fabulous views of Mitre Peak and Sutherland Falls.

InterCity and Fiordland Travel have daylong (12-hour) trips from Queenstown for NZ$95 and 9-hour trips from

Te Anau, including a launch trip on the sound run by either Fiordland or THC, for NZ$65 adults and NZ$32 children (lunch extra). The coach excursion leaves at 8:15 a.m. and returns at 5:45 p.m. Both the THC and Fiordland Travel operate launch trips on Milford Sound. With a lunch on board, the longer cruise costs NZ$20.

Sightseeing Highlights
▲▲ **Lake Te Anau**, branching into three landlocked fiords, offers an ideal introduction to the region's thickly wooded mountains. Set in a glacier-gouged trough, the South Island's largest lake has a backdrop of the Kepler Mountains and the Murchison Range running parallel to the north. "Te Anau" is a short version of a Maori word, *Te Ana-Au*, meaning "caves of rushing waters." The myriad mysterious shapes of greenish glowworms gleaming from 15,000 years of limestone accretions have made the recently discovered caves across the lake one of the most popular local attractions. Te Ana-Au Caves can only be reached by boat, costing NZ$24 adults, NZ$9 children. Book this 2½-hour round-trip at the Fiordland Travel Centre (at the intersection of Milford Road and Te Anau Terrace, tel. 7416), which, besides Park Headquarters, is the main source of travel information for the Te Anau-Manapouri-Milford Sound area. While you're there, pick up NZ$.50 tokens to visit the Te Anau Underground Trout Observatory, south along Te Anau Terrace across from Park Headquarters, where you can watch, feed, and photograph brown, rainbow, and native trout daily from 6:00 a.m. to 9:45 p.m. To find some easy walks along the lake, from the observatory continue south on Te Anau Terrace and turn right on the road along the lake toward Manapouri. Starting at the control gates, Riverside Walk and several extensions offer one- to five-hour one-way walks of varying difficulty around the lake, up Mt. Luxmore and to Lake Manapouri.

▲▲▲ **Milford Sound**—Cruise down the ten-mile-long, deeply furrowed glacial trough hemmed in by rock walls reaching from 900 feet underwater to almost a mile high.

This fiord cruise to the Tasman Sea passes Mitre Peak, soaring over 5,000 feet from its reflection in the dark waters straight up out of the sound, passes close enough to 450-foot Stirling Falls to feel the spray, and also passes Bowen Falls, cascading about 500 feet from a hanging valley over two or three tiers. Watch for dolphins, seals lying on Seal Point's rocks, and Fiordland crested penguins. From the hotel, it's just a short walk up a flight of steps to Lookout Track for excellent views of the sound, or continue farther up a steep ridge for higher viewpoints.

Itinerary Options—Overnight Stay at Milford Sound

A mile from the sound in a beautiful setting, spartan dormitory rooms in **The Milford Lodge** (P.O. Box 10, Milford, tel. 0229/80-71) rent for NZ$15 pp. Each room (some with showers) has nothing more than three beds, but after hiking the Milford Track, who needs more (except for the sauna)? There's a kitchen and a lounge with fireplace.

For trackers or just travelers, the culmination of a visit to New Zealand is seeing Milford Sound and also should include the experience of a splurge overnight at the **THC Milford Sound Resort Hotel** (Private Bag, Milford Sound, Fiordland, tel. 0229/79-26). That experience consists of the resort's total environment, from the magnificent lawns along the sound overlooking Mitre Peak to the atmosphere of glass-enclosed lounges with fireplaces, bar, and restaurant in the evening. Regular rates are NZ$130-$180 for rooms. Check with NZTP or Fiordland Travel Ltd. (tel. 0229/74-16) for a package that includes coach to Milford, one night's lodging for one or two, breakfast, a launch trip, and lunch—a minimum NZ$220 value for one person or NZ$310 value for two.

Bring a picnic lunch or plan to splurge on a complete seafood lunch at the **THC Milford** (tel. 0229/79-26) for NZ$21 while viewing the spectacular scenery.

DAY 18
TE ANAU—WANAKA

Leave Te Anau early, drive on Highways 94 and 6 to Arrowtown, and take Highway 89 up to the top of Crown Ridge for magnificent views overlooking Wakatipu Lake, the Kawarau River, Queenstown, and the Remarkables. Drive through Cardrona Valley to Wanaka for an afternoon of boating, fishing, hiking, or other activities in the Lake Wanaka area.

Suggested Schedule

7:00 a.m.	Breakfast and check out.
10:30 a.m.	Highway 89 to Wanaka.
12:30 p.m.	Lunch in Wanaka.
1:30 p.m.	Walk up Mt. Iron.
2:30 p.m.	Glendhu Bay and boat trip on Lake Wanaka, or Lake Hawea for trout fishing.
7:30 p.m.	Dinner at Ripples Restaurant.

Driving from Te Anau to Wanaka
Queenstown to Wanaka is 75 miles. Retrace your driving route on Highway 94 east to Mossburn, then north on Highway 6 to Queenstown. Lake Wanaka is two hours from Queenstown unless you drive on Highway 89, which could take longer depending on driving conditions and your speed up the mountain.

In good weather only (not in midwinter!), drive Highway 89 up the very steep unpaved road from Arrowtown to the top of the Crown Ridge for magnificent views overlooking Wakatipu Lake, the Kawarau River, Queenstown, and the Remarkables. This road passes through Cardrona Valley from Wanaka to Queenstown, 44 miles of slow-going, bumpy unpaved road (versus 57 miles following Highway 6 around the Pisa Range).

Sightseeing Highlights
▲▲▲ **Wanaka** is one of New Zealand's most underrated resorts because it is in the shadow of Queenstown, only

60 miles away. Lakes Wanaka and Hawea are famed for their fishing (brown and rainbow trout and landlocked salmon). They have the best weather and most sunshine days in the southern lakes. Many skiers from the United States and Europe prefer Treble Cone to Coronet Peak (Queenstown is still the apres-ski favorite). The Wanaka region has most of the same outdoor recreational choices as Queenstown. For panoramic views of Lake Wanaka and Mt. Aspiring National Park, walk up Mt. Roy (3 hours) or Mt. Iron (1 hour).

▲▲**Glendhu Bay**, west of Wanaka and Roy's Peak on Wanaka Aspiring Road, especially in autumn, is renowned for its seasonal beauty and views of Mt. Aspiring National Park.

Where to Stay

Just a few minutes from the lake, one of the best features of the **YHA Hostel** (181 Upton St., tel. 02943/7405) is its mountain bike rentals and outings or contacts for recreational outings (horseback riding, rockclimbing, skiing, etc.) The rate is NZ$12 pp for seniors, juniors half price (incl. GST). Eight miles from Wanaka, **Glendhu Bay Camp** on lovely Glendhu Bay, with especially beautiful sunsets over Mt. Aspiring, is the place to set up a tent (NZ$6.50) or rent a cabin (NZ$24 single/double, plus GST). At the end of the road to the bay (22 additional unpaved miles across many streams) is the starting point for climbs up Mt. Aspiring.

Less than a mile from the center of town, **Wanaka Motor Park** (212 Brownston St., tel. 02943/7883) offers cabins (NZ$14 pp in season, NZ$9 pp otherwise), caravan sites (NZ$8.50), and tent sites (NZ$7.50), all plus GST. **Pleasant Lodge Caravan Park** (Mt. Aspiring Rd., tel. 02943/7360) has tent and caravan sites (NZ$12 double) and cabins (NZ$17 double), all plus GST.

At **Creekside Guest House** (84 Helwick St., tel. 02943/7834) you get your own room with private bath and breakfast for NZ$25-$50 single/double (in season, plus GST). Among several other good B&Bs in Wanaka charging about the same rate is the **Country Lane B&B** (28 Dungarvon St., tel. 02943/8040). If you can get a special discount rate (normal rate NZ$65, plus GST) for the **THC Wanaka Resort Hotel** (P.O. Box 26, Lake Wanaka, tel. 02943/7826), consider making it your overnight stay.

Where to Eat
Kingsway Tea Lounge (21 Helwick St.) down the street from the Creekside is one of the best places in town for budget sandwiches, salads, soup, and light fare from 9:00 a.m. to 5:00 p.m. Open later (until 9:00 p.m.) with a more limited menu, **Aspiring Takeaways** (68 Ardmore St.) also sells groceries. **First Cafe**, also on Ardmore, with a more extensive menu is open from 6:00 until 10:00 p.m.

The dinner menu at the THC's **Storehouse Bistro** restaurant (Ardmore St., tel. 7826) includes everything you might want to eat in fish and meat at reasonable prices (NZ$10-$18). The decor with fireplace, crossbeams, and old photos of the hotel on the walls makes it one of the most comfortable restaurants in Fiordland.

You want tasty Indian, Greek, Mexican, and other food at reasonable prices? **Te Kano Cafe** (63 Brownston St., tel. 7208) is one of two local alternatives to Ripples (the other is Freshwater Cafe, below) for food lovers (especially those watching their budget). Expect to pay up to NZ$20 for main courses served from 6:30 p.m. until late. **Ripples** (Pembroke Village Mall, tel. 7413) is still one of the best restaurants on the South Island and worth a trip from Queenstown. In season it's open 6:30 to 10:00 p.m. seven days, and in summer it's open for lunch, too. Expect to pay up to NZ$45 for complete dinners (BYO license). In the same mall, **Freshwater Cafe** serves a delicious variety of main courses until 9:00 p.m. Leave room for equally good desserts.

For those who follow my suggested itinerary option and drive the Crown Range Road (Hwy 89) between Wanaka and Queenstown, the **Cardrona Restaurant** (tel. 8153) will reward you with the beautiful restored interior (circa the gold rush days) of the old Cardrona

Wanaka—Queenstown Region

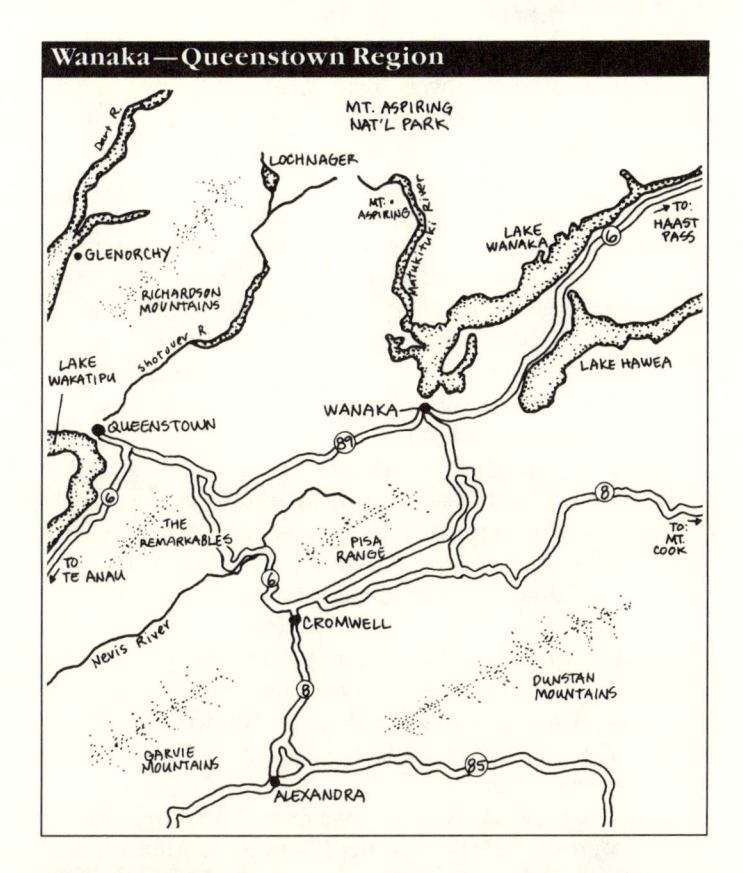

Hotel, delightful garden if you prefer, and superb dining accompanied by homemade sourdough bread. Expect to pay over NZ$20 for a complete meal, certainly an excellent value.

Itinerary Options
Alternate Routes from Te Anau or Queenstown
If you plan to travel to Te Anau to see Milford, and also want to see Dunedin, I'll suggest a counterclockwise circuit from Te Anau that also will take you to Invercargill and Stewart Island and along the coast to Dunedin and includes an alternative route for the return to Cromwell from Dunedin.

From Te Anau, it's only 70 miles to the coast and an equal distance on Highway 99 to Invercargill; Invercargill to Balclutha, on Highway 92 with a detour on Highway 9 and another detour off Highway 1 to the coast on the South Road from Taieri Mouth to Green Island, is over 200 miles. With these detours (not including Stewart Island), it's about 350 miles from Te Anau to Dunedin.

From Te Anau and Manapouri, continue south on Highway 99 following the Waiau River past Clifden (18 miles east of lovely Lake Hauroko) to Te Waewae Bay (take a side trip to beautiful white sand Blue Cliffs Beach), then along the coast to Riverton and Invercargill (Bluff and Stewart Island, see below).

For some of the best sightseeing on the South Island, continue to Balclutha on the slower Highway 92 to the golden sands of Porpoise Bay, the fossilized forest in Curio Bay and, between Chaslands and beautiful Tautuka Beach, the fascinating Cathedral Caves (if the tide is right). Picturesque Lake Wilkie, impressive Matai Falls and especially Purakaunui Falls, magnificent Jacks Bay beach, and spectacular Jacks Bay blowhole near Owaki are attractions on Highway 92 (instead of Highway 1) to Balclutha. Then take a right at Lake Waihola via Taieri Mouth (partly gravel) to Dunedin.

Return to Queenstown/Wanaka from Dunedin on one of two routes: (the longer route, 150 miles to Alexandra plus 57 miles to Queenstown) via Highway 87 to Middlemarch, Naseby/Ranfurly, and Highway 85 to Alexandra, Clyde, and Cromwell, then Highways 6 and 6A to Wanaka; or alternatively (the shorter route, 125 miles to Alexandra), backtrack on Highway 1 to Milton, then north on Highway 8 through Lawrence and Roxburgh along the Clutha to Alexandra. (Be sure to view the region around Alexandra from Tucker Hill Lookout.) Both ways, you see historic Alexandra and Cromwell. With only 25 miles difference, take Highway 85 and pass through Victorian **Naseby**, with a side trip to historic St. Bathans, some of the other old gold towns of Otago, and Blue Lake.

Day 18

This entire circuit—Te Anau-Dunedin-Queenstown—is close to 600 miles without additional side trips. Allow a day to Stewart Island, at least a day and two nights on the island, a day from Invercargill to Dunedin, two days in Dunedin/Otago Peninsula, and a day to Wanaka, without excessively early starts and late arrivals. In sum, allow a total of no less than six days and five nights. Contact the NZTP office (131 Princes St., tel. 024/740-344) or the Dunedin Visitor Centre (The Octagon, tel. 024/774-176).

Dunedin—Otago Peninsula—Stewart Island

Fueled by Central Otago's gold rush in the 1860s, Dunedin became Victorian New Zealand's wealthiest town. "The Edinburgh of the South" envisioned by its Scottish founders flourished as a planned city with more interesting, diverse architecture than any other in the country. Dunedin is framed by a greenbelt on the hills facing the harbor set between the rugged Otago Peninsula and the coast.

North of the City, Signal Hill and Mount Cargill offer sweeping panoramas of the harbor, or follow the four-mile Queens Drive through the Town Belt. Other viewpoints include Unity Park, Bracken's Lookout, Southern Cemetery, and Prospect Park.

The 35-room Jacobean-style Olveston Mansion, Dunedin's primary attraction, is a showcase of European antiques only matched by the Larnach Castle on Otago Peninsula. Visiting Olveston Mansion (42 Royal Terrace, tel. 024/773-320) is a must while you're in Dunedin, but you need a guide and a reservation. Admission NZ$5 adults, NZ$1 children.

The Otago Museum on Great King Street contains an extensive collection of early Maori, Chatham Islands, and Oceanic art and artifacts and the Mataatus meeting house from Whakatane on the North Island. Open Monday through Friday, 9:00 a.m. to 4:30 p.m., Saturday 10:30 a.m. to 4:30 p.m., Sunday 1:30 to 4:30 p.m.

The Otago Peninsula, northeast of Dunedin, offers high-contrast scenery between the Otago Harbour and

Pacific Ocean sides: serene and dotted with settlements on the harbor side, wild and rugged on the ocean side.

Larnach Castle (1871), a 43-room neo-Gothic "monument" set in 35 acres of gardens, contains a 3,000-square-foot ballroom crafted and furnished in grand style. Richly carved ceilings and Venetian glass, created by imported European craftsmen, decorate the rooms. The tower, over 1,000 feet above sea level, provides superb views of the peninsula and harbor. Open 9:00 a.m. to 5:00 p.m.; December-February until 8:00 p.m. (tel. 024/761-302). The most memorable overnight stay in Dunedin is at the **Larnach Castle Lodge** (tel. 761-302) in bunk rooms (NZ$20-$30 single/double) in an 1870 coach house, or in lodge house rooms with shared bath (NZ$48 single/double) or private bath (NZ$69). Continental and cooked breakfasts are extra. When all of the other tourists leave, you have the castle and grounds to yourself. From Highland Road, turn left on Camp Road and follow the signs.

The Royal Albatross Colony is the closest to a developed area of any nesting place for these huge birds. The breeding grounds can be visited with prior arrangement from November through September; December to May are the best viewing months. Chicks hatch in January.

Yellow-eyed penguins come ashore to nest in Penguin Bay and seals bask on a rocky islet (Seal Island) only 10 yards from shore.

From Bluff on the ferry *MV Wairua*, Stewart Island is two hours across the Foveaux Strait (or 20 minutes by air). With its brilliant dawns and sunsets, the Maoris call it Rakiura, "Island of the Glowing Sky." Most of the 500 people on this unspoiled 40-mile by 25-mile (425,000-acre) island, descendants of European whalers, live in Halfmoon Bay (Oban) and fish the often stormy Pacific and Antarctic waters. Visit the Rakiura Museum for Stewart Island's history (open only between 10:00 a.m. and 1:30 p.m. on ferry days).

With only 12½ miles of road on the northern coast, Stewart Island is for walkers, bird-watchers, and deer hunters. Bring waterproof clothing and boots. In particular, this island is an ornithologist's paradise: tui and bellbirds in spring, tomtit and rare wekas in summer, fantails in winter, and parakeets, kakas, fernbirds, dottrels, brown creepers, moreporks, and perhaps even kiwis year-round.

You can see all of the sights along the 12½ miles of paved road with Beryl Wilcox's one-hour minibus tour from Observation Point to Thule Bay. Beryl knows everything worth telling about the island. Contact **Stewart Island Travel** (Betty and her husband, Lloyd, P.O. Box 26, Stewart Island, tel. 021/391-269). They can arrange your accommodations and help with anything else you want to do on the island.

Launch cruise and self-charters visit Ulva Island's sandy beaches and wooded walking trails, Paterson Inlet, Ocean Beach, Port Adventure, and Port William. Enjoy short walks to Horseshoe Bay, Garden Mound, Ringoringa Beach, and Lee Bay. The northern part of the island offers weeks of hiking, but obtain local information and maps first, and avoid wandering off the beaten track.

DAY 19
WANAKA TO FOX AND FRANZ JOSEPH GLACIERS

Leave very early once more for an eight-hour drive (including stops) from Wanaka through the Makarora Valley to Haast Pass, descending to the two great glaciers of Westland National Park, Fox and Franz Josef. Thirteen miles apart, Fox and Franz Josef glaciers descend about six miles into rain forests 1,000 feet above sea level. The land rises to peaks over 10,000 feet high with incredible scenery. Today and tomorrow, take advantage of fabulous recreational opportunities, including glacier excursions and forest walks at both glaciers.

Suggested Schedule

7:00 a.m.	Breakfast and check out.
8:00 a.m.	Depart for Haast Pass.
12:00 noon	Picnic lunch near Haast Pass.
2:30 p.m.	Arrive at Fox Glacier.
3:00 p.m.	Climb to Fox Chalet Lookout for sunset views.
6:30 p.m.	Head for Franz Josef to check in, dine, and relax in front of a fireplace.

Wanaka to Fox and Franz Josef Glaciers
From Wanaka to Franz Josef is 180 miles. The Haast Pass Road (Highway 6) from Wanaka to Westland National Park passes through fabulous scenery. With many one-lane bridges and gravel sections, steep slopes, blind and sharp corners, magnificent scenery and view points, walking and picnicking opportunities, you can't hurry—and don't want to.

From Wanaka, continue to follow Highway 6, first along Lake Hawea and then along Lake Wanaka up the Makarora River Valley to Haast Pass. Drive through Mt. Aspiring National Park, named for the highest and most magnificent peak (over 10,000 feet), and over Haast Pass (1,700 feet). Mt. Cook is only 50 miles to the north.

Highway 6 skirts the western shore of Lake Hawea, another scenic gem known for its trout and landlocked salmon fishing, then crosses The Neck between Lakes Hawea and Wanaka, and follows Lake Wanaka to Makarora Gorge. One of the most scenic parts of the entire trip lies in Mt. Aspiring National Park, between the gorge and Haast Pass. The mountain after which the park is named rises west of Wanaka. Along Highway 6 to the 1,500-foot pass, the Makarora and other rivers flow in and out of hills and flats covered with sheep. Snow-capped peaks appear in the background. There are a few remaining stretches of bad gravel: 9 miles from Hawea for 5 miles, 3 miles beyond the Neck between Lakes Wanaka and Hawea for 6 miles, and 2 miles beyond Makarora through the beech forests up to the Haast Saddle.

From the pass, the Haast River drops through the gorge known as the Gates of Haast, where it roars through a gorge full of enormous boulders. The river is joined by the larger Landsborough in a wider valley along which you can drive down to the sea. You may want to stop in Haast, refuel, and stock up on food supplies before continuing. Cross Haast Bridge and travel north 15 miles to Knights Point, a headland fringed by golden sand beaches and rocky bays, where you may see seals playing offshore just south of Lake Moeraki, with glacial lake water and good fishing. Another good stop is Lake Paringa.

Sightseeing Highlights
▲▲▲ **Westland National Park**—Fox and Franz Josef glaciers are unique in that they push steeply down into rain forest within a few miles of the sea. The park contains over 60 named glaciers and beautiful lakes. Fox and Franz Josef glaciers can be visited easily from the Westland National Park Visitor Centres. To get to Fox Glacier from the village, backtrack south on Highway 6 a little over a mile to the Glacier Access Road. Watch for the Glacier View Road sign on the right. At the south end of Glacier View Road starts the 40-minute (one-way) Chalet

Lookout Track. The Cone Rock Track branches off the Chalet Lookout Track, climbing steeply 1,000 feet above the Fox River, a strenuous hour and a half on a steep switchback trail. The Chalet Lookout Track is much less strenuous. From Fox Glacier Hotel, a walking track to lovely Minnehaha Creek is just a 20-minute stroll through forest. Try it at night with a flashlight to see thousands of glowworms dangling in the rain forest.

Tomorrow in Franz Josef, stop at the Park Centre for brochures on short walking tracks in the area and general information on hiking in the glaciers. Franz Josef Glacier is less than four miles from the Centre. Head back south along Highway 6 for a few hundred yards to the turnoff onto the Glacier Access Road. From this road through the rain forest, many tracks branch out for from 30 minutes to three or four hours of moderate to strenuous walking. The Centre's brochures provide details on all of these tracks. Don't forget to bring rainwear and plenty of potent insect repellent in late spring and summer months. Tomorrow, also plan to see at least one of the beautiful nearby Lakes—Kaniere, Mapourika, Mahinapua, Mauapiurike, Matheson, Paring, Brunner, Ianthe, or Wahapo.

Where to Stay
Fox Glacier Motorcamp (tel. 41-821) has tents (NZ$13.50), caravan sites (NZ$15), nice cabins (NZ$24), tourist flats (NZ$44), and motel units (NZ$55), all double (incl. GST), and bunks for NZ$10. All accommodations include continental breakfast. On the premises, the **Alpine View Motel** (tel. 41-821) has rooms with kitchenettes from NZ$55-$72 double.

Franz Josef Glacier: One of the best hostels in New Zealand, **Franz Josef YHA Hostel** (24 Cron St., P.O. Box 12, tel. 754) has ten rooms for 60 travelers at NZ$13 seniors, juniors half price (incl. GST). Set in a beautiful forest, **Forks Lodge and Motorcamp** (P.O. Box 6, Okarito, tel. Whataroa 351) is 12 miles north of Franz Josef, about a mile off the main highway at the Forks. Three units sleep two to ten people at NZ$9 per adult, tent sites are NZ$4, and camper van sites are NZ$12 (all plus GST).

Franz Joseph Motor Camp (tel. 766), located on the main road about a half-mile south of Franz Josef, has one of the best views and nicest grounds of South Island's motor camps. If not for the outpouring of sandflies in summer, it would be heaven (repellent is a must!). Indoor swimming pool, kitchen facilities, communal bathrooms, dormitory-style cabins (NZ$8), roomy deluxe (NZ$14 pp) and renovated standard cabins (NZ$20 double), and family cottages with kitchens (NZ$33), all plus GST are all first rate.

If you can get the two-day special rate of NZ$99, **THC Franz Josef** (Private Bag, Hokitika, tel. 719) becomes much more affordable. Also consider the **Westland Motor Inn** (tel. 729) if you can get one of the budget lodgings, single beds in double and triple rooms for NZ$14-$25. Otherwise, for motel-type units, book at the **Bushland Court Motel** (Cron St., P.O. Box 41, tel. 757) with small and large units at rates starting at NZ$46 double (plus GST); or the more expensive **Motel Franz Josef** (Private Bag, Hokitika, tel. 742) on the main road three miles north of the village, with one- and two-bedroom units for NZ$60 single or double (plus GST).

Where to Eat
Fox Glacier: The **Hobnail Cafe** in the Alpine Guides complex has good lunches and home-baked goods for morning or afternoon tea. **Fox Glacier Hotel** serves soup, savory, and grill at reasonable prices.

Franz Josef: On one side of the souvenir shops, **Glacier Store and Tearooms** serves the usual inexpensive snacks and grills. On the other side, seven days from 10:30 a.m. to 9:30 p.m., **D.A.'s Restaurant** serves all types of main dishes and salads for under NZ$17.

The **Westland Motor Inn** (tel. 729) has a casual/dress-up restaurant for dining, nice decor, and views, with dinner prices around NZ$20 or higher. About a half hour walk from the village, **THC Franz Josef's Fern Room** (tel. 719) has a better view and less expensive prices for main dishes. Ask about the three-course special for under NZ$20.

Itinerary Options

At Fox Glacier, the Chalet Lookout Walk to the Cone Rock Walk is three to four hours up and down including sightseeing time. Within the suggested schedule, even an overnight fly-in (to a hut above the main icefall)/walk-out trip with Alpine Guides (P.O. Box 38, Fox Glacier, Westland National Park, tel. Fox 825) is possible. Instead of heading for Franz Josef tonight, another outstanding trip option is to drive (Cook Flat Rd.) to Lake Matheson, stay overnight at the tent, caravan, bunk, or cabin facilities of nearby Fox Glacier Motor Camp (tel. 821), or Alpine View Motel (tel. 839), for an early morning walk around the lake and a view of its justly famous reflections of Mt. Cook and Mt. Tasman. Two other alternatives are to drive five miles north of Franz Josef to beautiful Lake Mapourika where there's a free campground at McDonalds Creek or stop on the way to Fox Glacier at the Lakeside Motel (tel. 894) in Fox Glacier for fabulous trout fishing on Lake Paringa.

The Fox Glacier heli-hike, offered by Alpine Guides (tel. Fox 825), lets you ride a helicopter to the glacier and walk back down (2½ hours). The cost is NZ$65 adults, including boots, socks, and parkas.

Now that the 22 days around New Zealand are almost over, you can decide whether you have enough money left to spend NZ$98 pp to view unforgettable alpine scenery on the one-hour Mt. Cook Lines' skiplane flight from Franz Joseph to the top of the Tasman Glacier (in Franz Josef, tel. 714; at Fox, tel. 41-812).

DAY 20
FRANZ JOSEF—HOKITIKA—GREYMOUTH

Spend the morning in the Franz Josef area, then head north past scenic west coast lakes, visit a greenstone factory in Hokitika, retrace the region's gold mining era, and enjoy magnificent scenery before heading to Greymouth for the night.

Suggested Schedule

7:00 a.m.	Breakfast and check out.
8:00 a.m.	Franz Josef Glacier Valley Walk, or at 9:00 a.m., the four-hour guided Franz Joseph Glacier Walk.
12:00 noon	Leave for a picnic lunch and lake touring en route to Hokitika.
2:30 p.m.	Visit Hokitika's Greenstone Factory and local sightseeing.
6:00 p.m.	Dinner in Greymouth.

Orientation

Greymouth is 110 miles from Franz Joseph Glacier along Highway 6. The narrow strip called Westland, never more than 30 miles wide, is yet another climatically, topographically, and historically unique area of New Zealand. The last ice age, ending 14,000 years ago, covered the lowland areas that now consist of dense coniferous rain forests, alpine grasslands, shrublands, herb fields, coastal lagoons and lakes, and the wide gravel beds of glacier-fed rivers. Permanent ice and snow remain above 4,500 feet, a bluish-white mass spilling slowly downward, cracking into deep ravines and crevasses under its enormous mass and the force of gravity, slowly retreating as 600 species of trees, shrubs, ferns, and plants colonize the bare rocks in accordance with the altitude. The quantities of insects thriving on this kind of rain forest and wetland environment support comparably vast numbers and varieties of birds, which you'll hear constantly chattering and singing as you hike up to the glaciers or visit some of the beautiful lakes on the 85-mile drive to Hokitika.

The weather is relatively mild, with high rainfall south of the Westport area. Coastal growth like nikau palms and fern trees merges with coastal rain forests rising to mountain beech beneath the snow-capped peaks. The rain falls mainly at night, thereby allowing the region to match Auckland for sunshine hours.

Captain Cook followed Abel Tasman on the west coast, as he did on the north coast of South Island. Amazingly, between Cook's visit in 1770 and 87 years later, the west coast wasn't approached by sea despite the hardship that Thomas Brunner and other explorers experienced on overland routes. This exploration from the Nelson area in the 1840s sought sheep and cattle country, but the discovery of gold in 1859 between Greymouth, the largest Maori settlement along the coast, and Hokitika opened a new era of settlement. Gold lured over 10,000 miners to the west coast in the next five years—including an "invasion" of Australian gold seekers. Hokitika was founded in 1864, becoming the "Capital of the Goldfields" with a hundred hotels springing up, mostly on Revell Street.

The Arthur's Pass route, discovered by Sir Arthur Dobson, was opened as a coach road in 1866, when the population of the coast surged to 50,000. Greymouth and other harbors were jammed by ships bringing new miners and supplying prospectors and storekeepers. Logging and milling of local timber and the export of bituminous coal began at the same time. Coal export, centered around Westport to this day, expanded slowly for lack of port facilities and a railhead, and then grew rapidly after 1880 as gold mining declined in importance. The decline of gold mining left a string of deserted former boomtowns—Charlestown, Barrytown, Denniston, Stockton, and others. Shantytown, a historical reconstruction of a local gold settlement of the 1880s, is Greymouth's most popular attraction (see Day 21).

Westland National Park

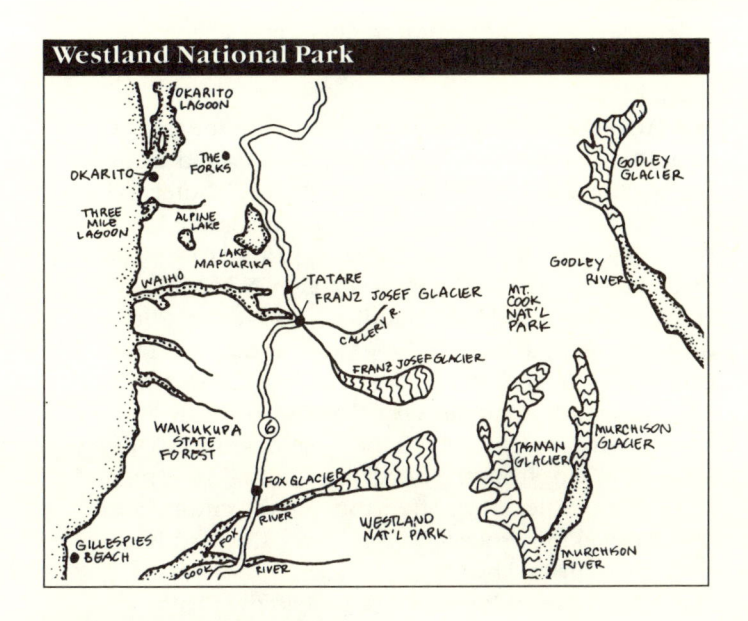

Sightseeing Highlights

▲▲▲ **Franz Josef Glacier Valley Walk** takes you by minibus to the glacier and then on a glacier walk (2 ½ hours). As an alternative to the drive up the glacier, there is a walking track of less than two miles on the north side of the Waiho River, going along the Callery River Gorge. At the suspension bridge where the track crosses to Glacier Road, a second track branches off to Roberts Point above the glacier. Sentinel Rock and Peters Pool on Glacier road are other easily accessible vantage points, as is Canavans Knob, which begins about a mile to the south off Highway 6. For this type of tour, contact Stan Peterson, Westland Guiding Service (tel. 750), NZ$27 adults and NZ$13 children.

The guided Franz Josef Glacier Walk, offered by the THC Franz Josef Hotel, departs at 9:30 a.m. and 2:00 p.m. for a four-hour tour. Be at the hotel at 9:00 a.m. to get your special boots, socks, and orientation. Experienced guides will lead you up and down icy pinnacles and over crevasses, for an unforgettable experience costing only

NZ$24 adults, NZ$12 children, including all equipment. Take a snack lunch along for nourishment while on the glacier.

▲▲ **Hokitika**'s claim to fame started with the discovery of gold in 1864. Within two years, the area had 50,000 people digging for gold and more than 100 hotels. The West Coast Historical Museum on lower Tancred Street recalls the gold mining era (open 9:30 a.m. to 4:40 p.m. weekdays, 1:30 to 4:00 p.m. weekends, NZ$2.50 adults, NZ$1 children, and NZ$7 families). Today, in addition to timber milling, several factories in Hokitika cut and polish greenstone (nephrite jade) from neighboring mountains and make it into jewelry. Greenstone is the Maori's sacred gemstone, for which they made perilous journeys across the Alps from the north and south. The Greenstone Factory (tel. 713), offers tours of the cutting and jewelry-making process on weekdays. Buy a souvenir rock or beautiful jewelry.

For magnificent local views, drive to the Plane Table Lookout north of Hokitika and the Sea View Lookout in a cemetery near the hospital. For a very picturesque view of the river mouth, walk down to Gibson Quay.

Take Blue Spur Road east of town to see the Vintage Farm Museum and Greenstone Factory (Westland Greenstone Co., Tancred St., tel. 713, and Len Provis's Greenstone Factory, Blue Spur, tel. 1785), open 8:00 a.m. to 5:00 p.m. every day; then visit the mine tunnels of the working Blue Spur Gold Mine.

About 12 miles south of Hokitika, the Lake Kaniere Scenic Reserve offers a scenic drive and walks second to none.

Where to Stay
A modern, well-maintained hostel (like Franz Josef) at the south end of Greymouth, **"Kainga-ra" YHA Hostel** (Cowper St., P.O. Box 299, tel. 027/49-51) has 43 beds in eight rooms rented at NZ$12 seniors, juniors half (plus GST). The closest motor camp to the city, about 1½ miles south, **Greymouth Seaside Motor Camp** (Chesterfield

St., tel. 027/66-18), offers the entire range of accommodations: tent sites (NZ$13.50 double), caravans (NZ$15), on-site caravans (NZ$29), cabins (NZ$26 double), tourist cabins (NZ$33 double), and tourist flats (NZ$48).

Stay at the **West Haven Tourist Lodge** (62 Albert St., tel. 027/56-05) and have breakfast or brunch elsewhere and your rates are only NZ$18-$34 single/double (incl. GST). **Golden Coast Guest House** (10 Smith St., tel. 027/78-39) caters to B&B enthusiasts. Gladys Roche's four guest rooms are as neat as can be, and you can rent with continental or cooked breakfast (NZ$38.50-$55 single/double) or without (NZ$45-50 double), all plus GST. If you're looking for some nice, moderately priced family units next to a beach, try **South Beach Motel** (318 Main South Rd., tel. 027/26-768), a Best Western, with NZ$59 rates (plus GST).

Where to Eat

The Raceway Carvery (Union Hotel, Herbert St., tel. 40-13) serves substantial main courses starting at NZ$10 seven days a week. The pricey surprise in town is the gourmet **Café Collage** (115 Mackey St., tel. 54-97), which serves a variety of delectable main courses from NZ$16 to $30. The cozy **Albion Bistro** in the Kings' Motor Hotel and the **J.B. Restaurant** in the DG Greymouth Hotel, 68 High Street (tel. 4361), are moderately priced. For big appetites, the international menu and portions at the **West Inn**, Paroa (tel. 732), should be a perfect remedy.

A **Cobb & Co.** restaurant is located in the renovated Revington's first floor (next door to a very lively bar). Revington's, built 15 years after the first gold strike in 1864, has rooms with a lot of character for NZ$55 double.

Itinerary Option

Twelve miles north of Franz Josef Glacier is the Fork (with a motor camp in an idyllic location, tel. Whataroa 351) where a nine-mile side trip leads to beautiful **Okarito Lagoon**. You'll find a youth hostel there that will tempt you to stay over.

DAY 21
GREYMOUTH—ARTHUR'S PASS NATIONAL PARK—CHRISTCHURCH

Begin the day by visiting Shantytown. Then start the spectacular 65-mile trip on Arthur's Pass Road (Highway 73). Crossing the Divide affords magnificent views and opportunities to explore Arthur's Pass National Park on the way back to Christchurch. Make steep ascents and descents along the twisting pathways of four glacier-fed rivers—Taramakau, Otira, Bealey, and Waimakariri—rushing through totally contrasting landscapes of mountains and foothills on the wet western and dry eastern sides of the highest highway across the Southern Alps. Scenic lookouts and both short and longer walking or hiking trails are easily accessible from the highway.

Suggested Schedule

7:00 a.m.	Breakfast and check out.
8:30 a.m.	Visit Shantytown.
9:30 a.m.	Arthur's Pass Road up to the Pass.
12:00 noon	Picnic or other lunch near Arthur's Pass Village.
1:00 p.m.	Scenic walks in the vicinity of the village.
4:00 p.m.	Descend to Christchurch.
7:00 p.m.	Dinner in Christchurch.

Sightseeing Highlights

▲▲ **Shantytown** is a faithful reconstruction of the old west coast gold mining town, complete with hotel, church, shops, jail and gallows, livery stables, steam engine, gem and minerals hall, and working gold claim where visitors can pan for their own. Open 8:30 a.m. to 5:00 p.m. NZ$4 adults and NZ$2 children.

▲▲▲ **Arthur's Pass National Park** is reached from the old gold-mining town of Kumara in Westland, at the junction of Highways 6 and 73. Highway 73 traverses the Main Divide to Springfield on the western outskirts of Christchurch. As you drive along this paved and well-maintained road, try to imagine a thousand workers with picks and shovels building first the road and then the railroad over Arthur's Pass in the middle of winter; Cobb & Co. stagecoaches madly racing for 36 hours to reach Westland's newly discovered gold fields; and the Maori using this route, without a road, to obtain precious greenstone in the riverbeds of the western mountains. Ascend steeply through lush grassland in the Taramakau River Valley, past the old railway town of Otira, and then cross the Otira River to Arthur's Pass. (Between Otira and Arthur's Pass, caravans and trailers are banned. The alternative for returning to Christchurch is Lewis Pass.) The road is surrounded by rugged snow-capped mountains with dense beech forests to the snow lines and deep glacier-carved gorges. Follow Bealey Valley and the Bealey River into the township of Arthur's Pass. The few miles before the village, Top of the Pass, is well worth walking to get the most out of the great mountain scenery.

Allow four hours for driving from Greymouth to Christchurch and the rest of the day for sightseeing activities. Stop by the Park Visitor Centre, open seven days, 8:00 a.m. to 5:00 p.m. (tel. Arthur's Pass, 500) in Arthur's Pass village for information, brochures, detailed maps, and to see a variety of fascinating exhibits on the history, flora and fauna, geology, and other background. Just a short walk from the Visitor Centre is the Devils Punchbowl Trail to the nearby Devils Punchbowl waterfall, pouring down a 400-foot gorge. The Bridal Veil Nature Walk to a view of Bealey Valley from the Bridal Veil Lookout, about an hour round-trip, starts near the Bealey footbridge. Another one-hour walk from the village, starting opposite the Dobson Memorial, winds through flower beds along Dobson Nature Walk.

From Arthur's Pass to Bealey, follow the mighty Waimakariri River within Arthur's Pass National Park. Watch for clearly marked walking tracks, picnic shelters, and camping sites. The Waimakariri River and parallel Highway 73 curve around the northern end of the tree-covered Craigieburn Range, which becomes bare, eroded hills around trout-filled Lakes Grasmere and Pearson. The landscape changes to the beech-covered Craigieburn Forest Park and then to the smooth round hills near Castle to begin a rather desolate descent from the 3,000-foot level around Porters Pass to the fertile Canterbury Plains.

Where to Eat
The Store and Tearooms in the village is open seven days a week. The **Chalet Restaurant** serves two moderately priced meals a day (dinner 6:00 to 7:45 p.m.).

Where to Stay
On Highway 73 in the middle of the village, **Sir Arthur Dudley Dobson Memorial YH** (tel. 89-230) consists of two dorms for 39 people. The rate is NZ$12 pp. The **Alpine Motel** (tel. 89-233) has units with cooking facilities and private baths for NZ$44 double.

Itinerary Options
For the return to Christchurch, you have a choice between Arthur's Pass (Hwy 73) and Lewis Pass (Hwy 7). The west side of Arthur's Pass is especially lush and beautiful. The Lewis Pass Road does not offer the scenic grandeur of Arthur's Pass National Park but does open up worthwhile side trips—to Hanmer Springs, for example. Just west of Lewis Pass is Maruia Springs, hot pools in an alpine setting. In midwinter, Lewis Pass may be easier to cross.

For those returning to the North Island on the Inter-Island Ferry, it's a four-hour drive from Westport to Picton, passing through the very scenic Lower Buller Gorge on Highway 6. This route opens up these options: Coaltown Trust Museum, which displays the history of Westport, the country's main coal shipping port (Queen St. South, tel. 8204, open daily, NZ$4 adults and NZ$2 children); a side trip to the Punakaiki Scenic Reserve, where Pancake Rocks and Punakaiki Blowholes jut into the sea midway between Westport and Greymouth. Stratified rock formations in lush greenery interlaced with rocky grottoes and blowholes; a side trip to the Abel Tasman National Park or the Nelson Lakes National Park.

DAY 22
CHRISTCHURCH—BANKS PENINSULA

Take an all-day trip to Banks Peninsula and Akaroa (50 miles from Christchurch), a charming village with French atmosphere. Afterward, return to Christchurch to relax and enjoy a special evening.

Suggested Schedule

7:00 a.m.	Leisurely breakfast.
8:30 a.m.	Leave for all-day trip to Banks Peninsula and Akaroa.
2:00 p.m.	Visit Okains Bay.
4:30 p.m.	Return to Christchurch for a celebration dinner.

Directions: Christchurch—Akaroa Round-trip

There are two ways to drive from Christchurch to Banks Peninsula: to Lyttelton through the road tunnel under Port Hills and via Summit Road, the route suggested for today.

From Cathedral Square, head west on Worcester Street, make a left on Montreal Street across the Avon River, right on Tuam Street and left on Antigua Street to Bletsoe Road to Wychbury Road. Go right on Glynne Road to Domain Terrace, and left into Lincoln Road to Highway 75 (Halswell Road) through the suburb of Halswell. Take the more scenic old Taitapu Road to the village of Taitapu. From Taitapu, drive along Highway 75 past Lake Ellsmere to Birdlings Flat, turn left to Little River, Duvauchelle, Robinson Bay, and finally Akaroa.

On the return, at Robinson Bay, turn right along Okains Bay Road to Summit Road, turn left and enjoy the marvelous views of both sides of the high (1,500-foot) ridge. Turn right on Kukupa Road to Pigeon Bay (3.5 miles), 5 miles of gravel to Port Levy, then on to Purau and Diamond Harbour on the outskirts of Lyttelton. Head around the harbor to Governors Bay.

Sightseeing Highlights

▲▲▲ **Banks Peninsula** is geologically as well as geographically set apart from its Canterbury surroundings. Formed by two extinct volcanoes, the peninsula is cut deeply by narrow bays that can be reached on steep roads off Highway 75. Akaroa is the closest the French came to colonizing New Zealand. In fact, it's just an accident of history that Christchurch is very English rather than Gallic. In 1835, Jean Langlois sailed the whaling ship *Cachalot* into what today is French Bay at the site of Akaroa to shelter from cold southerly winds. He managed to buy land from the Maoris, returned to France and organized colonists, and left France in March 1840 on the *Comte de Paris*. Britain annexed New Zealand on February 6, 1840. *Mon Dieu!* But at least Jean and the descendants of this frustrated French contingent (resting in the old French cemetery on L'Aube Hill) left their indelible imprint on Akaroa. Many street names and signs are in French. The Langlois-Eteveneaux House (1845), at the rear of which is a colonial museum, has been restored by the New Zealand Historic Places Trust. A walking tour should also include visits to St. Patricks (1864) and St. Peters (1863), The Domain, and views from side streets on surrounding hills above the harbor.

▲▲▲ **Walking Tour of Akaroa**—French beginnings and flavor are mixed with late Victorian style in Akaroa. Allow at least two hours for a leisurely walk through the town and its waterfront area. A good place to park is near the **Church of St. Patrick** on Rue Lavaud and walk from there first toward town and then up **L'Aube Hill**. Built of totara, black pine, and kauri, the picturesque church is the third Catholic church on the site, built in several stages in the second half of the nineteenth century. Walk up Rue Brittan past **Trinity Church** (1886) to **The Gallery**, one of the Christchurch area's finest art galleries. Walk up L'Aube Hill past the **Old French Cemetery** for the wonderful view from the Power Board reserve. Head down hill to Rue Lavaud to see the mid-nineteenth-century **Langlois-Eteveneaux House and Museum**,

Christchurch Peninsula

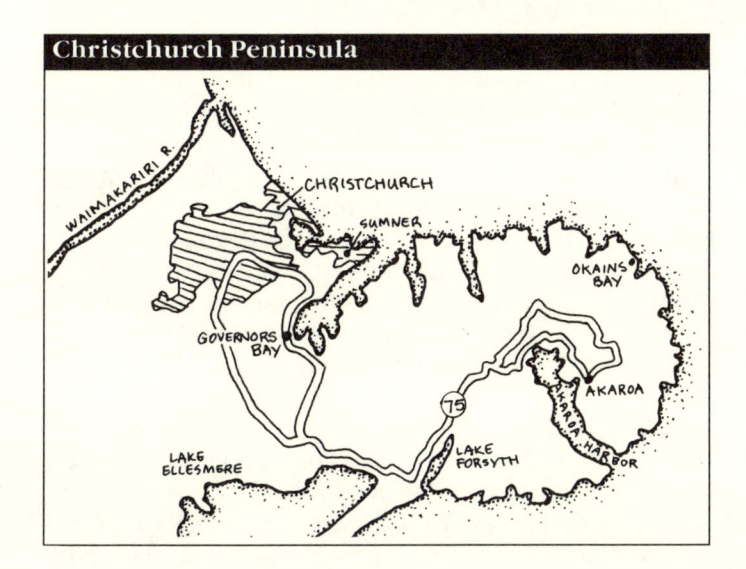

and the museum's collection from early French settlement (10:30 a.m. to 2:00 p.m.). The cottage itself is not open to the public, but peek through the windows. From here walk along the waterfront and enjoy the scenery in this delightful village.

On the way back to Christchurch, stop at one or more of the scenic towns, bays, and beaches along the north shore of Banks Peninsula: **Le Bons Bay**, with a sheltered beach and some fine old homes; **Okaina Bay**, also with a safe beach and an interesting and unpretentious **Maori and Colonial Museum** that actually includes a carved meeting house and restored colonial buildings—a cottage, stables, and a smithy shop, open 10:00 a.m. to 5:00 p.m., tel. 485—in addition to artifacts from both cultures; and, if there's time, **Little Akaloa**, with picturesque **St. Luke's Anglican Church** (1906) set in trees above the cove.

Where to Eat

On Beach Road in Akaroa, you have a choice of three places for a light lunch: the **Harbor View Tearoom**, the **Montarsha Tearoom**, and the **Akaroa Bakery**.

For travelers who are comfortable in a magnificent setting for dinner, tonight appropriately will be one of the best in New Zealand—**Grimsby's** (Cranmer Courts, Kilmer and Montreal sts., tel. 03/799-040). In an old stone building (1876), formerly a school, the medieval architecture, elegant decor and furnishings, classical background music, and exquisite table setting prepare you for an impressive menu offering rack of Canterbury lamb, beef Wellington, roast venison, and other superb main courses averaging over NZ$30. Dinner is served from 7:00 to 10:30 p.m. Monday through Sunday.

Itinerary Option
Stay over at the **Mount Vernon Lodge** (Rue Balgueri, tel. 0514/7180), on a lovely site overlooking Akaroa Harbour, in a two-level cottage for only NZ$13 pp, motel flats for NZ$38 double, or if you book far enough in advance and plan to spend a few days, the A-frame chalet for NZ$50 double. Or camp (NZ$12), rent a cabin (NZ$30 double) or a caravan site (NZ$15) at the **Holiday Park Campground** (Old Coach Rd., tel. 0514/7471).

Return to the United States
Christchurch International Airport is six miles from Cathedral Square. Most rental car companies will drive you to the airport at no charge (although a tip would be appreciated) when you drop off your car (call ahead and request this service). Otherwise, the airport coach leaves from Cathedral Square for NZ$2.10 (off-peak less), and the airport shuttle bus runs regularly from hotels and other lodgings for NZ$5 (tel. 669-660).

For those of you returning directly to the United States, depending on the time of your departing flight from Auckland, Air New Zealand, Mt. Cook, or Ansett will make the connection.

INDEX

North Island
Agrodome 94
Albert Park 48
Alladins Cave 71
Anaura Bay Walkway 100
Anaura Scenic Reserve 100
Aranui Cave 88
Aratakai Information Centre 55
Aratiatia Rapids 32,95
Auckland 31,36-52
Aupori Peninsula 78
Automobile Association (Auckland) 38
Awakino River 90
Awhi-o-te-rangi meeting house 84
Bay of Islands 31-32,57-72
Bay of Islands Maritime and Historic Park 62
Bay of Plenty 82,92
Bethells Beach 56
Blue and Green Lakes 94
Bluff Hill 110
Bridal Veil Falls 69
Brooksland Park 90
Bushy Park 112
cable car (Wellington) 119
Cape Brett 70
Cape Kidnappers Gannet Sanctuary 110-11
Cape Reinga 78,79; Walkway 79
Capt. Cook Cruises 41,46,51
Captain Cook Memorial Museum 63
Cascades and Kauri Park 56
Castor Bay 56
Cavilli Islands 72
Centennial Memorial Regional Park 55
Christ Church (Russell) 63
Clapham Clock Museum 67
Collard Winery 55
Coast-to-Coast Walkway 48
Cook Straits ferry 33
Corbans Winery 55
Cornwall Park 29, 37, 38
Coromandel Peninsula 32,73,75-78,80-87
Coromandel Walkway 87
Cream Trip 69-70
cruising or yachting (Bay of Islands) 67-68
cycle touring 39
Dargaville 32,73,74
Deep-sea fishing/Northland 52
Devonport Ferry 37,45,48
Devonport 37,45
Diving (Northland) 67
Drurie Hill 112
East Cape 100
East Coast Bays Cliff Walks 56
Ferry Building Information Centre 45
Fletcher Bay 81
Fuller Tours 78
Fuller's Captain Cook Cruises 46
game fishing 68
Gisborne 100-101
Government Gardens 93
Great Barrier Airlines 52
Great Barrier Island 47,52
Hahei Beach 82
Hamurana Springs 94
Haruru Falls 71
Hastings 110
Hauraki Gulf 36,45,46,47,51-52
Hauraki Gulf Maritime Park 38,47
Hawke's Bay 110
Hawke's Bay Museum & Art Gallery 77
Henderson Valley 53,54,55-56
Hicks Bay 72
Hinemoa's Hot Pool 71
Hipango Park 113
Holly Lodge Estate Winery 112
Hot Water Beach 82
Huka Falls 32
Huka Village 99
Hurunui River 95

Inter-Island Ferry 117
Jerusalem 115
John Hammond's River Road Tours 115
Kai-Iwi Lakes 79
Karangahake Gorge 81
Karikari Peninsula 78
Kauaeranga Valley 75
kauri trees 55,74-75
Kawau Island 60,62
Keith Park Memorial Airfield 50
Kelburn 116
Kelley Tarton's Underwater World 49
Kemp House 72
Kerikeri 32, 65,69; Inlet 69
Kerikeri Golf Club 72
Ketetahi Track 108
Lady Knox Geyser 95
Lake Okataina 98
Lake Rotoehu 98
Lake Rotoiti 98
Lake Rotomahana 95
Lake Rotorua 91
Lake Tarawara 99
Lake Taupo 32,91,96, 102
Lake Waikaremoana 99
Levin 112
Maketu 81,84
Maki Hill 63
Mangawhai Cliffs Track 60,62
Mangawhai Heads 60
Mangonui Harbour 78
Marakopa Falls 89
Marine Drive 116,118
Marineland 110
Marine Parade 110
Matakoke 73,75
Maoris 36,91-92; arts and crafts 22, 23
Maori Arts and Crafts Institute 93
Maori hangi 94
Mayor Island 82
Mercury Bay 82
Merrowvale 89
Miramar Peninsula 118
Mission Bay 52
Mohaka River 76
Mokau River 90
Mokoia Island 98
Motiti Island 84
Mototapu Island 51
Motu River 72
Motuihe Island 51
Mount Atkinson 55
Mount Bruce National Wildlife Centre 111
Mount Cook's Tiger Lily Cruises 56
Mount Eden Domain 46-47
Mount Egmont 89,90
Mount Maunganui 80,81,82-83
Mount Ngauruhoe 109
Mount Ngongotaha 68
Mount Paka 82
Mount Ruapehu Alpine Walk 109
Mount Tarawara 99
Mount Victoria (Auckland) 48
Mount Victoria (Wellington) 117
Muriwau 55
Museum of Shipwrecks 71
Museum of Transport & Technology 50
Napier 110
National Museum and Art Gallery (Wellington) 119
New Plymouth 89,90
New Zealand Government Tourist Bureau (Auckland) 38
Ngoiotonga Scenic Reserve 60
Ngongotaha 94
Ninety Mile Beach 78,79
Nocturnal Wildlife Centre 110
Northern Wairoa Maori, Maritime and Pioneer Museum 75

Northland Charter Boat Association 57
Ocean Beach 76,84
Ohaki Maori Village 89
Ohakune 73,102,104
Ohinemutu 94
Old Auckland Customhouse 47,49
Old Government Building 119
One Tree Hill 47
Onetangi Island 41
Opitiki 70
Opouture Beach 64
Opua 60
Orakei Korako 99
Orchard Railway 72
Origin Art & Craft Cooperative 72
Otorohanga Nocturnal Kiwi House 88
Otamatea Kauri & Pioneer Museum 59
Paekakariki 112
Paihai 63-64,66,70
Pakatoa Island 41
Pakinson's Lookout 55
Parliament 116,118-119
Parnell 30, 32, 37, 38
Pauanui 82
Penfolds Vineyard 42
Piercy Island 70
Piha 53,55
Pink and White Terraces 95
Pipiriki 109
Pipiriki Jet Boat Tours 109
Pohutu Geyser 93
Polynesian Pools 68
Pompellier House 63
Ponsonby 40
Poor Knights Islands 67
Port Fitzroy, 41
Prakei Korako 71
Pukeiti Rhododendron Trust 90
Pukekura Park 90
Pukematekeo Lookout 43
Queen Elizabeth Square 37
Queens Wharf 37
Raetihi 73
rafting 108,109
Rainbow and Fairy Springs 93-94
Rainbow Falls 72
Rakino Island 47,51
Rangitoto Island 47,51
Rawene 58
Rotorua 32,84-87,91-96,98-100
Rotorua Museum and Art Gallery 68
Round-the-Mountain-Track 77
Ruakuri Cave 88
Ruapehu 105
Russell 32,57,58,60,61,62-63,64-65,66
Sandspit 60
Sea Bee Air 52
St. Faith's Anglican Church 68
St. Heliers Bay 44
Stone Store and Museum 71
Stratford Mountain House 90
Taharoa Domain 79
Takapuna 52,56
Tamaki Drive 52
Tamatekapua Meeting House 22, 68
Taumarunui 103,109
Taupo 32,96-97
Tauranga 80,81
Te-Awhi-o-te-rangi meeting house 64
Te Mata Peak 110
Te Paki Coastal Park 79
Te Tokanganui-a-Noho Meeting House 89
Te Wairo 95
Thames 73
Tokanganui-a-Noho Meeting House 65
Tolaga Bay 100
Tongariro National Park 32,103-04,107-09
Tongariro Ngauruhoe 74
Tongariro River 108
Tongariro Trout Hatchery 103

Touristop Tourist Services 31
Trounson Kauri Park 74
Tudor Towers 93
Turangi 108
Turoa 102
Tutukaka Coast 67
Tuwhakairiora meeting house 72
Upper and Lower Hutt 116
Urewera National Park 99
Urupukapuka Island 70
Victoria Park Market 37,49
Virginia Lake 112
Wagener Museum 78
Waiheke Island 47,51,56
Waihi 76
Waikanae Beach 100
Waikareoana Track 71
Waikato River 66, 68
Waimangu Thermal Valley 95-96
Waimate North Mission House 78
Waiotapu Thermal Wonderland 96
Waipoua Kauri Sanctuary 32,73,74-75
Wairakei 68
Wairakei Geothermal Steam Power Station 66, 69,96
Waitaia Beach 87
Waitakere Scenic Drive 31,53-55
Waitangi National Reserve 66,70-71
Waitemata Harbor 36,37,52
Waitomo 87-89
Waiwera 54
Waiwera Hot Pools Leisure Resort 56
Wanganui 33,102-103,106-107,108,112-113
Wanganui River 33,113
Wanganui River Road 103,109
War Memorial Museum 46,49
Wellington 33,113-115,116-121
Wenderholm Regional Park 52
West Coast Beach 59
Whakapapa Village 104
Whakarewarewa Thermal Reserve 93
Whakatane 100
Whangarei Falls 62
Whangarei Deep Sea Anglers Club 52
Whangarei Falls 49
Whangaroa Bay 60,72,78
Whanharauru Peninsula 60
Whitecliffs Walkway 90
Whitianga 81
Winter Garden 46

South Island
Abel Tasman National Park 126,178
Akaroa 35,179,180-181
Arrow River Gorge 146
Arrowtown 143
Arthur's Pass and village 35,172
Arthurs Pass National Park 35,176-177
Arts Centre of Christchurch 131
Ashley Gorge 139
Avon River 127,128,130
Banks Peninsula 35,179-181
Blenheim 122
Blue Cliffs Beach 162
Blue Lakes 136
Bluff 164
Bob's Peak 144
Botanic Gardens (Canterbury) 131
Botanic Gardens (Nelson) 125
Bridle Path 132
Bridal Veil Nature Walk 177
Buller River and Gorge 178
Burke's Pass 134-135
Canterbury Museum 131
Cardrona Valley 34,135,158
Cardrona 106,146
Cathedral Caves 162
Cathedral Square 127,128,131
Cecil Peak Sheep and Cattle Station 144
Chalet Lookout Track 168

Index

Chaslands 162
Christchurch 33,35,120,121-25,127,134, 176-77
City Mall Complex 131
Cone Rock Track 170
Coronet Peak 144,146
Cromwell 161
Crown Ridge 115,135
Doubtful Sound 147-148
Dunedin 161-165
Eglinton Valley 154
Ferrier Fountain 131
Ferrymead Historic Park 132
Fiordland National Park 34,148
fishing 125,133,159,170,178
Fox Glacier 35,166,169
Frankton 138,139
Franz Josef Glacier 35,168,169,171; Valley Walk 35,173-174
Gibson Quay 123
Glendhu Bay 159
Blue Spur Gold Mine 174
Godley Head Walkway 132
Golden Bay 126
Greenstone 174
Greenstone Valley Walk 151,152
Greymouth 35,171,174-175
Haast Pass 35,166,167
Hadley Park 132
Halfmoon Bay (Oban)164
Hamner Springs 178
Harris Mountains 146
Havelock 126
Heaphy Track 126
Heliskiing 146
Hokitika 35,174
Hollyford Tourist & Travel Ltd. 152
Hollyford Valley and Walk 151,155
Homer Tunnel 154
Invercargill 162
Jacks Bay beach 162
Kaikaura Peninsula 121
Kaiteriteri Beach 126
Kawarau River 145
Keneouru Sound 125
Kenepuru Sound 125
Lake Brunner 168
Lake Coleridge 139
Lake District Centennial Museum 104
Lake Grasmere 177
Lake Gunn 154
Lake Hauroke 162
Lake Hawea 34,167
Lake Ianthe 168
Lake Kaniere Scenic Reserve 35,168,174
Lake Lyndon 139
Lake Manapouri 147,148-149
Lake Mapourika 168
Lake Matheson 168
Lake Mauapiurike 119
Lake Moeraki 167
Lake Oahu 137
Lake Paringa 167
Lake Pearson 177
Lake Pukaki 136
Lake Rotoiti 126
Lake Rotoroa 126
Lake Tekapo 136
Lake Te Anau 156
Lake Wahapo 168
Lake Wakatipu 143
Lake Wanaka 34,158
Lake Wilkie 162
Langlois Eteveneaux House 180
Larnarch Castle 164
Le Bons Bay 181
Lewis Pass 177
Lindis Pass 135
Little Akaloa 181
Lyttelton Harbor 132

Mackenzie Valley 136
Makarora Valley 35,167
Maori and Colonial Museum 181
Marlborough Sounds 125; Maritime Park 122
Maruia Springs 178
Mataatua Meeting House 101
Methven 133
Milford Sound 147,156
Milford Track 151
Mirror Lakes 154
Mitre Peak 154
Motueka 125,126
Mt. Aspiring National Park 159,167
Mt. Cook National Park 33,135
Mt. Cook Village 135
Mt. Hutt & Ski Area 133
Mt. Iron 34,159
Mt. Nicholas Sheep Station 144
Naseby 162
Nelson 125-126
Nelson Lakes National Park 126,178
Nga-Hua-E-Wha National Marae 131
North-West Nelson State Park 126
Okains Bay 35,179,181
Olveston Mansion 163
Otago 162-163
Otago Museum (Dunedin) 23, 163
Pelorus Sound 125
Picton 120,121
Plane Table Lookout 174
Port Hills 132
Provincial Government Buildings 90
Queen Charlotte Sound 84
Queenstown 34,137-139,142-146
Rakaia River & Gorge 133,139
Rakiura Museum 164
Rangitata River 133
Remarkables 144,146
Routeburn Walk 151,152; Ltd. 153
Royal Albatross Colony 164
Shantytown 172,176
Shotover River 145
Signal Hill 163
skiing 136-137,146
Skippers Canyon 145-146
S.S. Earnslaw 143
St. Bathans 162
Stewart Island 20, 164-165
Stirling Falls 157
Summit Road 132
Sutherland Falls 114
Takaka Hill 125
Tasman Bay 126
Tasman Glacier 170
Tautuka Beach 162
Te Anau 147,149-151,156
Town Hall (Christchurch) 131
Treble Cone 146,159
Tucker Hill Lookout 162
Ulva Island 102
vineyards 125-126
Vintage Farm Museum and Greenstone Factory 174
Waiau River 95
Waimakariri River & Gorges 133
Wairau River 133
Wairau Valley 89
Wanaka 34-35,146,158-161,162,166
West Arm 149
West Coast Historical Museum 174
Westland National Park 35,167-168
Westport 172

Other Books from John Muir Publications

Adventure Vacations: From Trekking in New Guinea to Swimming in Siberia, Richard Bangs (65-76-9) 256 pp. $17.95

Asia Through the Back Door, 3rd ed., Rick Steves and John Gottberg (65-48-3) 326 pp. $15.95

Being a Father: Family, Work, and Self, *Mothering* Magazine (65-69-6) 176 pp. $12.95

Buddhist America: Centers, Retreats, Practices, Don Morreale (28-94-X) 400 pp. $12.95

Bus Touring: Charter Vacations, U.S.A., Stuart Warren with Douglas Bloch (28-95-8) 168 pp. $9.95

California Public Gardens: A Visitor's Guide, Eric Sigg (65-56-4) 304 pp. $16.95 (Available 3/91)

Catholic America: Self-Renewal Centers and Retreats, Patricia Christian-Meyer (65-20-3) 325 pp. $13.95

Complete Guide to Bed & Breakfasts, Inns & Guesthouses, Pamela Lanier (65-43-2) 520 pp. $15.95

Costa Rica: A Natural Destination, Ree Strange Sheck (65-51-3) 280 pp. $15.95

Elderhostels: The Students' Choice, Mildred Hyman (65-28-9) 224 pp. $12.95 (2nd ed. available 5/91 $15.95)

Environmental Vacations: Volunteer Projects to Save the Planet, Stephanie Ocko (65-78-5) 240 pp. $14.95

Europe 101: History & Art for the Traveler, 4th ed., Rick Steves and Gene Openshaw (65-79-3) 372 pp. $15.95

Europe Through the Back Door, 9th ed., Rick Steves (65-42-4) 432 pp. $16.95

Floating Vacations: River, Lake, and Ocean Adventures, Michael White (65-32-7) 256 pp. $17.95

Gypsying After 40: A Guide to Adventure and Self-Discovery, Bob Harris (28-71-0) 264 pp. $14.95

The Heart of Jerusalem, Arlynn Nellhaus (28-79-6) 336 pp. $12.95

Indian America: A Traveler's Companion, Eagle/Walking Turtle (65-29-7) 424 pp. $16.95 (2nd ed. available 7/91 $16.95)

Mona Winks: Self-Guided Tours of Europe's Top Museums, Rick Steves and Gene Openshaw (28-85-0) 456 pp. $14.95

Opera! The Guide to Western Europe's Great Houses, Karyl Lynn Zietz (65-81-5) 280 pp. $18.95 (Available 4/91)

Paintbrushes and Pistols: How the Taos Artists Sold the West, Sherry C. Taggett and Ted Schwarz (65-65-3) 280 pp. $17.95

The People's Guide to Mexico, 8th ed., Carl Franz (65-60-2) 608 pp. $17.95

The People's Guide to RV Camping in Mexico, Carl Franz with Steve Rogers (28-91-5) 320 pp. $13.95

Preconception: A Woman's Guide to Preparing for Pregnancy and Parenthood, Brenda E. Aikey-Keller (65-44-0) 232 pp. $14.95

Ranch Vacations: The Complete Guide to Guest and Resort, Fly-Fishing, and Cross-Country Skiing Ranches, Eugene Kilgore (65-30-0) 392 pp. $18.95 (2nd ed. available 5/91 $18.95)

Schooling at Home: Parents, Kids, and Learning, *Mothering* Magazine (65-52-1) 264 pp. $14.95

The Shopper's Guide to Art and Crafts in the Hawaiian Islands, Arnold Schuchter (65-61-0) 272 pp. $13.95

The Shopper's Guide to Mexico, Steve Rogers and Tina Rosa (28-90-7) 224 pp. $9.95

Ski Tech's Guide to Equipment, Skiwear, and Accessories, edited by Bill Tanler (65-45-9) 144 pp. $11.95

Ski Tech's Guide to Maintenance and Repair, edited by Bill Tanler (65-46-7) 160 pp. $11.95

Teens: A Fresh Look, *Mothering* Magazine (65-54-8) 240 pp. $14.95 (Available 3/91)

A Traveler's Guide to Asian Culture, Kevin Chambers (65-14-9) 224 pp. $13.95

Traveler's Guide to Healing Centers and Retreats in North America, Martine Rudee and Jonathan Blease (65-15-7) 240 pp. $11.95

Understanding Europeans, Stuart Miller (65-77-7) 272 pp. $14.95
Undiscovered Islands of the Caribbean, 2nd ed., Burl Willes (65-55-6) 232 pp. $14.95
Undiscovered Islands of the Mediterranean, Linda Lancione Moyer and Burl Willes (65-53-X) 232 pp. $14.95
A Viewer's Guide to Art: A Glossary of Gods, People, and Creatures, Marvin S. Shaw and Richard Warren (65-66-1) 152 pp. $10.95 (Available 3/91)

2 to 22 Days Series

These pocket-size itineraries (4½" × 8") are a refreshing departure from ordinary guidebooks. Each offers 22 flexible daily itineraries that can be used to get the most out of vacations of any length. Included are not only "must see" attractions but also little-known villages and hidden "jewels" as well as valuable general information.

22 Days Around the World, Roger Rapoport and Burl Willes (65-31-9) 200 pp. $9.95 (1992 ed. available 8/91 $11.95)
2 to 22 Days Around the Great Lakes, 1991 ed., Arnold Schuchter (65-62-9) 176 pp. $9.95
22 Days in Alaska, Pamela Lanier (28-68-0) 128 pp. $7.95
22 Days in the American Southwest, 2nd ed., Richard Harris (28-88-5) 176 pp. $9.95
22 Days in Asia, Roger Rapoport and Burl Willes (65-17-3) 136 pp. $7.95 (1992 ed. available 8/91 $9.95)
22 Days in Australia, 3rd ed., John Gottberg (65-40-8) 148 pp. $7.95 (1992 ed. available 8/91 $9.95)
22 Days in California, 2nd ed., Roger Rapoport (65-64-5) 176 pp. $9.95
22 Days in China, Gaylon Duke and Zenia Victor (28-72-9) 144 pp. $7.95
22 Days in Europe, 5th ed., Rick Steves (65-63-7) 192 pp. $9.95
22 Days in Florida, Richard Harris (65-27-0) 136 pp. $7.95 (1992 ed. available 8/91 $9.95)
22 Days in France, Rick Steves (65-07-6) 154 pp. $7.95 (1991 ed. available 4/91 $9.95)
22 Days in Germany, Austria & Switzerland, 3rd ed., Rick Steves (65-39-4) 136 pp. $7.95
22 Days in Great Britain, 3rd ed., Rick Steves (65-38-6) 144 pp. $7.95 (1991 ed. available 4/91 $9.95)
22 Days in Hawaii, 2nd ed., Arnold Schuchter (65-50-5) 144 pp. $7.95 (1992 ed. available 8/91 $9.95)
22 Days in India, Anurag Mathur (28-87-7) 136 pp. $7.95
22 Days in Japan, David Old (28-73-7) 136 pp. $7.95
22 Days in Mexico, 2nd ed., Steve Rogers and Tina Rosa (65-41-6) 128 pp. $7.95
22 Days in New England, Anne Wright (28-96-6) 128 pp. $7.95 (1991 ed. available 4/91 $9.95)
2 to 22 Days in New Zealand, 1991 ed., Arnold Schuchter (65-58-0) 176 pp. $9.95
22 Days in Norway, Sweden, & Denmark, Rick Steves (28-83-4) 136 pp. $7.95 (1991 ed. available 4/91 $9.95)
22 Days in the Pacific Northwest, Richard Harris (28-97-4) 136 pp. $7.95 (1991 ed. available 4/91 $9.95)
22 Days in the Rockies, Roger Rapoport (65-68-8) 176 pp. $9.95
22 Days in Spain & Portugal, 3rd ed., Rick Steves (65-06-8) 136 pp. $7.95
22 Days in Texas, Richard Harris (65-47-5) 176 pp. $9.95
22 Days in Thailand, Derk Richardson (65-57-2) 176 pp. $9.95
22 Days in the West Indies, Cyndy & Sam Morreale (28-74-5)136 pp. $7.95

"Kidding Around" Travel Guides for Young Readers

Written for kids eight years of age and older. Generously illustrated in two colors with imaginative characters and images. An adventure to read and a treasure to keep.

Kidding Around Atlanta, Anne Pedersen (65-35-1) 64 pp. $9.95
Kidding Around Boston, Helen Byers (65-36-X) 64 pp. $9.95
Kidding Around Chicago, Lauren Davis (65-70-X) 64 pp. $9.95
Kidding Around the Hawaiian Islands, Sarah Lovett (65-37-8) 64 pp. $9.95
Kidding Around London, Sarah Lovett (65-24-6) 64 pp. $9.95
Kidding Around Los Angeles, Judy Cash (65-34-3) 64 pp. $9.95
Kidding Around the National Parks of the Southwest, Sarah Lovett 108 pp. $12.95

Kidding Around New York City, Sarah Lovett (65-33-5) 64 pp. $9.95
Kidding Around Paris, Rebecca Clay (65-82-3) 64 pp. $9.95 (Available 4/91)
Kidding Around Philadelphia, Rebecca Clay (65-71-8) 64 pp. $9.95
Kidding Around San Francisco, Rosemary Zibart (65-23-8) 64 pp. $9.95
Kidding Around Santa Fe, Susan York (65-99-8) 64 pp. $9.95 (Available 5/91)
Kidding Around Seattle, Rick Steves (65-84-X) 64 pp. $9.95 (Available 4/91)
Kidding Around Washington, D.C., Anne Pedersen (65-25-4) 64 pp. $9.95

Environmental Books for Young Readers

Written for kids eight years and older. Examines the environmental issues and opportunities that today's kids will face during their lives.

The Indian Way: Learning to Communicate with Mother Earth, Gary McLain (65-73-4) 114 pp. $9.95
The Kids' Environment Book: What's Awry and Why, Anne Pedersen (55-74-2) 192 pp. $13.95
No Vacancy: The Kids' Guide to Population and the Environment, Glenna Boyd (61-000-7) 64 pp. $9.95 (Available 8/91)
Rads, Ergs, and Cheeseburgers: The Kids' Guide to Energy and the Environment, Bill Yanda (65-75-0) 108 pp. $12.95

"Extremely Weird" Series for Young Readers

Written for kids eight years of age and older. Designed to help kids appreciate the world around them. Each book includes full-color photographs with detailed and entertaining descriptions of the "extremely weird" creatures.

Extremely Weird Bats, Sarah Lovett (61-008-2) 48 pp. $9.95 paper (Available 7/91)
Extremely Weird Frogs, Sarah Lovett (61-006-6) 48 pp. $9.95 paper (Available 6/91)
Extremely Weird Spiders, Sarah Lovett (61-007-4) 48 pp. $9.95 paper (Available 6/91)

Automotive Repair Manuals

How to Keep Your VW Alive, 14th ed., (65-80-7) 440 pp. $19.95
How to Keep Your Subaru Alive (65-11-4) 480 pp. $19.95
How to Keep Your Toyota Pickup Alive (28-81-3) 392 pp. $19.95
How to Keep Your Datsun/Nissan Alive (28-65-6) 544 pp. $19.95

Other Automotive Books

The Greaseless Guide to Car Care Confidence: Take the Terror Out of Talking to Your Mechanic, Mary Jackson (65-19-X) 224 pp. $14.95

Off-Road Emergency Repair & Survival, James Ristow (65-26-2) 160 pp. $9.95

Ordering Information

If you cannot find our books in your local bookstore, you can order directly from us. Please check the "Available" date above. If you send us money for a book not yet available, we will hold your money until we can ship you the book. Your books will be sent to you via UPS (for U.S. destinations). UPS will not deliver to a P.O. Box; please give us a street address. Include $2.75 for the first item ordered and $.50 for each additional item to cover shipping and handling costs. For airmail within the U.S., enclose $4.00. All foreign orders will be shipped surface rate; please enclose $3.00 for the first item and $1.00 for each additional item. Please inquire about foreign airmail rates.

Method of Payment

Your order may be paid by check, money order, or credit card. We cannot be responsible for cash sent through the mail. All payments must be made in U.S. dollars drawn on a U.S. bank. Canadian postal money orders in U.S. dollars are acceptable. For VISA, MasterCard, or American Express orders, include your card number, expiration date, and your signature, or call (800) 888-7504. Books ordered on American Express cards can be shipped only to the billing address of the cardholder. Sorry, no C.O.D.'s. Residents of sunny New Mexico, add 5.875% tax to the total.

Address all orders and inquiries to:
John Muir Publications
P.O. Box 613
Santa Fe, NM 87504
(505) 982-4078
(800) 888-7504